T0301549

Money, Investment and Consumption

To
Lorie Tarshis
Sir John Hicks
James Tobin

'Gentlemen, I have decided to change the title of my course of lectures from "The Theory of Money" to "The Monetary Theory of Production"'.

So went Keynes's announcement, as per the recollection of Lorie Tarshis, a young student and member of 'the Circus' in Cambridge, when he entered his first lecture in the first term of 1932 – a sober resonance, which at that moment made Tarshis tremble without knowing what it really meant.

Money, Investment and Consumption

Keynes's Macroeconomics Rethought

O.F. Hamouda

York University, Canada

Edward Elgar
Cheltenham, UK • Northampton, MA, USA

Published by
Edward Elgar Publishing Limited
The Lypiatts
15 Lansdown Road
Cheltenham
Glos GL50 2JA
UK

Edward Elgar Publishing, Inc.
William Pratt House
9 Dewey Court
Northampton
Massachusetts 01060
USA

A catalogue record for this book
is available from the British Library

Library of Congress Control Number: 2009937752

Mixed Sources
Product group from well-managed
forests and other controlled sources
www.fsc.org Cert no. SA-COC-1565
© 1996 Forest Stewardship Council

FSC

ISBN 978 1 84542 979 9 (cased)

Printed and bound by MPG Books Group, UK

Contents

Figures

Preface

This book is dedicated to the memories of three great scholars and fine gentlemen, Lorie Tarshis, John Hicks, and James Tobin, three different interpreters of John Maynard Keynes, one of the most creative economic thinkers of the twentieth century. The first, Lorie Tarshis, was an ardent and true student of Keynes. Having brought me to York University, he was my delightful and dear colleague for more than six years in whom the satiation for our daily luncheon discussions about the *Treatise*, *The General Theory*, war reparations, national debts, and the fate of the developing economies was never reached. The second, Sir John, was a man of an exceptional depth of knowledge whom I had the chance to know during the last six years of his life. In the process of reading his work for my dissertation critical about his contributions, I learned more about economics and its purpose than I ever acquired from the classroom. My subsequent meetings with the private Hicks, at his home at Blockley, in my travels with him in Oxfordshire, and during our time spent together when he came to Glendon College in Toronto for a month gave me a chance to appreciate immensely the depth of his intellect and to correct my misconceptions about his economic writings. The third, James Tobin, was an eclectic and original Keynesian, whom I met only a couple of times but whose writings among those of all the Keynesians are the most original and close to Keynes's interest in money and finance.

During the summer of 1988, while Sir John was visiting us at Glendon College, Tobin, on his way to Ottawa for some consultations, accepted, as a good friend of Lorie's, to stop in Toronto and join an impromptu gathering in honour of Sir John. A few other distinguished scholars, Ron McKinnon, Sam Hollander, David Laidler, Bernard Wolf, and John Crow, then Governor of the Bank of Canada, were invited to join the small group for an informal day of discussion.

On the evening before the memorable workshop, I had the chance at the informal dinner in honour of Hicks and Tobin, which Lorie and I organized, to sit around the table and listen to these three very humble men discuss money, inflation, policies, and of course Keynes. Obviously Tarshis, Hicks, and Tobin had different theoretical understandings of Keynes, but like Keynes, each in his own way was socially compassionate and commanded respect and admiration for his scholarship. Disagreements among thinkers help foster and advance knowledge. Differences about understanding and interpreting economic theories, however, also raise questions particularly pertinently as to why and how many interpretations and conclusions can emerge from the reading of Keynes. The eclectic, dynamic discussion during that informal dinner between just these three very remarkable men stimulated me all the more to write about what it is in Keynes's theoretical contribution that has aroused in economists, adversaries or supporters, so many different readings.

Ideas explored in a series of papers and lectures, which I have given over the last ten years, have now coalesced into this monograph. The early rush to interpret Keynes before understanding him was from different angles their shared subject. I had become increasingly persuaded that it was the controversies over semantics that derailed the innovative contribution of one of the most prolific economists ever. The enormous writing generated by Keynes's verbal expression has, it seems to me, had very little to do with his actual ideas. Only piecemeal have a few scholars grasped their intricacies and importance.

The purpose of this book is thus to demonstrate that, despite the convictions of those who derailed Keynes's theory from the start, notably Robertson, Hayek, and Hicks, primarily because they were puzzled by Keynes's semantics, Keynes provided a novel, general theory different from that of the Classicals and neoClassicals to whom they grafted him. The goal here is to spell out Keynes's model, with a new diagrammatic representation, to highlight his unique vision pertinent not only to the circumstances of his time but also to those well beyond, applicable to situations of recession and stagflation, as well as to full employment. It will be shown that the main stumbling block to understanding Keynes's ideas was semantic. Robertson's and Hayek's objections to the substance of Keynes's theory in the *Treatise* were therefore *baseless* and Hicks's interpretation and the ensuing IS-LM apparatus for *The General Theory* (see Figure 5.9), which became the surrogate for Keynesians new and old, is in fact *antithetical*. The alternative model, based on a straight reading of Keynes's theoretical core, found in the *Treatise*, in the drafts of *The General Theory*, and in *The General Theory* itself, provided here (see Figure 5.8), shows the contrast of Keynes's own theory to the theory behind the IS-LM.

Most of the ideas in this book have been percolating in my head since, as a student, I attended the Keynes Centenary Conference at King's College, Cambridge in 1983, an unprecedented gathering of scholars, members of the Circus as well as later generations of those both pro- and anti-Keynes.[1] The writing of the various chapters of this book is the much more recent outcome, and many of the ideas were presented in the following lectures:

- 'Views on long-term investment and finance: Keynes' hetero-doxy co-opted', given at the conference 'Politiques économiques: Perspectives de l'Hétérodoxie Keynesienne', University of Dijon, May 2002
- 'Keynes, Hayek, Hicks: money, prices, and the co-ordination of savings and investment' given at the John Hicks Centenary Workshop, University of Bologna, October 2004[2]
- 'Money and cyclical production: who was right, Keynes or Hayek?', given at the International Conference on the Cambridge School of Economics, Hitotsubashi University, Tokyo, February 2005
- 'Institutional framework, credit management, and managerial responsibility: Keynes, Hayek, Hicks', given at the Workshop on the Development of the Cambridge Economic Tradition, Graduate School of Economics, Kyoto University, March 2005
- 'Responses to the social welfare impacts of inflations and deflations: Wicksell, and Keynes, Hayek, and Hicks', given at the History of Economic Thought Seminar, Sophia (Jouchi) University, Tokyo, March 2005
- 'Woodford's Neo-Wicksellian Theory', given at the Economics Seminar, Rikkyo University, Tokyo, March 2005
- 'Hicks' Mr Keynes' *General Theory of Employment* reconsidered', given at Hitotsubashi University, Tokyo, March 2006
- 'Shackle's early contribution to business cycle theory', given at the conference, 'Shackle's Heritage in Economics: Micro and Macro Aspects', University of Padua, May 2006.

I would like to take this opportunity to thank the many people who invited me to give the lectures above and to participate in the various gatherings: Claude Gnos and Bernard Schmidt in Dijon, Stefano Zamagni and Roberto Scazzieri in Bologna, Toshiaki Hirai, Tamotsu Nishizawa, and Ryuzo Kuroki in Tokyo, Ludovic Frobert in Lyon, and Michel Bellet and Abdallah Zouache in Saint Etienne, and Sergio Rossi in Fribourg, and Ferdinando Meacci and Fulvio Fontini in Padua. My particular thanks are expressed to colleagues Toshiaki and Tamotsu for inviting me in two sequential years to Japan and for giving me the opportunity to try out many of the ideas found in this book. There are many with whom over the years I have had scholarly exchanges and whom I would also wish to thank for their thoughts: Geoff Harcourt, Robin Rowley, Harald Hagemann, Marina Colona, André Lapidus, Sheila Dow, Vicky Chick, Ingrid Rima, John Smithin, Syed Ahmad, Bob Dimand, Doug Mair, Malcolm Sawyer, Pierre Dockès, Michael Trautwein, Yoshio Inoue, Daniel Diatkine, Michiel deVroey, Larry Boland, Carlo

Zappia, Jack Birner, Roger Middleton, and the late George Shackle, Tom Asimokopoulos, and Jack Weldon. My deepest appreciation is for the invaluable comments and discussions with my partner Betsey Price over the course of the writing of the papers and the book manuscript.

OFH
Toronto, Ontario, Canada
September 2008

NOTES

1. The gist of the substance of that gathering was edited by David Worswick and James Trevithick.
2. This paper benefited from substantial comments, made at the John Hicks Centenary Workshop in Bologna, October 2004, by Mauro Baranzini, Carlos Casarosa, Rainer Masera, Robert Solow, and Erik Streissler. An understanding of this paper will be immensely enhanced by an accompanying reading of the workshop contributions of these authors published in Scazzieri et al. (2008).

Introduction

For experience seems to show that people are divided between the old ones whom nothing will shift and are merely annoyed [*sic.*, amazed, (sent letter of August 30, 1936, Keynes 1987, p. 85)] by my attempts to underline the points of transition so vital in my own progress, and the young ones who have not been properly brought up and believe nothing in particular. . . . I have no companions, it seems, in my own generation, either of my earliest teachers or of earliest pupils . . . (Keynes to Harrod, draft letter of August 27, 1936, cited by Clarke 1988, p. 259)

Judging by any standard in economics, John Maynard Keynes was truly an exceptional, innovative scholar, who made a significant contribution to economics. His was a contribution not in the ordinary sense of adding a little here or transforming things a little there within the established corpus, contributions which luckily will be simply a footnote in the annals of knowledge. It was rather a contribution like those of Adam Smith, Ricardo, and Marx, which have in essence shaken the corpus, a contribution that will last. Whatever the merits of Keynes's work, it transformed thinking in economics. Throughout his career as an economist, Keynes was above the crowd in his abilities to theorize, to shape the intellectual agenda, and even more astonishing, to be able to participate in a unique way in government decision-making in public affairs. One could reiterate that to be a good economist, one must be a good philosopher, historian, mathematician . . . Keynes had all the attributes of the ideal economist.

In fact Keynes managed to contribute in multiple fields and to attract attention from beyond the economics profession. By the very harsh critics, who did not like or agree with his ideas, he was depicted as a charlatan, but of course over the years he has also had many promoters. The literature on Keynes is enormous. There are biographies, for example, those of Roy Harrod, Robert Skidelsky, Don Moggridge, and Gilles Dostaler, among others, which give accounts of a fascinating man. Numerous books and articles by economic historians, for example, Sue Howson, Roger Middleton, and Peter Clarke, reveal the importance of Keynes's involvement in public affairs and his participation in the shaping of public policy, whether British or international. Rod O'Donnell, Terrence Hutchinson, Anna Carabelli, and Brad Bateman have brought to light influences that drove Keynes's philosophical thinking.

It is on Keynes's economic theory that this book is focused, and specifically as it was developed in *A Treatise on Money* and *The General Theory*. Although other aspects of his works are admittedly integral to the man's thinking, it is not the intention here to study all facets of Keynes's various contributions. Nonetheless, as background for the present study, the variety of works on Keynes, too numerous to mention, are extremely important to understanding the development of Keynes's theory. Such works are a *sine qua non* to putting Keynes's technical theoretical treatment of economics into perspective. For this reason, the authors just named and many more are to be found in the final select bibliography.

While the biographers, economic historians, and historians of philosophy have done their job in analysing Keynes within their own areas of interest, economists and particularly historians of thought, save for a few exceptions, have failed miserably in assessing Keynes's complete theory. Despite the enormous literature and the institutionalization of Keynes, his generalized General Theory has yet to see the light. The so-called Keynesian Revolution was more a controversy over bits and pieces of Keynes's ideas than a product of their comprehensive whole. Keynes's work was recognized from the beginning as expressing an unusually challenging terminology and a new methodological approach, which in themselves posed enormous difficulty in comprehension. Not knowing how to evaluate Keynes's distinctiveness, the first reactions of the orthodoxy were to attempt to figure out his fit within the mould.[1]

By readjusting his terminology, twisting his premises back to the ordinary understanding, and trivializing the novelty of his theory, very early on Keynes was made Keynesian. The outcome was established by consensus, and Keynes's desired revolution was stifled. In a publication by an outstanding Keynes scholar, timed coincidentally quite closely with this book, Luigi Pasinetti has touched on a similar observation: 'The great majority of those theories that we now call "Keynesian" have in fact little to do with the theoretical "revolution" that Keynes had in mind in the 1930s' (2007, p. xiv). In looking back, the failure to recognize Keynes's theoretical contributions on their merits stemmed first from the harsh criticism of the antagonistic reviewers, and second from the protagonists who were so defensive that they made matters worse. What started as personal attacks by Hayek and Robertson on Keynes's scholarship gave any subsequent commentator an almost obligatory caricature of his attributes and then the 'licence' to remedy the perceived deficiencies.

The myth developed that Keynes was a 'bad', 'sloppy', 'careless' writer, that he 'did not read' or 'understand' much of the Classics, that he was 'ignorant of Austrian and Swedish theories', and that he was 'confused and inconsistent about his own ideas'. To give just a few examples of this mythology, which, as will be shown in Chapter 3, Hayek and Robertson established as the footprints to follow, see Klein[2] in his abundant use of 'the confused state of Keynes' ideas at the time . . . the seeming contradiction . . . the principal fault of the *Treatise* . . . inadequate formal theory . . . exceedingly superficial' (*passim*); Patinkin's repetitions, 'the ineffectualness of the "fundamental equations" . . . obscurities . . . Keynes failed to realized . . . Keynes' failure . . . Keynes not only failed . . . his failure to explore' (1976, 1982, *passim*); and Leijonhufvud's condescension,

> Keynes was not entirely successful . . . another omission may be more glaring . . . his model was not logically watertight . . . the *General Theory* was in several respects, as has frequently been said, 'a badly written book'. . . the defects of organization and presentation were disappointing . . . it is the defects of the model that are serious . . . when a model contains logical errors, later interpreters are given considerable freedom in deciding where 'repairs' should be undertaken

like plumbers called upon to fix a leaky pipe (1968, *passim*). Neither did Keynes's ardent pupils, in a state of defensiveness in the face of such criticism, help others understand their teacher during his lifetime, and especially not thereafter. The irony is in fact that they did not but add to the myth. Here again, as Pasinetti has rightly pointed out, '[T]he result is that Keynes's pupils, taken all together, appeared more cohesive as a group of critical thinkers than as a group of theoretical founders' (2007, p. xvii).

As apologists for what others saw as Keynes's deficiencies, Keynes's pupils also fell into the absurd mode of caricaturing. It is astonishing to read the presumptuous, famous statement by Joan Robinson, 'There were moments when we had some trouble in getting Maynard to see what the point of his revolution really was' (1988, p. 256)[3], or the mildly modest one of Richard Kahn, 'Schumpeter's suggestion that my "share in the historic achievement cannot have fallen very far short of co-authorship" is clearly absurd' (1984, p. 178). More study, especially of the exchanges between Keynes and his pupils, particularly those in the immediate circle, 'the Circus', is needed to appreciate the role of those caught in the fervour of the controversies between Keynes and his staunch opponents, yet equally unable to interpret the essence of their teacher's ideas on his own terms. Witness Keynes's paralleling them to 'the old ones' in his impressionistic letter to Harrod, cited at the beginning of this Introduction, and even his comments about Harrod himself: 'Your preoccupation with the old beliefs – and much more so in the case of other people – would prevent you from seeing the half of what I am saying' (letter to Harrod, August 27, 1935, CW, XII, p. 548). There are numerous instances in the correspondence, where Keynes reacted directly in the same manner to other members of the Circus, which are yet to be explored.

Even though his pupils were bright and had their hearts in the right place, their impact on the formation of Keynes's vision has been vastly exaggerated by them and by others. There seems to be confusion in identifying the inspirations of Keynes himself with the stimulation a teacher like Keynes could obtain from his students. Keynes was in a league of his own to which his students were no match. He undoubtedly needed a platform from which to diffuse his ideas and did have great hope in and patience with the younger scholars. The timing of Pasinetti's *Keynes and the Cambridge Keynesians* is fortuitous for this work and will no doubt be of great help in re-evaluating the first generation of the Cambridge Keynesians.

The exercise of assessing the merits of Keynes's own work – from his own text and on its own terms – has, generally, evaporated. While the target discussion of this book is narrowed down especially to Hayek and Hicks, a general point is worth stating: the first generation of economists, whether critics or proponents, did not do enough for the next to help steer the discipline into the intricacy of Keynes's theory. It is simply incredible that the persona of Keynes in economics as a whole is exemplified by the myth that Keynes was confused, sloppy, wrote badly, and so on. Since it has become such a part of common parlance, the tacit conclusion is that any good understanding of Keynes must come from second-hand interpretation, such as Hicks's very powerful IS-LM. The literature on Keynes continues thus to perpetuate a consensus contaminated with a warped perception of Keynes's theory.

The purpose of this book is to return to the initial controversies that led to the misconceptions about Keynes's theory, in short, to address the myth. It will be shown that Keynes had a command of the language unsurpassed by his critics and commentators. He read carefully among the Mercantilists, the Classicals and the neoClassicals. Despite the colossal amount of work and the multitude of duties he imposed on himself, Keynes was lucid, coherent, and almost obsessive about defining and clarifying terms and concepts in his written work, particularly as concerned the core of his theory, developed in *A Treatise*, the various drafts of *The General Theory*, and in *The General Theory* itself. It will be shown that Keynes developed a coherent and complete theory, which ran from the *Treatise* through *The General Theory*. It is asserted even further that Keynes's theory is applicable not only to the situation of the slump but also is capable of explaining any phase of the trade cycle.

Keynes made two major breakthroughs in economics: one in the theory of value, the other in monetary theory. Along with the myth that commentators and critics developed about Keynes's semantics, there was also their wondering where his theory fit within the moulds of economics. His theory of value did not depend on labour as did the Classicals nor on utility as does neoClassical theory. It had to be recognized that his concept of value is a hybrid, based on average cost and market fluctuations embedded in the discrepancies between savings and investment, and that his price-level is an index embodying both a monetary component, usually associated with income, and a component related to liquidity shifts. It is with this price-level index that Keynes showed the way out of the Quantity Theory of Money.

Keynes's commentators and critics were set to wondering what the source of Keynes's inspiration had been. Misunderstanding the thrust of Keynes's own references, Hayek and Hicks both forced Wicksell upon him as his prime source. In the eyes then of others as well (for example, Klein, Patinkin, and Leijonhufvud), Wicksell became the 'official' inspiring author for Keynes. It will be shown in this book that there is very little evidence that this is the case and that in fact the results of the theories of Wicksell and Keynes are actually quite opposing. While for Wicksell, the ultimate goal of his theoretical endeavour was to show that price stability is required for containing income inequality, for Keynes, price changes, through the various inflationary and deflationary pressures, are necessary for sustaining employment and redistributing income.

The present book was completed in September 2008. Just as it was making its way to the publisher, the world underwent the outright meltdown of the financial system in the latest economic crisis, reviving, for many, thoughts of the similar financial crisis of the 1930s and the circumstances during which Keynes wrote his theory. Many have seen parallels between the two crises and a new appropriateness of theoretical links to Keynes, a revival of Keynesianism. Even as it delayed the release of this study of Keynes, it became imperative to take into perspective these latest developments in economic thinking. Chapter 1, 'The financial crisis of 2008 and the unKeynesian Keynes' has thus been added, to use the crisis of 2008 to illustrate how Keynes's own and the Keynesian perspective are different in both their explanations of the causes of economic crisis and the means they feel are needed to cure the problem. The core of the book remains the same and is found in Chapters 5 and 6. In Chapter 5 an alternative model is presented, Keynes's Efficiency of Capital/Supply Price model (EC-SP), distilled from a straight reading of the theoretical core of the *Treatise*, the drafts of *The General Theory*, and *The General Theory* itself. It is shown why the Hicksian IS-LM is inconsistent with Keynes's theory and that the EC-SP model is the corrective counter to the popular and erroneously well-established IS-LM.

In Chapter 1, 'The financial crisis of 2008 and the unKeynesian Keynes', Keynesian application of the concepts of Aggregate Demand and Aggregate Supply, derived from the IS-LM model, and Keynes's Effective Demand, derived from the EC-SP model of Chapter 5, are used as illustrations to explain the difference between the management of Aggregate Demand and that of Effective Demand. The core, interdependent components of Keynes's theory, namely Money, Investment, and Consumption, are all conceived and analysed from the firm's perspective, and not dichotomized into Aggregate Demand and Aggregate Supply, as by the variants of Keynesianism. Keynes was a supply theorist, in the sense that his economic policies derive from a macroeconomic production theory in which the profit motive and entrepreneurs' investment decisions are the key to the determination of employment. Keynes's economy is production, not demand-driven. To advocate demand expansion in every phase of the business cycle is not Keynes; consumerism promoted as the only way out of a financial crisis is not Keynes. The attempt in Chapter 1 is to shed light on the respective appropriateness of Keynes's and Keynesianism's tools to remedy economic crisis.

For the balance of the book, highlighting Keynes's generalized General Theory is the purpose. Keynes provided a novel, general theory different from that of the Classicals and neoClassicals, a theory yet unrecognized as being behind both *A Treatise on Money* and *The General Theory*. Contrary to the commonly perpetuated belief that Keynes's theory was only appropriate to a depression, his generalized model encapsulates a unique vision, pertinent not only to those circumstances of his time but applicable also to each and every economic situation well beyond: recession and stagflation, as well as full employment. Keynes's unique liquidity theory emphasized the role of banking and credit in sustaining economic activity but also showed how shifts in financial assets, due to excessive bullishness and bearishness, cause economic instability and potentially violent fluctuations. The extremely important distinction Keynes made between unproductive consumption (associated with investment in fixed capital) and productive consumption (linked to investment in working capital) that has gone unnoticed is brought to light.

A further important and unexploited characteristic of Keynes's theory is that for him unemployment goes hand in hand with income distribution. Cyclical fluctuations are by definition a reallocation of resources, whether through shifts in the factors of production from one sector to another, in financial liquidities from one form of asset to another, and/or in the level and/or composition of output. There are bound to be movements in prices corresponding to these reallocations. When Inflation or Deflation of the general price-level is decomposed into the various Inflations and Deflations (commodity, wage, income, capital, profit, and raw material), changes of relative prices and earnings (or relative purchasing power) are revealed to be occurring at every phase of the cycle across an economy, where different varieties of Inflation or Deflation run ahead or behind one another, offsetting one another or accumulating to create acceleration or deceleration in economic activity. Inflations and/or Deflations can result in a Slump, Stagflation or True Inflationary phase of the credit cycle.

In relation to one variable or another, income redistribution is for Keynes a permanent feature of the business cycle. Even at the extreme highs and lows of the cycle, Inflations will coexist with Deflations. Adjusting the various Inflations and Deflations is key to his economic policy. The interest rate is only one tool, which in some circumstances on its own is not sufficient to achieve the desired level of economic activity. To advocate, thus, as Wicksell did or as is now the practice of the central banks, a stabilization of the currency and hence the price-level, arrests addressing all the causes of unemployment or disparities of earnings. Keeping the general level of price constant does not guarantee that its components will remain unchanged. Keynes, in *A Treatise*, showed that unless inflation is decomposed and its various components analysed, the overall price does not reveal much and can be very misleading.

Although Keynes's theory and policy are presented here in a new light in Chapters 5 and 6, the challenge of confronting Keynesianism in its totality is a serious one. Some more groundwork is necessary to undertake that questioning, and this is provided in Chapters 2 through 4 and the Appendix. The overall goal of the book is to demonstrate that the convictions of those who derailed Keynes's theory, from the very start, notably Robertson, Hayek, and Hicks, stemmed primarily from their puzzlement over Keynes's prose. The main stumbling block to understanding Keynes's ideas was semantics, not substance. Most of Robertson's and Hayek's objections to Keynes's *Treatise* were theoretically *baseless*. Hicks's later interpretations and the ensuing IS-LM apparatus for *The General Theory*, which became the surrogate for Keynesians new and old, was in fact *antithetical* to Keynes.

After Chapter 1, the book is organized as follows:

Chapter 2, 'Money, price, and interest', puts Keynes's own theory of money in perspective. It is explained how:

1. the controversies about what money is and how money, prices, and interest rates interrelate, which all predate Keynes, are part of the evolution of what divides the Banking from the Currency School;
2. Keynes countered earlier treatments of interest-rate theory, as reflecting the characteristics of money as a commodity, in the tradition of Marshall-Pigou-Fisher;

3. the three characteristics Keynes uniquely attributed to money stem from his novel approach to defining the interest rate in *The General Theory*. Through Keynes's attempt to show that the special characteristics of money set it apart from commodities, it is revealed that these ideas exposed in *The General Theory* link it back directly to the *Treatise*.

Both Chapters 3 and 4 are devoted entirely to the dissection of the semantics and the theory behind the Fundamental Equations of *A Treatise on Money*.

Chapter 3, 'Keynes's semantic shifts', is directed to his contemporaries' objections to the use of terms and concepts, such as money, income, investment and saving, profits, and capital, found in the *Treatise*.

1. It is devoted to a discussion of the disagreement over semantics and a justification for rejecting Hayek's and Robertson's criticisms of the *Treatise* as baseless.
2. It explains that, while Keynes's concepts share some affinity with Wicksell's, the two authors are diametrically opposed in terms of their theories and policies.
3. The chapter develops into a full exposition of Keynes's macroeconomic model deriving from his Fundamental Equations, encapsulating both his monetary theory, from Chapter 2, and his capital theory, newly presented.

In Chapter 4, 'Keynes's theoretical shift', Hayek's Austrian period-of-production theory is spelled out and contrasted to Keynes's capital theory of the *Treatise*. It is shown that Keynes and Hayek started from different premises, but that:

1. they both developed a trade-cycle theory. Both analysed the real economy as having virtually the same structure of production, Hayek seeing that process as horizontal; Keynes, as vertical;
2. here again they differed dramatically on the notion of money itself and the impact of monetary policy, for example, on what would result from a policy of manipulating the money supply.

The ambitious objectives of Chapter 5, 'Keynes's causal relations', are multiple. It sets out:

1. to show that Keynes's two works, the *Treatise* and *The General Theory*, are intimately connected, that there is in fact a traceable,

straight line of development in Keynes's theoretical analysis from the *Treatise* to *The General Theory*, with the Fundamental Equations extending their use into *The General Theory* (with a slight modification in formulation, but with components comprising the same type of variables), and further, that the concluding chapters of *The General Theory* hark back directly to the business-cycle concerns of *A Treatise* to form a generalized General Theory;

2. to demonstrate where Hicks's conception of *The General Theory* went astray and to explain why his assessment of Keynes is, at best, simply a misrepresentation, at worst, a wrong analysis. Hicks's assessment of Keynes's *General Theory*, which led to the IS-LM model, is shown to be both classic and theoretically antithetical to Keynes.

By Chapter 6, 'Inflation/Deflation and the policy of the general *General Theory*', the last chapter in the book, Keynes's contribution to the analysis of inflation and deflation can be read as deriving from the combination of his ideas in the *Treatise* and *The General Theory*, thus from the perspective of Keynes's generalized General Theory. It is demonstrated throughout this book that the Fundamental Equations, so crucial to the *Treatise*, are also critical to *The General Theory*. Further, it will have already been shown in Chapter 5 that the Fundamental Equations extended their use into *The General Theory*.

1. It is recognized as true that discussion of inflation is found in much more detail in the *Treatise* than in the first four books of *The General Theory*, but it is asserted now that Keynes's earlier work is taken as their backbone and Chapter 21 as their distillate.
2. It is illustrated how, in terms of policy, stabilizing the currency was not Keynes's target as it had been Wicksell's.
3. Analysis of inflation and deflation stems from the Fundamental Equations of the *Treatise*, already introduced in Chapter 4, in which decomposition of the price-level is shown to lead to changes in profits, income, wages, and the prices of capital, commodities, and raw materials.
4. In Chapter 6, in light of the EC-SP model, the various inflations and deflations in the dynamics of Keynes's credit cycle are analysed as deriving from the components of the Fundamental Equations.

The Appendix, 'False novelties', addressed to those interested in the development of economic ideas and premises, is a synopsis or an attempt to identify and highlight what makes Keynes's theory unique and accessible. It provides:

1. a bare-bones list of various characteristics and theoretical premises that make Keynes's theory distinct from those of the neoClassical and Classical schools;
2. his original perspective on the distribution of income, an aspect of Keynes not usually described as novel. Keynes sympathized with the approach of the Classicals, but had his own theory of income distribution in which a mechanism permits the economy to be brought pre-emptively to a 'near-full' employment equilibrium.

In conclusion, it is maintained that Keynes provided a complete set of macroeconomic relations and the ingredients of a new theoretical model, much more reflective of and analytically appropriate to the corporate world of the twenty-first century, than those on which current macroeconomics is based. Keynes ought no longer to be encapsulated in the IS-LM, which is damaging at present, witness the responses of Keynesianism to the crisis of 2008. Presented in this book are the premises of Keynes's contribution. Current macroeconomics needs a new generation of economists to readdress his ideas and orient the discipline in a new direction.

NOTES

1. In *The Keynesian Revolution* (1966), Klein, on the opening page, asserts boldly 'Keynes was always a classical economist.'
2. Contrast Klein's assertion that Keynes accepted Schumpeter's position on technological change without reservation (1966, p. 16) with Keynes's own statement on fixed capital in *A Treatise on Money* (1930, II, p. 100). Also, as will be shown here further on, Klein's claim that Keynes intended to keep prices stable and his bold statement that 'the fundamental equations were not the essential contribution' of the *Treatise* (1966, p. 17) are both indications that Klein missed the point.
3. Cited by Clarke (1988), p. 256.

1 The financial crisis of 2008 and the unKeynesian Keynes

Resurgence of the name of Keynes has never caught more attention among journalists and politicians nor provoked such debate worldwide than since the start of the current financial crisis. What is presumed under the name of Keynes is, however, in fact Keynesianism – in sum, government interventionism in the form of three policies, all geared to promote consumerism in order to sustain employment: (1) there must be aggregate Demand management; (2) monetary and fiscal policies should be used to sustain Demand; (3) High Demand must be achieved, even if it means Budget Deficits. There is so much written about Keynes that one would have thought everything about his theory would be known by now. Ongoing economic policy controversies attest, however, to the contrary.

Keynes was indeed an extremely prolific writer and a fierce debater whose use of the language presented the world with many quotable quips. If one leaves, however, his analogies, cynical twists, and self-deprecating humour to the cartoonists, and focuses on a thorough reading of the core of his theory, as found in *A Treatise on Money* and *The General Theory*, one would find that no part of the triad above resembles what Keynes's theory proposed. Keynesianism itself is a product of neoClassical economics of whose very foundation Keynes was critical. Keynesianism old and new would have been an anathema to Keynes. A return to the theory of Keynes himself would set remedies to the 2008 economic crisis in a different light.

Economists have recently pointed quite correctly to indebtedness as the cause of the 2008 crisis. For example, Harvard professor Niall Ferguson gave a good account, in the London *Financial Times* on December 19, 2008, 'The age of obligation', of the enormity of the size and significance of current debt. Dominant macroeconomic theory does not, however, have appropriate policy recommendations to address curing the problem. In its extreme form, the Chicago School, it is offering nothing but a hands-off attitude. In its interventionist form, the Keynesian approach (alien to Keynes), it proposes badly conceived policies, which might aggravate the problem of debt. Massive amounts of taxpayers' money are being allocated to government spending. The consequences of the economic policies ensuing from present macroeconomic theory, many taken in the name of

11

Keynes, pose serious potential danger to the very foundation of the free-market economy he had at heart.

While corrective monetary and fiscal policies are features in both Keynesianism and Keynes's theory, they are applied through two fundamentally different models and yield entirely different analyses and consequences. The approach taken by the US Federal Reserve System under Ben Bernanke, a representative Keynesian, is one in which fiscal policy is subjugated to monetary policy and monetary policy itself is constrained by the objective of containing inflation. Inflation of the general level of price was not an issue for Keynes. Using fiscal and monetary policies to adjust an economy's sub-inflationary and sub-deflationary pressures was instead the key to Keynes's theory. In Keynes, monetary and fiscal policies are intertwined, and, for him cyclical fluctuations are by definition a reallocation of resources. For Keynes a permanent feature of the economics of cyclical fluctuation was to rebalance the variety of inflations and deflations, to readjust employment and income redistribution.

The remainder of this book will embark on an in-depth analysis of when, why, and how Keynes's theory was derailed and an explanation of the ways in which the IS-LM model, the core of neoClassical theory, is an anathema to Keynes's EC-SP model, reconstructed from the *Treatise* and *The General Theory*. It has been deemed helpful, however, in this first chapter to explore some differences and similarities in the economic settings, and social and political environments of the two acute financial crises of interest: Keynes's of the early 1930s and ours of 2008–9. In both instances, (1) economists were caught by surprise, (2) the collapse in the market economies was precipitated by a financial crisis which quickly spread internationally into industrial sectors, (3) bleak economic prospects engendered social fear and political instability, and an appeal to government for help, and (4) the responses providing ideas about economic policy remedies came mostly from Cambridge and London then and from Cambridge and Washington now. In this first chapter, the contrast between the impacts of monetary and fiscal policies as they derive from the Aggregate Demand of the Keynesian IS-LM model and from the Effective Demand of Keynes's EC-SP model is introduced to shed light on their relative appropriateness as tools to reveal the remedy of the current crisis.

1.1   SIMILARITIES BETWEEN THE CRISES' CONTEXTS: 1930s AND 2008–9

Of course, the economic world of the 1930s was structurally different from that of the early 2000s. Knowledge, especially that derived from gathering data about how markets function, has grown enormously. Relegating the study of the economy to its various component, independent micro- or sector markets, macroeconomics post-World War II has in fact produced very little in-depth, comprehensive analysis. In many respects, the fundamental premises, about what drives economic agents, whether speculators, entrepreneurs, or workers, continue to be the same, based on the simple rule of cost–benefit analysis whose measuring stick is price. Individual prices themselves are simply an outcome of demand and supply analysis. The presuppositions about 'market force' resource allocation, in terms of efficiency and equity, are also still the same. The questions of yesterday about production (how and what to produce) and distribution (who should get what) are the questions of today and will remain acute. Controversies about what ought to or should be are still what drive the policies.

Today's theoretical models should encompass those of yesterday. If in principle, there has been advancement and accumulation of theoretical as well as empirical knowledge, why would one bother with an author of the past, like Keynes? Has there, however, been any advance? It seems, historically at least, that, instead of building from era to era, in economics, it takes crisis points to create progress, to shake up the discipline and make economists pause and rethink their theories.

As the joke goes, the financial crisis of 2008 caught economists and analysts by surprise, just as have virtually every fifteen of the ten sudden overturns of the recent past, including the one of 1929. Yet from a glance at any current macroeconomics textbook, used in teaching and consequently in macroeconomic policy advising, one is amazed by the confidence of macroeconomists in their model's ability to explain and predict the course of economic events. By 'predicting', macroeconomists really only mean, however, that a model does well on the whole in tracing the path from the past into current events. When an acute economic crisis, such as that of 2008, strikes and the evidence shows that something has gone wrong in the functioning of the economy, a form of quick explanation is provided. Take, for example, the explanation by Edmund Phelps (*Financial Times*, November 5, 2008, 'Keynes had no sure cure for slumps'): speculators anticipated poorly one market, that of housing, thus '[T]he prime cause was [their] forecasting with badly mistaken models'.

The main 'predictive' model of present macroeconomics is made up of two constituents: a policy-making institution, understood to be Government (Big Brother, acting for good or ill) and the Economy, whose market structure is premised on rational behaviour by hedonistic *homines economici* (consumers and producers). Macroeconomic analysis seems to focus primarily on the impact of Government policy on the course of the

Economy, and it is as if Government is the main player and the spoiler or stabilizer of economic activity, depending on whether seen through the eyes of monetarists or Keynesians. Keynesians, advocating that government has some role to play in circumstances such as the crisis of 2008, draw their policies from a basic form of the macro-model found in virtually any macroeconomics textbook today. In one text in particular, by Olivier Blanchard (2005), the author presents in an epilogue, chapter 27, in less than a dozen pages, the life story of macroeconomics running right up to the current theories of the Real Business Cycle, the New Keynesians, and the New Growth. Blanchard has rendered great service in encapsulating the essence of how the sub-field of macroeconomics evolved from Keynes and divided through neoClassical synthesis and Rational Expectations into the most current developments.

Leaving aside the technical and mechanical complexities of today's macroeconomic models, it does not in fact take more than a few pages to describe the slim advances in any fundamental reshaping of macroeconomics in the 70 years since Keynes. Blanchard concludes his overview with a summary paragraph of beliefs he considers common to all macroeconomists. It is striking what can be inferred from the epilogue:

1. Keynes is in name the resounding reference for virtually all macroeconomists, those both pro- and anti-Keynesianisms.
2. 'Keynesianism' became the legacy of Keynes, seen through Hicks, while 'anti-Keynesianism' became monetarism, the legacy of Hayek.
3. The cast of characters around Keynes at Cambridge and Hayek at the London School of Economics, with Hawtrey at the Treasury, is being echoed by the cast around Samuelson (and his neoClassical Synthesis) at Massachusetts Institute of Technology (MIT) and Friedman and Lucas at Chicago, with now Bernanke at the Federal Reserve.
4. Keynesianism and anti-Keynesianism still have a single preoccupation: does or does not the action of government impact the level of output?

It is undeniable that Keynes is to be credited with steering economics from micro to macro perspectives, at least in that part of economics concerned with employment, inflation, and public finance. Many of his theoretical concepts, such as liquidity preference, marginal efficiency of capital, and marginal propensity to consume, have become the cornerstone of present macroeconomics. Keynes's conceptualization of macroeconomics, from the start, has, however, by now been so corrupted that what is understood as Keynesianism is not to be found in his work.

Well-rounded macroeconomists with keen capabilities of observation and analysis are rare, and their supply has dried up in the last couple of decades. In the last few centuries, the United Kingdom produced three great economists: Adam Smith, David Ricardo, and John Maynard Keynes. All three had a wide and in-depth understanding of the economic, social, and political environment of their world. All three combined a balanced blend of theoretical analysis with pragmatism, whose conclusions provided guidance to those who wished to apply their thinking to socio-economic issues.

In 1776 Adam Smith provided a treatise that became the reference for liberalism. It played a major role in shaping the economic attitudes that jumpstarted the Industrial Revolution. Ricardo and Keynes were successful stock exchange investors, who knew the banking setting of their time inside and out. Both understood the important roles of investment and entrepreneurs in sustaining production and economic growth. Ricardo was concerned by the precariousness of the entrepreneur's profits, squeezed by both rising rent-seeking and wage bill increases under Malthusian population pressure.

Ricardo's awareness and insight derived in part from his having lived amid the technological inventions and innovations and introduction of machinery at the turn of the nineteenth century. It provided him with a rather optimistic perspective on periodic productivity bursts, which elevate profits. Although preoccupied with the survival of the entrepreneur under the law of diminishing profit, Ricardo was nonetheless not terribly concerned by its dire implications. The Industrial Revolution, free and unregulated in its golden era, created huge prosperity.

The Industrial Revolution led as well to extreme disparities. Given the burdens imposed on the working class, it did not take much for socialist ideas to mature. Soon after Ricardo's death, his labour theory of value, in the hands of Marx, produced a serious rival doctrine to the liberal ideas of Smith that were to become the cornerstone of neoClassical economics.

Thus, by the 1930s, two rival economic doctrines, stemming from Smith and Ricardo, were well entrenched in their camps. Appeal for, and experience with, central planning began to be put into application in Russia. Political turmoil and bleak economic prospects in Europe rendered the social fabric fragile and amenable to doctrinal manipulation, whether fascist or socialist. Keynes, who was part of the privy political circle of the English senior civil servants and a Cambridge academic, a student of Alfred Marshall, was well placed and well trained to observe the dynamics of the economics and politics of his time and the danger of instability. A firm believer in individual and market freedoms, he was persuaded that safeguarding economic prosperity and relatively fair income equality was the only way to prevent an economy from swinging to either of the political extremes.

Keynes, while writing *A Treatise on Money* (1930), was already convinced that the dominant economics, that of Marshall and Pigou, was ill conceived for a monetary, entrepreneurial economy of the twentieth century and that it needed rethinking. Just as for Ricardo, for Keynes, in a true free-market monetary economy, the role of the entrepreneur is central to production, employment, and growth. It is the entrepreneurs who run the show; they decide production, and thus employment and wages. Also, for both, profits, an essential incentive, motivating production and competition, are constantly liable to cost squeeze from rents and the wage bill. For Ricardo, capital was still Land, which was scarce, and thus, in the early nineteenth century there was little one could do to lower rent.

What does the analysis of past economists have to do with the current crisis? Keynes came to realize that from the time of Ricardo to his own, capitalism had evolved. In the world of the first quarter of the twentieth century, although scarcity of Land as capital was no longer the issue, scarcity of the new form of capital, finance or money, was. Vital to production, money capital in the hands of rentiers could still demand higher returns when scarce. For Keynes, however, the scarcity of capital could be circumvented, and thus, economic prosperity and stability meant making financing so available that its returns could not squeeze the profits of the entrepreneurs very much and its availability would let production expand to the point of near to full employment.

Just as Keynes sought to avoid the potential squeeze on production from scarcity of capital, so too did he address the potential squeeze from the side of labour. As long as an economy is not at the level of full employment, he asserted, labour has little or no leverage on wages *per se*. Thus, although market competition can make wages rise in an economic upswing, since wage inflation is only to be feared when an economy reaches full employment, Keynes advocated just under full employment. This would avoid what he termed 'true inflation', inflation that includes the sub-inflation of wages. Keynes's type of economy would provide then a double achievement: employment and the more equitable distribution of income among investors, entrepreneurs, and workers.

A casual reading of *The General Theory* has led to the conclusion that the main concern of Keynes was how to get an economy out of the slump, but Keynes's economics actually provided a blueprint for a general *General Theory* which could address the problematic circumstances at any phase of the business cycle. His work reveals in fact that his true concern was how to keep an economy from sliding into rather than having to climb out of a slump. Keynes's general *General Theory* is articulated around three main relationships: investment (marginal efficiency of capital), consumption (marginal propensity to consume), and finance (liquidity preference). Correspondingly, it features three sets of players: two active economic agents, the financiers (banks, speculators, traders, and shareholders) and the entrepreneurs (firms and producers), and the passive player, labour.

1.2 MANAGEMENT STRATEGIES: AGGREGATE DEMAND VS EFFECTIVE DEMAND

It will be explained in Chapter 5 how Keynes's *General Theory* was misinterpreted by Hicks to become summed up in the IS-LM model. For now the results of this transformation, running from the hands of Alan Hansen through all following generations of Keynesians, are depicted in Figure 1.1(a), with the Aggregate Demand (**AD**) and Aggregate Supply (**AS**) curves as the focal points. Both curves relate the general level of price, **P** to the national production or gross domestic product (GDP), **Y**. One of the fundamental characteristics of the Keynesian model is the dichotomy it establishes between the two aggregates. Money, consumption, and investment (the elements of Keynes's liquidity preference, marginal propensity to consume, and marginal efficiency of capital) are all built into the Keynesian **AD**, leaving **AS** to be derived entirely from cost factors and technology.

Consequently any Keynesian monetary or fiscal policy filters its impact through **AD**, which thereby impacts the level of price. The effect will not impact **AS**, regardless of whether one assumes a Keynesian or a monetarist posture toward money. Assuming money as a neutral medium of exchange in the model means that the role of finance and financiers

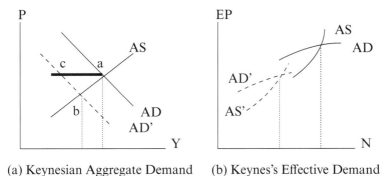

(a) Keynesian Aggregate Demand   (b) Keynes's Effective Demand

Figure 1.1   The distortion of Keynes's aggregates

becomes benign, an assumption of which Keynes was vehemently critical. Extreme forms of neoClassical economics assume **AS** to be vertical and any upward manipulation of demand, ineffective and inflationary.

Keynes, for his part, did not conceive his model in terms of an interaction between the desires of those who demand goods and services, and those who supply them. His macroeconomic analysis was instead entirely focused on business behaviour and the viability of investment. It is the firms who decide what amount of labour to hire and what they require in terms of finances. Keynes's curves of the Aggregate Demand, **AD** and the Aggregate Supply, **AS** relate expected revenue (or proceeds) to the level of employment.

As Keynes conceived his model (Figure 1.1(b)), in order to produce, firms take into account the availability and costs of finance and labour. If firms expect to increase employment, their need for finance rises and so do their costs, yielding the **AS** curve. The **AD** curve, on the other hand, expresses the firms' expected revenue from selling their products if they were to hire a certain amount of labour. Firms will continue to hire labour so long as their expected revenues exceed their costs, that is, up to the point where the two curves meet. This intersection or equilibrium Keynes termed the Effective Demand.

Improvement of employment was the central concern of Keynes. In a market economy, that goal can only be achieved through the active participation of businesses whose operations are viable. Investment and profits were thus for Keynes the fundamental variables for expanding production and employment. His monetary and fiscal policies were targeted to improve both productive investment and profits. Unlike the Keynesian model, in Keynes's theory, both **AS** and **AD** are simultaneously affected by monetary and fiscal policies.

The theories of the Keynesians and of Keynes are fundamentally different, and the targets their policies aim to reach are also different. The 2008 financial crisis can illustrate the different approaches, just as it has allowed the neoClassical approach to be expressed. To start it might be said that neither perspective would accept Phelps's curious account that the financial crisis was caused by an overreaction in a specific market, which led merely to a localized bubble, nor the implication that in time the market will correct itself. Phelps's equating millions of ordinary homebuyers with speculators, seeing the crisis as an imperfection in a particular market, and presuming that the market will come around again, while it has done little to comfort the many small investors and pensioners who have now lost their life savings and the thousands who have lost their employment, not to mention the politicians, journalists, and others who look to economists for guidance, may have done its part to fuel the modest frenzy for alternate responses. Phelps's subsequent redirecting of the subject of the crisis to target Keynes is, however, once again a sign of the blurring of the important distinctions here under clarification.

Keynesians would explain the current credit crunch as a reduction of liquidity, which led to the collapse of Aggregate Demand and thus to a reduction in both GDP and employment. Since the economy's overall price level has not changed much, it means, turning back to Figure 1.1(a), that **AD** must have shifted to the left and that the intersection of **AS** and **AD** remains at the same level of price, at point C. The costs of production have also not increased, which otherwise would cause **AS** to shift backward. The only possible explanation consistent with what is happening (loss of liquidity yet no price change) is that the **AS** curve to the left of the **AD** curve has become horizontal, which mirrors the flat part of the demand-for-money curve. Furthermore, since the policy of interest rate reduction is not proving effective, there is the suggestion that the economy is in a liquidity trap.

In Keynes's theory, shrinking credit means less finance available for the running operations of firms. At the same time, firms suffer a collapse of their marginal efficiency of capital and lower expected returns from smaller projected investment due to scarce financing, despite the government's policy of bringing the interest rate down. Thus in Figure 1.1(b), both the **AS** and **AD** curves shift as shown.

From Figure 1.1(a) and 1.1(b), it is clear that the Keynesian theory and Keynes's own are conceived from two entirely different perspectives. It is thus also the case that their policy prescriptions for how to bring the economy back to its level prior to the 2008 economic crisis are not the same. What mechanism does each approach suggest would allow for a positive reversal?

For Keynesians, the economy is *demand driven*, in the sense that markets react to the desires of the components of Aggregate Demand, which include consumption, investment, and government and (net) foreign goods and services. Monetary and fiscal policies consist thus in causing shifts in Aggregate Demand through impacts on its components. If there is a collapse in the consumption component and inventories are piling up, then the remedy for Keynesians is to look to Government spending as the way to increase Aggregate Demand.

Keynes was instead a *supply theorist*, in the sense that for him the economy is production driven. It is the producers or entrepreneurs who decide how much to invest, given the cost of finance and the amount they expect to sell if they employ a certain amount of labour. Keynes's monetary and fiscal policies, which consist in managing Effective Demand, are directed exclusively toward rendering business in general viable by channelling money to firms. Keynes's emphasis on the role of banking and credit in sustaining economic activity yielded a unique liquidity theory; he showed how shifts in financial assets, due to excessive bullishness and bearishness, cause economic instability and potentially violent fluctuations.

Keynes made an important qualification of entrepreneurial investment, which has gone completely unnoticed. Entrepreneurial 'consumption', **AS**, was for Keynes only 'productive' if linked to investment in working capital and thus employment; otherwise he considered it 'unproductive', as associated predominantly with investment in fixed capital. Keynes thus closely linked the fraction of the entrepreneurs' expected generated income devoted to employment to anticipated consumption by labour. That consumer consumption, in **AD**, is what is taken by entrepreneurs as an indication of spending/savings and hence as a signal for investment. Keynes's Aggregate Supply is thus intimately connected to Aggregate Demand, and thus Effective Demand.

There are many aspects of the Keynesian approach that do not derive from Keynes. Two have been noted thus far. (1) Advocacy of Government spending as the way to increase Aggregate Demand was one of them. Nowhere in the *Treatise* or in *The General Theory* did Keynes explicitly include government spending in any of his variables. (2) In the Keynesian demand-driven economy, Aggregate Demand reflects consumer preferences, while Aggregate Supply indicates the willingness to work rather than to be at leisure. The two aggregates are assumed to be independent, the only economic agents in the picture are the same rabbits, which wear the consumer hat when they pop out on the Demand side and the producer hat when they stick their heads out on the Supply side. Such a dichotomizing of the aggregates is alien to Keynes.

A third aspect is revealed in the pragmatic implications of the two approaches. Bernanke, in his Stamp Lecture at the London School of Economics (January 13, 2009) affirmed that the current crisis, whose cause lay in the credit tied up in the housing market, transcended into other credit markets and broke down the entire lending system. He underlined various policies that the Federal Reserve System (the Fed) has under its jurisdiction to implement: adjustment of the interest rate (exhausted), policy communication, direct liquidity provision to borrowers and investors in the credit market, and purchase of longer term securities. He quickly assured his audience that Inflation is under control and that in fact the Fed's approach is that of 'credit easing' (lowering the quality of purchased securities), instead of 'quantitative easing' (lowering the Central Bank's reserves). Finally he expressed the Fed's willingness to establish a much stronger supervisory and regulatory system. As far as the US

Government's fiscal policy, without rejecting it, he noted that it is has to be left to the legislators and that at best it can only be part of the short-term answer to the current problems.

Developing stimulus policies that are not inflationary, as has been pursued by central banks, is not consistent with Keynes's theory. For him, creating employment is the prime objective, and if and when stimulus is needed, it must come through production in the form of productive investment. In any economy there is only one interest rate. Its monetary authority cannot devise various interest rates to be applied depending on the needs and objectives at the same time in different industries or different sectors, or for external or domestic purposes. Advocating stabilization of the currency and hence of the price level, as Wicksell did or as is now the practice of the central banks, is thus very constraining.

There is no doubt that resolution of the crisis of 2008–9 requires some action, but the issue is what kind of action. Bernanke's talk aimed to summarize the Fed's response to the crisis. While it is certainly not the Chicago approach, it is to a large extent very consistent with Keynesian policies. It seems that rescuing part of the financial industry, which has been in need of restructuring for a while, is what is getting the attention. From the perspective of Keynes's theory, it is, however, the production industry (the creators of added value) that should be the focus. It is curious that at a time when there is idle and ample liquidity, there are massive cutbacks in much needed production and employment.

Using fiscal and monetary policies to adjust the various Inflations and Deflations is key to Keynes's theory. Unlike the approach underlined by Bernanke, where fiscal policy is subjugated to monetary policy and monetary policy itself is constrained by the objective of containing inflation, in Keynes the two policies are intertwined and inflation of the general level of price in itself is not an issue. The interest rate, in many circumstances not sufficient on its own to achieve the desired level of economic activity, is, however, only one policy tool. Keynes, in the *Treatise*, showed that the overall price does not reveal much and in fact can be very misleading, unless it is decomposed into its various components. Keeping the general level of price constant does not guarantee that its components will remain unchanged.

When, however, the general price level is decomposed into the various Inflations and Deflations (commodity, wage, capital, and profit), changes of relative prices and earnings (or relative purchasing power) are revealed to be occurring at every phase of the cycle across an economy, where different varieties of Inflation or Deflation run ahead or behind one another, offsetting one another or accumulating to create acceleration or deceleration in economic activity. An important and unexploited characteristic of

Keynes's theory is that for him cyclical fluctuations are a reallocation of resources, whether through shifts in the factors of production from one sector to another, in financial liquidities from one form of asset to another, and/or in the level and/or composition of output. There is bound to be movement in prices corresponding to these reallocations causing a variety of Inflations and Deflations, which can result in a Slump, Stagflation or True Inflationary phase of the credit cycle. Even at the extreme highs and lows of the cycle, Inflations will coexist with Deflations.

For Keynes, rebalancing the components of the overall price is the objective of policies to keep the economy at a satisfactory level of employment and to provide a balance in the relative share of earnings between financiers, entrepreneurs, and labour. Profits, in the sense of earnings, are fundamental to the workings of a market economy. Not *the end* in themselves, they are instead *the means* by which to achieve and sustain employment. Thus, depending on the state of the economy, incentives and deterrents in the form of subsidies and taxes ought to be applied to profits, capital, commodities, and wages, respectively and differently in different industries and sectors, all with the objective of encouraging productive investment and sustained employment.

In the production-driven economy of Keynes's era, the chain of causation, or the way the economy functioned, was the following. From the use of given resources and available credit, production and employment ensued. They generated income that would finally be spent for consumption. Credit was mainly geared to investment in production. It allowed for spending on equipment and resources before production and on some expenses during the process.

In monetary, entrepreneurial economies, like the ones in which the developed world is functioning, finance is still vital to the production of commodities and services and to the generation of employment. For Keynes, money, particularly as credit, was not, however, the same as any other commodity or service. It has special characteristics. Being neither productive nor consumable, it does not produce added value or employment. Its prime purpose is to facilitate exchange and production. As a public good that could be produced *ad infinitum* at almost no cost, money, particularly as credit, must be managed.

From Keynes's perspective, if money, and hence the financial industry, does not itself create any added value, within the economy as a whole, the earnings of the financial sector derive ultimately from a share of the added value generated by production. The greater the size of and collusion within the financial industry, relative to that of the production sector, the more likely will be the pressure from the former to squeeze more 'rent' out of entrepreneurs' profits. Aligning the financial industry to the needs of production, while imperative, does not require State takeover but simply the reintroduction of strict regulations. A clear distinction has to be maintained between the counterbalancing functions of the banking system (the commercial and the central banks) and of the financial institutions. While it is understood that within the banking system commercial banks are private, under the direct supervisory umbrella of the Central Bank, credit can be controlled, and financial institutions for their part, if operating in separate fields of specialization, can be efficient sources of credit allocation.

The most recent new phenomenon to affect the way a monetary, entrepreneurial economy functions has been the explosion of credit for consumption. When an economy's demand for credit is high, it becomes profitable and attractive to lenders. What better way to let the supply of desired credit grow and competition among lenders flourish than to deregulate the financial market? Indeed, the neoClassical economists' policy response since the early 1980s was (1) to allow all players in the financial industry – the commercial banks and near banks, the insurance and mortgage companies, the trust and pension funds, and so on – to enter and operate in any of the others' specialized areas, (2) to relax the reserve requirements of the banks, and (3) to let new players emerge to offer credit in their own markets for automobiles, retail purchases, travel, and so on. As in any crowded market, in the fast-growing financial industry, the companies, all striving to make money from lending money, faced stiff competition from one another, so much so that the relaxation of qualification requirements for loans, and concentration and takeover became the routes many resorted to in order to get control of more market share.

In the present demand-driven economy, economic attitudes and the causal ways in which the economy functions are thus to some extent quite different from those in the time of Keynes. With credit for consumption not only easily obtainable but with reminders of its availability all too frequently provided through telemarketing, display advertising, and credit-card enticements, the temptation to use it – to 'buy now, pay later' – is there. In the neoClassical world of Rational Expectations, consumer credit seemed magically to permit everyone to get all they wanted when they wanted it. With plenty of available consumer credit, a significant portion of consumption spending has, however, now come to precede the receipt of the income that is expected to be generated by future production. Yet credit is no more without cost now than it ever was and, like other commodities or services, its price is the result of demand and supply.

The financial sector's expansion of credit to consumption has affected dramatically the entrepreneurial economy in less than obvious, pass-through ways. Within the new causal chain is the added cost to the consumer of the interest or rent on spending with credit. Thus, although credit to consumers stimulates demand, it erodes domestic savings through committed spending. The necessary backing for consumer credit, which domestic savings cannot cover, was derived partly from fictitious insurances and partly from inflows of international capital (witness the consistent US balance-of-payment deficits). Much of current developed-world demand for mass-consumption goods has been satisfied through trade deficits with low-wage economies.

Tremendous pressure on profits in a production industry unable to compete with the low-wage economies has pushed it to find ways of producing more quantity more cheaply. Entrepreneurs have turned to investment in fixed capital (Keynes's unproductive consumption) and are participating thus in the erosion of employment in favour of more capital-intensive technologies. According to Smith and Ricardo, in the world of comparative advantages, eventually the lower wages will rise and the terms of trade will reverse themselves. From a more pragmatic perspective, however, if low-wage economies prefer to freeride on the more advanced nations' development of capital-intensive technologies and after adopting them, sustain downward pressure on the wages of their own labourers, even as international growth in goods and services continues, the whole world will be caught in an 'unemployment trap'. Expansionary policies of easing credit to mass consumption may end up in these circumstances diminishing the disparities among nations, and yet at the same time, this is likely to occur at the expense of increased disparities within countries.

The relationship whereby consumption depended on income, as in Keynes's theory, has thus now been reversed, such that income depends on consumption. Loans for consumption, determined by the financial industry, had come to be based on the assumption that future economic production would generate sufficient employment and hence income to repay the loans. With the crisis of 2008, the burden of these loans has, however, been shifted from private debt into taxpayer debt. As per the Fed's policy response, the bulk of its money is not aids to fine-tuning the production economy but was earmarked as financial industry bailouts. As the money is released, some of it might filter to the production industry, but it remains to be seen how much will be spent in the domestic realm, and how much will become productive and how much unproductive investment. Furthermore, there is risk that some of it may vanish completely in speculation, as occurred during the 2008 crisis.

One final comment is in order. Even if the sequence of events leading up to the respective financial crises has not been the same, there are similarities between Keynes's world of the 1930s and ours. One in particular is the presence of fear about a bleak economic future. The social fabric is again amenable to political doctrinal manipulation. The fear infecting the market is transforming itself into a fear economy, which has been exacerbated in the post-9/11 era. The production economy, unable to generate sufficient, sustained employment, has been tempted, as a substitute, to resort to creating occupations, services, and gadgets related to security, defence, and protection. While rational and well-thought-out precautions and some safety measures are necessary for a nation's stability and order, overreaction – which leads to the employment of part of society as the watchdog over the other part – entails the potential dangers of eroding the individual freedoms and trust necessary for the functioning of the free-market system. The economy of fear, although it will undoubtedly run its course, might not, in the interim, be all that conducive to redirecting investment and strength into the production side of the economy, the key to resolution of any economic downturn.

Here, then, are just a few thoughts which demonstrate that Keynes's theory, which is different from what it is understood to be, is far from ubiquitous, is still unexploited, and has much to offer.

2 Money, price, and interest

Magnum aliquid est commercium illud reconditum, atque implexum, quo humana Respublica, pecuniae occulto gyro, non secus, ac sanguinis circuitus, florens atque incolumis perpetuo servatur. Sed hujus circuli naturam explorare difficillimum est, nec aliter possumus, nisi quaedam ponantur geometrarum more, ex quibus doctrinae ratio, & rei summa certis limitibus coerceatur. (Ceva 1711)[1]

Il [Locke] a bien senti que l'abondance de l'argent enchérit toute chose, mais il n'a pas recherché comment cela se fait. La grande difficulté de cette recherche consiste à savoir par quelle voie et dans quelle proportion l'augmentation de l'argent hausse le prix des choses. (Cantillon 1755; 1931, p. 161)[2]

For Keynes,[3] money was not just a medium of exchange. It has implicit characteristics that differentiate it from its conception by the quantity theorists to yield the Quantity Theory of Money. In Keynes's model, that theory is described simply as an extreme, special theoretical case of money. The Quantity Theory of Money, as expressed in the equation of exchange, widely used by economists, might, he thought, be a useful tool and classroom device for explaining a fictitious monetary equilibrium in a static state, but in a dynamic theory and in relation to the real world, he felt it did not say much. Fundamentally, the matter turns on two questions, posed in the simplest terms: (1) is there a one-to-one, unique relationship between changes in money and changes in price level and (2) does variation in money filter into the economy through the interest rate to impact the price level, even if without any definite proportionality? From a policy perspective, this controversial issue of the impact of money on prices still remains.

Money is the cornerstone of Keynes's theory. Of all the conceptual controversial issues (for example, value, capital measurement, and invariance), which have absorbed economists over time, the concept of money has proved to be one of the most difficult. Thus, understanding how and by what mechanism money is related to the level of prices is an absolute prerequisite to grasping Keynes's and others' conception of macroeconomic connections between variables, such as employment and unemployment, and production, investment, and savings. The issue of the role of money in exchange actually goes to the core of economics quite generally. Only one subgroup, the Quantity Theorists, seems to have obtained any consensus on the relationship of money quantity and the level of prices.

Some early monetary theorists, for example, Ceva and Cantillon responding to Locke, were perceptive as to the difficulties posed by the analysis of money, particularly regarding transmission of the impact of the amount of money in circulation on the level of prices and any proportional relationship. Ceva felt the circulation of money was mysterious, hidden, and complex and could only be grasped by a methodology that imposed constraints on its analysis. Even before the mid-eighteenth century, the concerns regarding money had already been expressed, as reflected in Cantillon: 'by what route is money channelled?' and 'what is the proportional relationship between the (quantity of) money and the level of prices?' One would think after centuries of searching, analysing, discussing, and arguing the issues that they would have been resolved, but it does not seem to be the case.[4] What was set as the agenda then is still being pursued, for example, into the recent work of Woodford (2003).[5]

Many pre-World War II economists, Fisher, Wicksell, Keynes, Hawtrey, Hayek, and Hicks, among others, were aware of these questions and would echo the same concerns as Ceva, Cantillon, and Locke.[6] The starting point behind their early controversies was disentangling the differences between the Currency and the Banking or Credit Schools. At the heart of the issue, which had originated with the Bullion Controversy of the early nineteenth century, was whether or not paper notes should be freely convertible on demand or, stated differently, whether credit can or cannot be managed. Debate of the theoretical arguments pro and con led to the current formulation of the Quantity Theory of Money. Thus, to begin, a quick look will be taken at what is meant by the Quantity Theory of Money. It will be followed by presentation of different formulations of the Quantity Equation and the many objections to and perceived limitations of the Quantity Theory of Money. Keynes's own position will then be introduced.

2.1 DEFINITIONS

The puzzling inflation of Europe in the mid-sixteenth and seventeenth centuries led some thinkers of that period, like Locke and Petty, to begin to articulate ideas about a correlation between money and prices. David Hume, in his essay, 'On money', which appeared in the mid-eighteenth century, seemed to have attracted the most attention for his description of the impact of money on prices:

though the high price of commodities be a necessary consequence of the encrease of gold and silver, yet it follows not immediately upon that encrease; but some time is required before the money circulates through the whole state, and makes its effect be felt on all ranks of people. At first, no alteration is perceived; by degrees the price rises, first of one commodity, then of another; till the whole at last reaches a just proportion with the new quantity of specie which is in the kingdom. (1752; 2003)

In my opinion, it is only in this interval or intermediate situation, between the acquisition of money and rise of prices, that the encreasing quantity of gold and silver is favourable to industry. When any quantity of money is imported into a nation, it is not at first dispersed into many hands; but is confined to the coffers of a few persons, who immediately seek to employ it to advantage. Here are a set of manufacturers or merchants, . . . (1752; 2003)

These statements by Hume about the effective proportionality between money and price describe a process through time, but became eventually attributed to I. Fisher as the Quantity Theory of Money, and eventually distilled by him into the Fisherian equation. Fisher himself acknowledged, '[T]his theory, though often crudely formulated, has been accepted by Locke, Hume, Adam Smith, Ricardo, Mill, Walker, Marshall, Hadley, Fetter and Kemmerer and most writers on the subject' (1911; 1963, p. 14, fn. 1). While Fisher's algebraic formulation was already to be found in S. Newcomb, Fisher identified Ricardo as the one who 'probably deserves chief credit for launching the theory' (1911; 1963, p. 26). Marget, on the other hand, attributes to Walras the '"equation of exchange" which was in all respects equivalent to equations of the so-called "Fisherian" type' (1931, p. 573).

In a thorough review of the literature on theories of the velocity of circulation, Holtrop (1929) identified, in addition to the English contributors, those of many others including Boisguillebert, Baccaria, DePinto, Busch, Say, and most of the Utopists and Marx. The goal here is not to examine each of these authors, but simply to narrow down the field of economists engaged in the theoretical discussion about money and price to determine what has been understood by the Quantity Equation and to show how, even within the proposed narrow selection of authors, that understanding differs sharply. Although most widely understood as Fisher's equation of the Quantity Theory (Figure 2.1(ii)), in addition to his there were two others: the Cambridge Quantity Equation, credited to Marshall and Pigou[7] (Figure 2.1(i)), and Keynes's Real-Balance Equation (Figure 2.1(iii)). In his *Tract on Monetary Reform*, Keynes suggested a slightly different expression of the Cambridge Quantity Equation, which he called the Real-Balance Quantity Equation, before turning to developing the alternative money equation found in *A Treatise on Money* and *The*

(i) <u>The Cambridge Quantity Equation</u> (Marshall–Pigou)

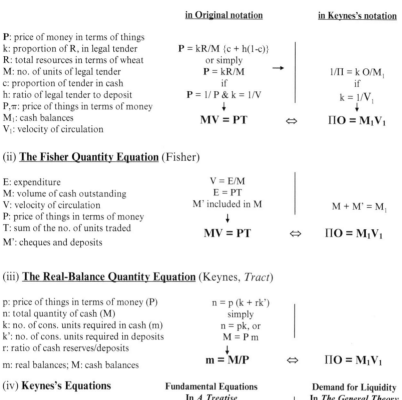

P: price of money in terms of things
k: proportion of R, in legal tender
R: total resources in terms of wheat
M: no. of units of legal tender
c: proportion of tender in cash
h: ratio of legal tender to deposit
P,π: price of things in terms of money
M_1: cash balances
V_1: velocity of circulation

in Original notation

$P = kR/M \{c + h(1\text{-}c)\}$
or simply
$P = kR/M$
if
$P = 1/P$ & $k = 1/V$

$$MV = PT$$

in Keynes's notation

$1/\Pi = k\,O/M_1$
if
$k = 1/V_1$

$\Leftrightarrow$ $\Pi O = M_1 V_1$

(ii) <u>The Fisher Quantity Equation</u> (Fisher)

E: expenditure
M: volume of cash outstanding
V: velocity of circulation
P: price of things in terms of money
T: sum of the no. of units traded
M': cheques and deposits

$V = E/M$
$E = PT$
M' included in M

$$MV = PT$$

$M + M' = M_1$

$\Leftrightarrow$ $\Pi O = M_1 V_1$

(iii) <u>The Real-Balance Quantity Equation</u> (Keynes, *Tract*)

p: price of things in terms of money (P)
n: total quantity of cash (M)
k: no. of cons. units required in cash (m)
k': no. of cons. units required in deposits
r: ratio of cash reserves/deposits

m: real balances; M: cash balances

$n = p\,(k + rk')$
simply
$n = pk$, or
$M = P\,m$

$$m = M/P$$

$\Leftrightarrow$ $\Pi O = M_1 V_1$

(iv) **Keynes's Equations**

Π: price level of output as a whole
E: total money income
O: total output, Y: income
I: investment
S: savings
M_1, L_1: transactional money
$M_2; L_2$: speculative money
r: interest rate

**Fundamental Equations
In *A Treatise***

$E = M_1 V_1$
$\Pi = E/O + (I - S)/O$
$O\Pi = E + (I - S)$
when $I = S$

$$O\Pi = M_1 V_1$$

**Demand for Liquidity
In *The General Theory***

$M = M_1 + M_2$
$M = L_1(Y) + L_2(r)$

$L_1(Y) = Y/V = M_1$
if $Y = OP$ and $M_2 = 0$

$\Leftrightarrow$ $MV = PT$ $\Leftrightarrow$ $OP = M_1 V_1$

Figure 2.1   Alternative Quantity Equations (or equations of exchange)

General Theory. In Figure 2.1 the three Quantity Equations are presented both in their original notation and, in a parallel column for the sake of comparison and discussion, in a translation of them into Keynes's later notation.

2.2   ALTERNATIVE QUANTITY EQUATIONS

Although the observations Hume made in his distillate of the proportional relationship between money and commodity prices were ones asserting that the 'price of commodities [must] be a necessary consequence of the increase of gold and silver' and that over time, with price increases affecting commodity after commodity, there will be 'a just proportion' between money and all prices, such statements were progressively linked to what was to become known as the equation of exchange. That equation is usually recognized in its boldest terms as MV = PT. It has become the basis of the Quantity Theory of Money. One author recently popularized the connection in a story that has become standard in macroeconomics textbooks:

> if T and the equilibrium value of V_T are taken as constants, we arrive at the proposition that the equilibrium price level is determined solely by, and is proportional to, the quantity of money. These further assumptions permit us to translate our identity, the *equation of exchange*, into the *quantity theory of money*, a theory of the determination of the price level which can be written

$$M_S \overline{V}_T = P\overline{T}$$

> with the bars over V and T signifying that they are constants.
> Though not stated as such by Fisher, this is equivalent to the following theory of the money market put in supply and demand terms. (Laidler in his youth, 1977, p. 56, original emphasis)

However, this story does not match the evolution of the attempts after Hume to deal with the relationship between money and prices, and the main goal of the investigation, the price-making process itself. The first set of challenges for the authors to whom Fisher himself eluded, and many others, was to explain the conditions needed to establish the proportionality observed.

Near the turn of the twentieth century, at least three different, important equations of exchange were generated. As far as the Quantity Theory is concerned, it is interpreted through the alternative Quantity Equations in Figure 2.1. They are presented in their original notation and in a parallel column, for the sake of comparison and discussion, translated into Keynes's later notation. For comparison purposes, the various alternative equations in Figure 2.I have been captured in symbolic components of apparently similar expression. In fact, however, embodied in each of them was a quite different perspective on the elements of Hume's description: 'specie', 'quantity of specie', 'price of commodities', 'commodity', and so on.

The Cambridge Quantity Equation

The Cambridge Equation is often referred to as the Marshall–Pigou equation. Although Marshall had written about it as early as 1879,[8] it is its expression found in Pigou's 'The Value of Money' of 1917–18 (p. 165) that is under examination here. This equation P = kR/M (leaving aside the portion of it describing allocations to cash or deposits) expresses the level of price, P, in terms of things or commodities, R: what proportion of wheat produced at t, (kR) is equivalent to a unit of legal tender (M)? In other words, how many bushels of wheat would it take to get one unit of legal tender? (Legal tender is defined by Pigou as coins, notes, and cheques.)

If one considers the inverse corollary of this equation, that is, P = M/kR, the equation then expresses the level of price, P, in terms of money, M: how many units of legal tender does it take to get one bushel of wheat? In other words, what is the volume of legal tender (M), in unit terms, that is equivalent to the proportional amount of wheat available for exchange? It is this inversion of the Cambridge Equation, which, when the proportion k is interpreted as 1/V, something which Pigou himself proposed,[9] can be expressed as the Fisherian equation, MV = PT.

The Cambridge Equation thus starts from the real sector of the economy taking into consideration (1) how much wheat is produced, (2) what proportion of it is allotted to transactions, and (3) how this reflects a commodity supply–demand dynamics. The equation determines the value of the unit of legal tender in terms of the real economy's available bushels of wheat. Its accepted inverse determines the value of the unit of commodity in terms of its price.

The Fisher Quantity Equation

The M in Fisher's equation is defined by him as '*what is generally acceptable in exchange for goods*' (1911; 1963, p. 8, original emphasis). Its distinguishing characteristic is 'its general acceptability', which, reinforced by law, renders it 'legal tender'. Just as for Marshall and Pigou, for Fisher, money (M) in the context of exchange is currency, which includes coins, notes, and cheques. The equation of exchange for Fisher is 'simply the sum of the equations involved in all individual exchanges in a year. In each sale and purchase, the money and goods exchanged are *ipso facto* equivalent' (1911, p. 16, original emphasis).

The equation's algebraic statement derives from the equating of the sums on both sides of the exchange: money and goods. Fisher defines V, the velocity of the circulation of money, as the ratio of E, the total amount of money expended for goods in a given year, over M, the average amount of money in circulation during the same year. On the money side, 'E may be expressed as MV'. The other side of the equation, the goods side, 'consists simply in *adding together the equations for all individual purchases within the community during the year*' (1911, p. 26. original emphasis). That sum in symbols, $\Sigma p^i q^i$, is simplified by Fisher in terms of P and T, where P is the weighted average of all p^is and T, the volume of trade of all q^i transactions.

The equation thus becomes MV = PT. In fact, written in this way, the Fisher Quantity Equation holds only if M is understood to be cash in circulation. The inclusion of cheques or deposits, M' complicates the equation, as it has to take into account a bank reserve requirement, such that the equation becomes MV + M'V' = PT.

The Real-Balance Quantity Equation

Keynes was well acquainted with both versions (i) and (ii) of the Quantity Equation. He read first-hand the account of Fisher's equation of exchange when he reviewed *The Purchasing Power of Money*, in 1911, at the same time as he was beginning to form his own ideas within the Cambridge monetary tradition in which he was immersed.[10] In *A Tract on Monetary Reform* (1923; 1971), he formulated his own exposition of the Quantity Equation following 'the general lines of Professor Pigou' (1923, p. 63, fn. 1) rather than those of Fisher: let k be the consumption units, n, the quantity of money in circulation, and p, the price of each consumption unit (or an 'index number of the cost of living'):

> it follows from the above that $n = pk$. This is the famous quantity theory of money. So long as k remains unchanged, n and p rise and fall together; the greater or the fewer the number of currency notes, the higher or lower is the price level in the same proportion. (1923, p. 63)

When the cash in circulation includes bank deposits k', the 'equation then becomes $n = p(k + rk')$' where r is now some reserve ratio.

Both previous Quantity Equations conceptualize the totality of all exchanges of goods for money, or vice versa, for a given period of time. The causal relations embodied in each are, however, framed slightly differently. Fisher asks, 'what is the purchasing value of a given amount of money in terms of a given volume of transactions?'. For Marshall–Pigou, the question is posed for a given volume of transactions: 'what is its equivalence in terms of the medium of exchange?' In both cases, what is given, as a thing, in the exchange is the equivalent or reflected mirror image of what is received, in terms of something else.

The Marshall–Pigou Quantity Equation monetizes exchanges in the real economy. For Marshall and Pigou, both the value and the quantity of money derive from the quantity and (relative) value of real goods. Theirs is not a monetary economy *per se*; it is consistent with Ricardo's wheat model of the Classical economy. Exchange is expressed first in real terms and money is tagged on (in an equivalence). For Fisher, the existence of money is assumed *a priori*; thus his M is an entity separate from any counterpart. In exchange, M is expressed as an equivalence of real goods.

It is perhaps Fisher's definition of money as something separate from its purchasing power in terms of real goods, which triggered enough interest in Keynes for him to devote several books to the nature and value of money in *A Treatise on Money*. Sometime between the writing of the *Tract* and *A Treatise on Money*, Keynes came to realize that the relation between price and money cannot be explained simply by the components of the Quantity Equations (Figure 2.1(i), (ii), or (iii)). On the one hand, the definition and creation of money had to be looked at in an entirely different perspective from the simple, broad assertion that M is currency in circulation. On the other hand, Keynes felt strongly that the interest rate, albeit recognized by Fisher, was an important missing variable in the equations of his 'price-making process'. In the *Treatise*, through the Fundamental Equations, Keynes thus introduced a new approach to capturing the relationship between prices and money.

In chapter 14, Book III of volume I of the *Treatise*, Keynes describes analytically his turning from his early Quantity Equation of the *Tract* (Figure 2.1(iii)), to Fisher's equation, and then to his own Fundamental Equations (Figure 2.1(iv)). It is interesting to note that while, at the outset, Fisher defined money in the most general terms, as what is acceptable in exchange, he quickly directed the reader to A.P. Andrew for a more nuanced definition of money.[11] Keynes, for his part, started with Knapp's concepts of state money (Figures 2.2 and 2.3), and after elaborating them, stated his own understanding of money (as will be discussed in Section 2.4).

> Formerly I was attracted by this [Fisher's] line of approach. But it now seems to me that the merging together of all the different sorts of transactions – income, business and financial – which may be taking place only causes confusion, and that we cannot get any real insight into the price-making process without bringing in the rate of interest and the distinctions between incomes and profits and between savings and investment. (1930, I, p. 229)

The Equation of Exchange Derived from the Fundamental Equations and the Demand for Liquidity Equation

In Keynes's (Fundamental) Overall Price Equation,

$$\Pi = E/O + (I - S)/O \qquad (2.1)$$

the level of Price, Π is determined by two factors: (1) cost of production, expressed as an average, E/O, earnings per unit of output, where E is earnings, but also, as in Fisher, corresponds to expenditure, and O is output, and (2) windfall profits per unit of output, expressed as $(I - S)/O$, where I is investment and S is savings. When $I = S$, and when earnings are expressed in money, then

$$O\Pi = E = M_I V_I \qquad (2.2)$$

Keynes took this formulation (Figure 2.1(iv)) to be equivalent to the Fisher Quantity Equation (1930, p. 150) (Figure 2.1(ii), in Keynes's notation). In *The General Theory*, Keynes redefined M, the amount of money held by individuals, to be made up of M_1, the amount of money needed for transaction purposes, and M_2, the amount needed for speculative purposes. While M_1 depends on the level of income, Y, M_2 depends on the interest rate, r.

In his formulation in *The General Theory* (1936, p. 199), Keynes's money equation is:

$$M = M_I + M_2 = L_I(Y) + L_2(r) \qquad (2.3)$$

When $M_2 = 0$, $Y/M = V$, and $Y = OP$, where P is now the level of Price, then Keynes's equation of the demand for liquidity, M, becomes $OP = MV$ (Figure 2.1(iv)), which, as in the *Treatise*, Keynes notes as being equivalent to Fisher's equation (1936, p. 209).

Keynes's Fundamental Overall Price Equation of *A Treatise* and his total Demand for Liquidity Equation of *The General Theory* share thus symbols similar to those of the other Quantity Equations of Figure 2.1. Clarification of what is meant by the 'Quantity Theory of Money' is now sought. First and foremost to be stated is that the Quantity Theory is *not* synonymous with the Quantity Equation. What is, however, of intriguing interest here is that across the broad spectrum of pre-World War II monetary theorists, with very differing views, including Wicksell, Fisher, Hayek, and Keynes, what Harrod referred to as the 'essence' of the Quantity Theory, 'that the value of *P* is the resultant of changes in *M*' (1969, p. 160), seemed worthy of acknowledgement.

Perhaps not surprisingly, the essential aspects of the Quantity Theory were laid out explicitly in the writings of the theorist most closely associated with the Money Equation, Irving Fisher. Witness:

The so-called 'quantity theory of money,' *i.e.* that prices vary proportionately to money, . . . is correct in the sense that the level of prices varies directly with the quantity of money in circulation. (1911; 1963, p. 14) the price level varies [in the equation of exchange] (1) directly as the quantity of money in circulation (*M*), (2) directly as the velocity of its circulation (*V*), (3) inversely as the volume of trade done by it (*T*). *The first of these relations is the most important. It constitutes the 'quantity theory of money'.* (emphasis added, 1911; 1963, p. 29)

Also near the turn of the twentieth century, another influential monetary theorist, Knut Wicksell, concerned by looming deflation, explored possible theoretical correlations between prices and money. In the author's preface of 1898 with which he introduced his *Geldzins und Güterpreisen*, translated later, in 1936, into English as *Interest and Prices*, Wicksell affirmed that 'The Quantity Theory is correct in so far as it is true that an increase or relative diminution in the stock of money must always *tend* to raise or lower prices' (1936, p. xxviii, original emphasis). He slightly modified his reason for its 'correctness' by the time he reached chapter 5 of the work, 'The Quantity Theory and its opponents' (1936, pp. 41–2, emphasis added): 'The Theory provides a real explanation of its subject matter, and in a manner that is *logically* incontestable . . .'

Keynes for his part defined the 'old-fashioned quantity equations' as the direct 'relationship of the purchasing power of money (or price-level of consumption-goods) and of the price-level of output as a whole to the quantity of money and the velocity of circulation'. He thus found himself agreeing, in *A Treatise on Money*, with the lines of Wicksell's argument, that, from a position of pure logic, there could indeed exist a situation in which: 'there is a unique relationship between the quantity of money and the price-levels of consumption-goods and of output as a whole, of such character that if the quantity of money were double the price-levels would be double also' (1930, I, pp. 146–7). In *The General Theory*, albeit in a footnote, Keynes stated outright, 'If we had defined V, not as equal to Y/M_1, but as equal to Y/M [where M includes M_1 and M_2], then, of course, the Quantity Theory is a truism which holds in all circumstances' (1936, p. 209, fn. 1).

Hayek was another influential author in the sphere of monetary theory, representative of the majority of the Austrian School economists. Contrary to Fisher, Wicksell, and Keynes, even as a principle, Hayek rejected aggregation as a meaningful tool – in this case, thus, every component of the Quantity Equation, P, T, and V. Nonetheless, he too was very willing to acknowledge the usefulness of the Quantity Theory:

The best known instance, and the most relevant case in point, is the resuscitation by Irving Fisher some twenty years ago of the more mechanistic form of the quantity theory of the value of money in his well-known 'quantity of exchange'. . . . I do not propose to quarrel with the positive content of this theory: I am even ready to concede that so far as it goes it is true, and that, from a practical point of view it would be one of the worst things which could befall us if the general public would cease to believe in the general proposition of the quantity theory. (1931, p. 3)

While, on logical grounds, it seems that these four authors, and, if representative, all monetary theorists of every stripe seem to have had the same understanding of the Quantity Theory of Money, that it could capture Hume's money–price proportionality. What is interesting are their differing assessments of the degree of usefulness of the theory with regards to its necessity to have any number of conditions be fixed for it to hold as an equilibrium (or truism, to borrow from Keynes).

2.3   OBJECTIONS TO THE QUANTITY THEORY

Having agreed on the logical possibility of a Quantity Theory of Money, all four authors, including Fisher, expressed nonetheless serious reservation, if not outright objection as far as the usefulness of the Theory to say anything meaningful about a 'real' correlation between price and money. Once the move is made to the functional aspects of the Equation of Exchange, or as Fisher put it, 'to inquire how far these propositions are really *causal* propositions' (1911, p. 151, original emphasis), the problems arise. Despite Fisher's conviction in the Quantity Theory, it is clear, he wrote, that the 'equation of exchange of itself does not affirm or deny these propositions' (1911; 1963, p. 152), of the proportionality between a change in money and a change in prices. Fisher was quite explicit that 'the fact that the strictly proportional effect on prices of an increase in M is only the *normal* or *ultimate* effect after transition periods are over' (1911, p. 159, original emphasis). With, however, transition periods linked to the trade or business cycle, which Fisher was persuaded was of a ten-year periodicity,[12] 'periods of transition are the rule and those of equilibrium the exception, [and] the mechanism of exchange is almost always in a dynamic rather than a static condition' (1911; 1963, p. 71).

Two more observations are pertinent concerning Fisher's Quantity Theory. The first regards the impact on the interest rate of rising or falling prices during the periods of transition. Fisher recognized that the change in money that brings about the change in price does affect the interest rate and showed that it is 'the peculiar behavior of the rate of interest during transition periods [which] is largely responsible for the crises and depressions in which price movements end' (1911; 1963, p. 56). The second point is Fisher's insistence that '*the price level is normally the one absolutely passive element in the equation of exchange*' (1911; 1963, p. 172, original emphasis). Despite Fisher's recognition that the Quantity Theory is a special case and does 'not hold true strictly and absolutely during transition periods' (1911; 1963, p. 161), he chose to spend a great deal of his attention in his influential book on that very special case of equilibrium, hammering again and again on the importance of the proportionality, which depends vitally on his assumption of the constancy of both velocity and trade transactions.

The very Quantity Equation itself, even in the situation of equilibrium, raises questions, which, for different reasons, bothered its critics. Wicksell, in the strongest terms, saw the whole Equation condemned by the cautionary conditions placed on it by Fisher, 'that the *velocity of circulation* of money is, as it were, a fixed, inflexible magnitude, fluctuating about a constant average level' (1936, p. 41, original emphasis):

> The Quantity Theory is *theoretically* valid so long as the assumption of *ceteris paribus* is firmly adhered to. But among the 'things' that have to be supposed to remain 'equal' are some of the flimsiest and more intangible factors in the whole of economics – in particular the velocity of circulation of money, to which in fact all others can be more or less directly referred back. (1936, p. 42, original emphasis)

Wicksell explained how undermining to the validity of the Equation were its many assumptions: 'an almost completely individualistic system of holding cash balances', 'that everybody maintains, or at least strives to maintain, his balance at an average level that is constant (relatively to the extent of his business or of his payments)', 'that an almost constant *proportion* of all the business of exchange, even if not the whole of it, is transacted by means of money in the sense of coin or notes', 'that the portion of the total stock of metal which is employed in actual circulation can be sharply differentiated from the portion which is kept in the form of hoards against future needs or which, in the form of ornaments and jewellery, is withdrawn from use as money' (1936, pp. 41–2, oroginal emphasis). To make the story short – it is not Wicksell who is under study here, but rather Keynes – in Wicksell's words, the Quantity Theory is based 'on assumptions that unfortunately have little relation to practice, and in some respects none whatever' (1936, p. 41) and '[I]t is consequently impossible to decide *a priori* whether the Quantity Theory is *in actual fact* true – in other words, whether prices and the quantity of money move together in practice' (1936, p. 42, original emphasis). It is worth noting that in Fisher, it is the change in money that effects changes in prices and those changes in turn influence interest rates. Wicksell saw the change in money affecting first the interest rate and then prices.[13] This too was a distinction in Keynes and a crucial point in understanding how Keynes was not alone in this criticism of the Quantity Theory.

Hayek rejected from the outset Fisher's insistence that the price-level must and can be studied independently of individual prices (1932, p. 175):[14]

> neither aggregates or averages do act upon one another, and it will never be possible to establish necessary connections of cause and effect between them as we can between individual phenomena, individual prices, etc. I would even go so far as to assert that, from the very nature of economic theory, averages can never form a link in its reasoning. (1931, pp. 4–5)

> that money affects individual prices only by means of its influence on the general price level seems to me to be at the root of at least three very erroneous opinions (1931, p. 7)[15]

(More will be discussed in Chapter 3 about Hayek's average period of production, explained entirely in terms of relative prices and rates of profit without his needing to make reference to price-level.) Further, Hayek found a position like Fisher's, that the statistical data that can show that the conditions of the transition periods do not undermine the causal effect of money on prices, not only ludicrous but also counter-productive:

> This theory, with its apparatus of mathematical formulae constructed to admit of statistical verification, is a typical instance of 'quantitative' economics . . . What I complain of is not only that this theory in its various forms has unduly usurped the central place in monetary theory, but that the point of view from which it springs is a positive hindrance to further progress. Not the least harmful effect of this particular theory is the present isolation of the theory of money from the main body of general economic theory. (1931, pp. 3–4)

Although Keynes's position was opposite to Hayek's scepticism about the usefulness of aggregates, he expressed nonetheless an opinion extremely close to Hayek's, at the opening of chapter 21 of *The General Theory*, about the tolerance of a dichotomy in the study of economics, which left money grafted superficially onto macroeconomics.

Keynes agreed with Fisher, that the Quantity Theory of Money would not hold outside equilibrium, whose set of conditions he defined in greater detail than Fisher:

> i.e., when the factors of production are fully employed, when the public is neither bullish nor bearish of securities and is maintaining the form of savings-deposits neither more nor less than the 'normal' proportion of its total wealth, and when the volume of saving is equal both to the cost and to the value of new investments. (1930, I, pp. 146–7)

Like Wicksell, Keynes, however, also believed, that the equilibrium conditions would likely never be met. Furthermore, in a dynamic environment,
where the pertinent variables are changing, such as the volume of savings
relative to the cost of investment and liquidity preferences, their incon-
stancy brings about the virtual impossibility of linking causes and effects,
particularly, as Keynes noted:

> the fundamental price-levels can depart from their equilibrium values without
> any change having occurred in the quantity of money or in the veloci-
> ties of circulation. It is even conceivable that the cash-deposits remain the
> same, the saving-deposits remain the same, the velocities of circulation may
> remain the same, the volume of monetary transactions may remain the same,
> and the volume of output may remain the same; and yet the fundamental
> price-levels may change. (1930, I, pp. 147)

This proposition of Keynes negated entirely the Quantity Theory of
Money and illustrated a potential frustration, kindred with Wicksell's
despair, of any tight correlation between money quantity and its impact.
Keynes also expressed Hayek's impatience with Fisher's appeal to statistics: 'The Fundamental Problem of Monetary Theory [is] not merely to
establish identities or statistical equations relating (*e.g.*) the turnover of
monetary instruments to the turnover of things traded for money' (1930,
I, p. 133).

Such correlations, even if they were possible, would not address the
context of money in the economy:

> The reader will have perceived by now that the relationship of the purchasing
> power of money (or price-level of consumption-goods) and of the price-level of
> output as a whole to the quantity of money and the velocity of circulation is not
> of that direct character which the old-fashioned quantity equations, however
> carefully guarded, might lead one to suppose. (1930, I, p. 146)

The challenge which Keynes felt remained to monetary theory was: 'to
treat the problem dynamically, analysing the different elements involved,
in such a manner as to exhibit the causal process by which the price-level is
determined, and the method of transition from one position of equilibrium
to another' (1930, I, p. 133).

From the above short overview of the pros and cons of the Quantity
Theory of Money, several points become clear. (1) The difficult monetary
questions which Keynes attempted to address in both *A Treatise* and *The
General Theory* were not those of an author working on the spur of the
moment and counter to the general wisdom; he was treating issues which
were part of a controversy on monetary theory that had been running for
centuries. (2) As far as the conditions compromising the validity of the

Quantity Theory, Keynes was in agreement with Fisher, Wicksell, and Hayek. (3) It seems quite generally that the pre-World War II monetary economists agreed that in the dynamics of an economy, money interacts with prices, but there is difficulty in establishing theoretically, and – even greater difficulty – in affirming empirically, definite correlations between prices and the quantity of money (that is, what exactly that relationship is at every instant, whether money may or may not affect prices, or whether it is ever possible for prices to change without change in the money quantity and/or vice versa).

In sum, these four authors considered Fisher's following recapitulation correct: the Quantity Theory is reflected in the Quantity Equation only under given conditions, *'provided the velocity of circulation of that money and the volume of trade which it is obliged to perform are not changed'* (1911; 1963, p. 14, emphasis added). Further, however, as Harrod noted, 'acceptance of the quantity equation *does not* make one a "quantity theorist"' (1969, p.159, emphasis added).[16]

Many of the post-World War II proponents of macroeconomics, be they neoWalrasians[17] or Keynesians,[18] have taken for granted the Quantity Theory of Money and adopted its distillate Fisher's Quantity Equation, as recounted, for example, in the popular version of Laidler, above. Serious pre-World War II monetary economists, however, whose primary goals were to understand the effects of inflation and deflation, found the Quantity Theory of little help in a dynamic economy. From Wicksell and Fisher on, it was the interest rate that was presented as the explanation for continuing linkages between money and prices outside of the equilibrium position, in which the proportionality of money and prices no longer seems to hold. For the Classicals, however, the rate of interest had begun to exist as the rate of discount on real capital. Thus, a connection between the interest rate and the relationship of prices and money was not immediately obvious: 'the rate of interest is not regulated by the abundance or scarcity of money, but by the abundance or scarcity of that part of capital, not consisting of money' (Ricardo 1952, II, pp. 88–9).

Differing views on the impact of the interest rate on the relationship between money and prices are illustrated well in the positions of Ricardo and Keynes. For Ricardo, the interest rate is determined in the market by the supply and demand for capital. It is 'regulated chiefly by the profits that may be made by the use of capital, it cannot be controlled by any bank, nor by any assemblage of banks' (1952; 2005, IV, p. 333). The opposite position would be that of Keynes, for whom control of the rate of interest is in the hands of the bank. The bank can stipulate the rate of discount which 'means, in substance, that the control of prices is exercised in the contemporary world *through the control of the rate of investment'* (1930, II, p. 211, original emphasis).

These issues were so live as to create a serious wedge between Keynes and Robertson. In their debate over the *Treatise*, Robertson accused Keynes of 'over-exalting' the rate of interest 'at the expense of the quantity of money' (1931, pp. 404–5). He was targeting thereby Keynes's passage in volume II of the *Treatise*:

> if the rate of investment can be influenced at will, then this can be brought in as balancing factor to effect in any required degree, first of all the price-level of output as a whole, and, finally, as a response to the effect of prices on profits, the rate of money-earnings of the factors of production. (1930, II, pp. 211–12)

It seems the controversy about the determination of the rate of interest and more importantly its impact (or lack thereof) on prices had its root in the understanding of what is money.

The distinctions between Robertson and Keynes would be the very parallel to the earlier contrast between Ricardo as representative of the Currency School and Tooke, of the Banking or Credit School. Contrast Ricardo's assertion, above, with the following statements of Tooke:

> the ambiguity of the term value of money or of the currency, when employed indiscriminately as it is, to signify both value in exchange for commodities, and value in use of capital, is a constant source of confusion. (1844, p. 77)

> On the Stock Exchange, and in the Money Market, the term money is used synonymously with capital. *Abundance and cheapness of money mean abundance of capital seeking employment, and the low rate of interest as the consequence*; as, on the other hand, scarcity of money, and tightness of the money market, mean comparative scarcity of disposable capital, and a consequent advance in the rate of interest. (1844, p. 76–7, emphasis added)

> a low rate of interest is almost synonymous with a high price of securities; while, as I have shown, its necessary tendency is to reduce the prices of commodities by diminishing the cost of production. (1844, p. 86)

For Keynes, money, as in the Credit School, is not simply a 'medium of exchange'. Nor is there any guarantee that it will stand as a 'store of value', even if it is already quantified. The concern for Keynes was the fact that, when non-barter transactions are conducted, money becomes operative. The different characteristics Keynes ascribed to money implicitly and explicitly differentiate his monetary model from those of the quantity theorists, theirs being based on money solely as 'medium of exchange'.

2.4   KEYNES'S MONETARY THEORY IN *A TREATISE ON MONEY* AND HIS THEORY OF INTEREST IN *THE GENERAL THEORY*

Once he had compared the three preceding versions, to help distinguish between them and his own, Keynes continued to explain the circumstances required to derive the equation of exchange from his own formulation and to demonstrate the Quantity Theory of Money reduction to be an extreme, special case.

Very little can be said about the interaction between money, price, and the interest rate without a clear understanding about what money is. Since money is the 'thing' that is used in exchange and that thing changes over time, the name 'money' can apply to different things at different times. Furthermore, another complication is that for different authors what is included under the notion of money is different. It has already been mentioned that however important money was to the discussion in Fisher, he chose to incorporate only a very vague definition of his own, relying on Andrew to provide the specifics.[19] Keynes, on the other hand, in *A Treatise on Money*, devoted over a third of volume I to the clarification of money in terms of its history and current meanings.

There are two aspects of Keynes's analysis of money. One is an overview of what had been said about money: as deposits, in circulation (coins, notes, and so on), purchasing power, debts and credits, and so on. The other is Keynes's own classification. With respect to the first aspect, of interest here is the legal status of money with which Keynes started, inspired by Knapp. Keynes launched directly into a discussion of the institutional setting that defines money, a setting which, by the writing of Hicks in 1969, would be identified as the 'Age of Keynes'!

For Keynes, what defined a modern economic system was fundamentally State control over money: its form, its guarantee, its supply, its distribution, and its discount rate. To Hicks's mind, that control 'which for long ages was so imperfect, has become complete,' by Keynes's time (1969, p. 96). Figure 2.2 has been prepared to summarize Keynes's overview. Keynes linked all aspects of money, not historically but conceptually, starting from a relatively unique, but fundamental concept for him, Money of Account, and ending up at the various divisions of Current Money. Figure 2.3 is an extension of Keynes's own tables in the *Treatise*. It provides a schematic view of the relationship of his concepts of M_1, M_2, and M_3 to the larger discussion on money.

The core of Figure 2.2 is found in *A Treatise on Money*, volume I, chapter 1, as two separate genealogical trees, on pages 9 and 10. They have been joined here to highlight the connections between the two, but,

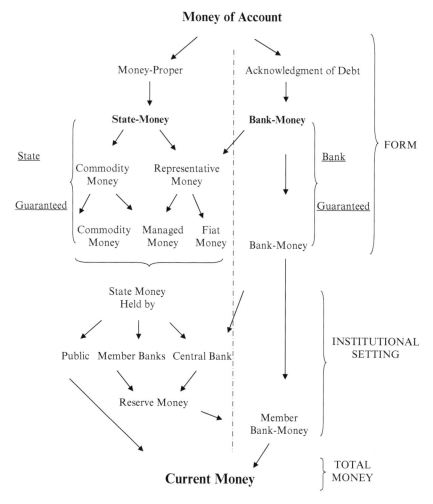

Figure 2.2   Keynes's Money (from A Treatise on Money*)*

as captioned, the upper part distinguishes the Forms of money, while the lower schematic represents the Institutional Setting for holding money. The combination of the two leads to the possibility of understanding Keynes's definition of money, Current Money, and its types, found in a third genealogical tree in the *Treatise*, on page 11. Figure 2.3 is dedicated to the typology of Current Money, guided by Keynes's perspectives in both the *Treatise* and *The General Theory*.

For Keynes, Money of Account is 'that in which Debts and Prices

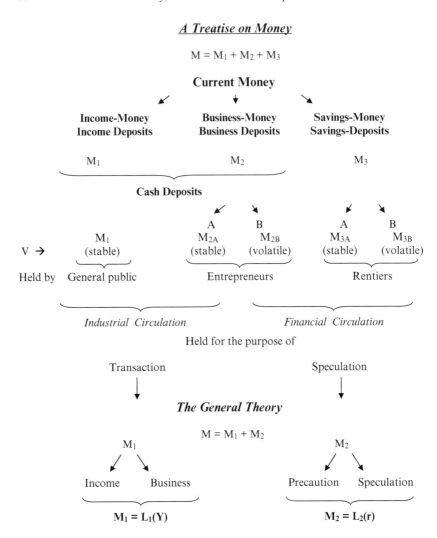

Figure 2.3   *Keynes's Money (from* A Treatise on Money *and* The General Theory*)*

and General Purchasing Power are *expressed*; it is a '*description* or *title*' of money the 'thing' (1930, I, pp. 3–4, original emphasis). It can take two forms, either a tangible (Money-Proper), or an intangible (Acknowledgment of Debt) form. Inasmuch as the first is something physical, the second can be just a signal (a handshake, a mark on a ledger sheet, and so on). With the sophistication of finance and credit in the more developed economies, the latter became integrated into the institution of the bank and subsequently recognized by the State. Money-Proper has for its part become universally acknowledged as money, by virtue of its connection to the State, either as a Commodity Money, 'composed of actual units of a particular . . . commodity which happens to have been chosen for the familiar purposes of money' (1930, I, p. 7), or as Representative Money, units which are themselves not commodities, either with or without a commodity as its standard, Managed Money and Fiat Money, respectively.

From his description of the forms of money, Keynes moved to a discussion of the institutional distribution of State Money and Bank Money. Bank-Money is defined as 'an acknowledgment of a private debt, expressed in the money-of-account, which is used by passing from one hand to another . . . to settle a transaction' (1930, I, p. 6). The definition highlights the potential, and certainly historical, autonomy of the institution of the private bank from the State's money-minting and printing, distributing, and reserve-holding roles. State-Money, defined as that money which the State has determined 'should answer as money to the current money-of-account' (1930, I, p. 5), is described by Keynes as being in the possession of three different institutions: the Public, the Member Banks, and the Central Bank. While Figure 2.2 reveals virtually only the relationship between the Central Bank and Member Banks, in the following passage from Hicks, one might see Keynes's description of the institutions of money:

> It is not just a matter of the introduction of paper money, so much cheaper to produce than the old metallic money . . . There is no longer a danger of the State's defaulting, on debt expressed in its own currency, since it is always possible for it to borrow from the banking system; the banks are not able to refuse to lend, since they can always create money to finance their loans. The power that thus passes into the hands of the State is very great, but by itself it is not unlimited. . . . this is the point in our story when we come to the Age of Keynes. (1969, p. 96)[20]

It is out of this institutional setting that Current Money derives. However important this institutional setting is as the environment in which money circulates, for Keynes, an absolutely fundamental element in his theory of money is that 'the total quantity of Money of all kinds [is] in the hands of the public; and it often makes but little difference whether the money in question is State-Money or Bank-Money. The aggregate of both may be called Current Money' (1930, I, p. 9). In Figure 2.3, it is Current Money that is analysed as to its components and their functions.

In Figure 2.3, Current Money, M, which is all money, is defined as having three components: Income Deposits, M_1, Business Deposits, M_2, and Savings Deposits, M_3. 'The *Income-deposits* and the *Business-deposits* together make up what we shall call the *Cash-deposits*' wrote Keynes (1930, I, p. 35, original emphasis), based on a distinction he seems to have found in Adam Smith (ibid., n. 1). While Income Deposits are deposits of individuals held for the purpose of transactions, Savings Deposits are held by them for speculative purposes. Business Deposits cover two types of transactions: (A) payments to factors of production and payments between firms for intermediary goods, and (B) speculative transactions in capital goods or commodities and financial transactions, such as 'the redemption and renewal of Treasury Bills, or changes of investment' (ibid., p. 45). Keynes called Income Deposits and Business Deposits of type A, *Industrial Circulation*. Business Deposits of type B and Savings Deposits, he called *Financial Circulation*.

Industrial Circulation corresponds to the money that is needed for 'the business of maintaining the normal process of current output, distribution and exchange and paying the factors of production their incomes . . .' (1930, I, p. 243); *Financial Circulation* includes 'Stock Exchange and Money Market transactions, speculation and the process of conveying current savings and profits into the hands of entrepreneurs' (ibid.). The volume of *Industrial Circulation* as a whole 'will vary with E, the aggregate of money incomes, *i.e.*, with the volume and cost of production of current output' (1930, I, p. 248). Keynes made both M_1 and M_2 relate to their respective velocities V_1 and V_2, but it is only Part A of the Business Deposits, M_2, or M_{2A}, which he linked to transactions, and thus to *Industrial Circulation* (money for factors of production – if it is for future transactions, in Keynes's terms, it is *Commodity Speculation*). Part B of Business Deposits, M_{2B}, is part of *Financial Circulation*.[21] The main distinction between the money held as M_{2A} rather than in M_{2B} resides in the fact that the former is linked to the amount of production and changes therefore with its level, while the latter is not and does not: 'the pace at which a circle of financiers, speculators and investors hand round one to another particular pieces of wealth, or titles to such, which they are neither producing nor consuming but merely exchanging, bears no definite relation to the rate of current production' (1930, I, p. 47).

These various categories reflect both the form in which money is held for a specific purpose, whether transaction or speculation, and the parties which hold the money. The parties are identified in Figure 2.3 as the General Public, the Entrepreneurs, and the Rentiers. For Keynes, the main purpose of making all these distinctions was to be able to pinpoint the sources of fluctuation in the monetary sector. Once distinguished, he could then show how fluctuations affect the total amount of money, where money is held, and the stability of prices, investment, and so on.

Thus, Savings Deposits are defined by Keynes as having two categories of savers: A, the holders of wealth, M_{3A} and B, the professional investors or 'financiers', the most active being a 'class of persons who borrow from the banks in order to finance a larger holding of securities than they can carry with their own resources', M_{3B} (1930, I, pp. 249–50).

There is a distinction to be made in the role of decision-making by the different categories of money-holders: the public in general, comprised of consumers and savers, the entrepreneurs, who decide where to place their money, and the rentiers, whose speculation makes the money turn over. For Keynes, financial dynamism comes from the actions of the entrepreneurs and the rentiers. The entrepreneur plays the central role with his decisions regarding investment in production or speculation, decisions which themselves are affected by the stock market activity of the rentiers or financiers. While the Income Deposits, M_1, and the Savings Deposits, M_{2A}, both of the general public, show some stability, Part B of the Business Deposits, M_{2B}, and especially Part B of the Savings Deposits, M_{3B}, through 'the effect of bullish or bearish sentiment in the financial markets' (1930, I, p. 255), are the source of financial fluctuations, in some respects independently of what is happening in the production sphere.

We conclude, therefore, that changes in the financial situation are capable of causing changes in the value of money in two ways. They have the effect of altering the quantity of money available for the Industrial Circulation; and they may have the effect of altering the attractiveness of [new] investment. (1930, I, p. 254)

The volatility of M_{2B} and M_{3B} is for Keynes the key financial source of the dynamics of the trade cycle.

The differences between the analysis of Fisher, above – with its Money Equation, $M_1V_1 + M_2V_2 = PT$, and dichotomy and proportionality between M_1 and M_2 – and Keynes's approach to money in Figures 2.2 and 2.3 should now be able to be seen even more clearly. 'For anyone brought up in the old Quantity-of-Money, Velocity-of-Circulation schools of thought, whether it be Cambridge Quantity Equations or Fisher Quantity Equations, this seems to be, for some obscure reason, a difficult transition to make' (Keynes's response to Hayek's review of the *Treatise*, 1931b, p. 390). The major difference between Fisher and Keynes was that their respective M_1 and M_2 are differently defined. For Fisher, M_1 and M_2 are for transaction purposes and correspond to some extent to Keynes's M_1. There is no counterpart to Keynes's M_2 in any of the Quantity Equations. Even if one could draw a parallel between Fisher's distinctions, M_1, Income Deposits and M_2, Loan Deposits, and Keynes's *Industrial Circulation* (M_1 in *The General Theory*) and *Financial Circulation* (M_2 in

The General Theory), Keynes's two Ms respond to different forces from Fisher's. Keynes's M_1 is relatively stable, but his M_2 is volatile (Figure 2.3). In Keynes, it is the impact of M_2 that makes M, total money, volatile.

Another major difference between Keynes and the Fisherian approach is the manner in which the interest rate enters their analyses. In Fisher, change in the interest rate is a consequence of a change in prices, which, through changes in velocity, effects variations in all the components of his Money Equation. Fisher uses this to show how the '*normal* or *ultimate*' proportionality between M and P is re-established. In short, Fisher's is an explanation of how a change in M, as would result from 'an increase in the amount of gold' (1911, p. 60), makes the currency deposits, M_1 and M_2, in terms of gold, adjust and lead to a new level of prices. Fisher's M_1 corresponds to Keynes's M_1, while Fisher's M_2 corresponds to Keynes's M_{3A}. Keynes's M_{2B} and M_{3B}, which are volatile and affect the rate of interest, are absent from Fisher.

The monetary framework described above is that of the *Treatise*. The ways in the *Treatise* in which Keynes saw money, price, and interest rate, on the one hand, and investment and savings, on the other, interacting and impacting one another will be discussed in Chapters 3 and 4. It might be asked, however, in what way his discussion of money in *A Treatise* made its way into *The General Theory*. It has already been asserted here that Keynes's two main works are one. Even if Keynes made some adjustments in terminology and perspective, his definitions, classifications, forms, and institutional settings, and so on, regarding money, as laid out in Figures 2.2 and 2.3, are overall alike in both works.

Keynes reintroduced money in *The General Theory* as being virtually the same entity as in *A Treatise*: 'As a rule, I shall, as in my *Treatise on Money*, assume that money is co-extensive with bank deposits' (1936, p. 167, fn. 1). As can be seen from Figure 2.3, 'In my *Treatise on Money* I studied the total demand for money under the headings of income-deposits, business-deposits, and saving-deposits, and I need not repeat here the analysis which I gave in Chapter 3 of that book' (1936, pp. 194–5). Keynes did make some changes, however, in his divisions of M, or total money, from three parts in the *Treatise* to two parts in *The General Theory*. It is in the context of his discussion of the motives determining liquidity preference that his two-part division of money in *The General Theory* takes shape.

M_1, as in the *Treatise*, still encompasses in *The General Theory* Income Deposits and a part of Business Deposits, defined as *Industrial Circulation*. Of great liquidity, M_1 is emphasized as being held for the purpose of transactions. Both its deposits are directly related to the level of income, now expressed as $M_1 = L_1(Y)$. M_2 in *The General Theory* is now also comprised of two parts, which respond to two distinct liquidity-preference motives: the precautionary and the speculative. The precautionary holdings encompass M_{2B} and part of M_{3A} of the *Treatise*; the speculative holdings envelop the balance of M_{3A} and all of M_{3B} of the *Treatise*. This link is alluded to in *The General Theory* as follows:

> Whilst liquidity-preference due to the speculative-motive corresponds to what in my *Treatise on Money* I called 'the state of bearishness', it is by no means the same thing. For 'bearishness' is there defined as the functional relationship, not between the rate of interest (or price of debts) and the quantity of money, but between the price of assets and debts, taken together, and the quantity of money. (1936, pp. 173–4)[22]

Although implicitly expressed still as the state of expectations, M_2 is, in *The General Theory*, newly expressed explicitly as a function of the interest rate: $M_2 = L_2(r)$.

It seems thus that the monetary settings of *The General Theory* and the genesis of Keynes's liquidity theory derive from the rich development his monetary theory had already undergone in *A Treatise*. When, further, the monetary theory of *The General Theory* is contrasted to that of the *Treatise*, it is striking to see how the demand for liquidity of the 1936 work is similar to the Fundamental Equation of 1930. In *The General Theory* money is defined as:

$$M = M_1 + M_2 = L_1(Y) + L_2(r),$$

when, as above M is replaced by Y, V, O, and P, then

$$M = \frac{Y}{V} = \frac{OP}{V} = M_1 + M_2$$

which becomes

$$P = \frac{M_1 V}{O} + \frac{M_2 V}{O}$$

When money held for transaction is equalized with expenditure $E = M_1 V$ and the money held for speculation is equalized with the discrepancy between investment and savings $(I - S)$, then

$$\Pi = \frac{E}{O} + \frac{I - S}{O}$$

There is a striking parallel between the Fundamental Equation of the *Treatise* and the Demand for Money Equation of *The General Theory* (Figure 2.1(iv)). It can be now seen how in the *Treatise*, short-term market forces affect the second component of the Fundamental Equation, I − S/O, the profit ratio. It is the discrepancies between I and S that are the cause of cyclical fluctuations. As discrepancy between I and S materializes, profits change, and the level of price changes; that creates fluctuations. Chapter 3 will analyse in depth the role of the Fundamental Equation in explaining the trade cycle. Chapter 4 will substantiate in detail *The General Theory*'s emphasis on how the bullishness and bearishness of the market affect the interest rate, which in turn affects the marginal efficiency of capital through the second component of the Fundamental Equation, and then the level of employment.

2.5 FROM KEYNES'S FUNDAMENTAL EQUATION TO HIS DEMAND FOR LIQUIDITY EQUATION

As will be seen, based on the same underlying monetary theory, *A Treatise* is in general an analysis of the causes of cyclical fluctuations in business and trade, while *The General Theory* is more focused on the forces that determine a specific level of employment.[23] For Keynes, the marginal propensity to consume, the marginal efficiency of capital, and the liquidity preference are the key determinants of the level of employment. Liquidity preference is crucial to determination of the interest rate. Feeling that the interest rate had been insufficiently developed in *A Treatise on Money*, Keynes dedicated some chapters in *The General Theory* to the further discussion of money. In point of fact, in Book IV, 'The Inducement to Invest', chapters 13–17, all but one chapter is devoted to an in-depth analysis of the relationship of money to the interest rate.

It is that very switch in *The General Theory* to emphasis on the interest rate which shows that, for Keynes, understanding it as a constituent part of money became fundamental to distinguishing a monetary, or entrepreneurial economy from a barter, or cooperative one. Money in the latter type of economy is simply a *numeraire*. Any object as money, whether cow or corn, can serve to determine the interest rate. In an entrepreneurial economy, however, only M (money), with three special characteristics, can be the unique determinant of the interest rate. It manifests no elasticity of production, elasticity of substitution, or variation in yield due to liquidity (par excellence).

Keynes's identification of three new characteristics of money, specific to its role in an entrepreneurial economy, stemmed from his novel approach to determining the interest rate in *The General Theory*. Trying to counter earlier treatments of interest rate theory, all reflecting the characteristics of money as a commodity in the tradition of Marshall–Pigou–Fisher, he initially evoked the implications of using commodities as the standard scale for interest-rate determination. These ideas in *The General Theory* regarding the special characteristics of money, which set it apart from commodities, link back directly to Keynes's discussion of money in the *Treatise*. Two of his 'entrepreneurial' characteristics of money, its inelasticity of production and its invariability in yield due to changes in liquidity, are found among the Institutional types of Money (Figure 2.2). They are shared by two of the possible forms of State Money as Representative Money: Fiat Money and Managed Money. '[M]oney has, both in the long and in the short period, *a zero, or at any rate a very small, elasticity of production . . .* In the case of an inconvertible *managed currency* this condition is strictly satisfied' (1936, p. 230, emphasis added) Although the liquidity characteristic of money is more general in *The General Theory* than in Keynes's description of it in his liquidity preference discussion of the *Treatise*, that characteristic is now more directed to the relationship between the quantity of money and its value: 'beyond a certain point money's yield from liquidity does not fall in response to an increase in its quantity' (1936, p. 233).

In his discussion of the *Exchange Standard* (1930, I, pp. 18–22), Keynes may also have alluded in *A Treatise* to another characteristic of entrepreneurial money, which he describes in *The General Theory* as follows:

> The second *differentia* of money is that it has an *elasticity of substitution equal, or nearly equal to zero*; which means that as the exchange value of money rises there is no tendency to substitute some other factor for it . . . its utility is solely derived from its exchange value. (1936, p. 231, second emphasis added)

In any case, he asserted that it was money's value invariance, enhanced by its other special characteristics, which leads 'to its own-rate of interest in terms of itself as standard being more reluctant to fall as output increases than the own-rates of interest of any other assets in terms of themselves' (1936, p. 229). Just as all commodities have their own prices and rates of interest, as had already been noted by economists, money too has its value and interest rate.

So it was that Keynes determined the three noted characteristics of money as elevating it above other commodities as the standard for an economy's interest-rate determination. Further, he noted that the rate of interest 'cannot be a return to saving or waiting as such' (1936, p. 167). It is not 'the "price" which brings into equilibrium the demand for resources to invest with *the readiness to abstain from present consumption*. It is the "price" which equilibrates the desire to hold wealth in the form of cash with the available quantity of cash' (1936, p. 167, emphasis added).

The implications of Keynes's discussion of money for his interest rate theory was also crucial to his theory of employment, in which employment depends on the anticipated costs and returns of new investment: 'the *rate of interest on money* plays a peculiar part in setting a limit to the level of employment, since it sets a standard to which the marginal efficiency of a capital–asset must attain if it is to be newly produced' (1936, p. 222, original emphasis).

For Keynes, due to the special characteristics of money, its market is not the same as any other. Unlike any commodity or service, money can be produced at almost no cost ad-infinitum. Money is neither productive nor consumable. It does not produce value-added or employment. Its prime role is to facilitate exchange and production. Yet, in a monetary entrepreneurial market economy, such as the one in which we function, the finance afforded by money is vital to the production of added value in all commodities and services and to the generation of employment.

NOTES

1. Translated into English: 'That trade of money, by whose concealed circuit, not different from the circulation of blood, the whole prospering human State is perpetually served, is something great, hidden and complicated. It is, however, very difficult to explore the nature of its circuit, nor are we able to do so other than if certain things are posited in the fashion of geometers, by whom the reasoning about and the amount of the subject matter are constrained within certain limits.' Ceva (1711).
2. Translated into English: 'he [Locke] has clearly seen that the abundance of money makes every thing dear, but he has not considered how it does so. The great difficulty of this question consists in knowing in what way and in what proportion the increase of money raises prices.' Cantillon (1755; 1931, p. 161).
3. As others of the Credit School, see Appendix, Section 3.
4. The literature of authors who have analysed the ideas and the history of monetary theory is enormous, and it is not the purpose here to review it.
5. The very few theorists noted here illustrate simply the point that the topic was and is still alive.
6. There is a certain irony here, for either the monetary issues regarding transmission and proportionality are irresolvable – in which case, it is not at all surprising that the same discussions keep recurring – or the issues are real and simply not yet resolved – in which case, monetary economists have consistently been showing themselves incapable of tackling them head on, simply hiding their difficulties, pretending that they have gone away, and offering recommendations of rules of thumb, for example, the Taylor rules. Despite an attitude that sees the current generation as being more knowledgeable than earlier generations, fundamentally, current monetary analysis is theoretically weak, as revealed in the context of the 2008 crisis.
7. 'the machinery that I shall suggest in the following pages is quite different from that elaborated by Professor Irving Fisher in his admirable *Purchasing Power of Money* . . . He has painted his picture on one plan, and I paint mine on another' (Pigou 1917, p. 39).
8. For more on Marshall on money, see Eshag (1964).
9. This transformation, of k to V and R to T, raises certain issues of its own.
10. By 1913 Keynes had completed his work on Indian currency and finance.

11. A careful reading of Fisher, particularly this passage from his Chapter 1 on Definitions, shows, however, that instead of pursuing a discussion of the characteristics of money independent of goods, he turned to the following description, in which M' is left completely aside: 'When a certain quantity of one kind of wealth is exchanged for a certain quantity of another kind, we may divide one of the two quantities by the other, and obtain the *price* of the latter. For instance, if two dollars of gold are exchanged for three bushels of wheat, the price of the wheat in gold is two thirds of a dollar per bushel; and the price of the gold in wheat is one and a half bushels per dollar. It is to be noticed that these are ratios of two physical quantities, the units for measuring which are quite different from each other. One commodity is measured in bushels, or units of volume of wheat, the other in dollars, or units of weight of gold. In general, a price of any species of wealth is merely the ratio of two physical quantities, in whatever way each may originally be measured' (Fisher, *The Purchasing Power of Money*, chapter 1, 'Primary Definitions' (1911, p. 3, original emphasis). Although from this passage Fisher's approach might appear quite similar to Marshall–Pigou's, as Keynes saw them, the equation of the latter is one of Cash-Balances, that of the former, one of Cash-Transactions (1930, p. 238).

12. 'In most cases the time occupied by the swing of the commercial pendulum to and fro is about ten years' (1911; 1963, p. 70).

13. 'The Quantity Theory is correct in so far as it is true that an increase or relative diminution in the stock of money must always tend to raise or lower prices – by its opposite effect in the first place on rates of interest' (1936, Author's Preface, p. xxviii).

14. 'Such anomalous conditions do not negate the general thesis that prices are the effect and not the cause of currency' (1932, pp. 173–4).

15. '*Firstly*, that money acts on prices and production only if the general price level changes, and, therefore, that prices and production are always unaffected by money, – that they are at their 'natural' level, – if the price level remains stable. *Secondly*, that a rising price level tends always to cause an increase of production, and a falling price level always a decrease of production; and *thirdly*, that "monetary theory might even be described as nothing more than the theory of how the value of money is determined"' (Hayek, 1931, p. 7 is quoting Hawtrey, 1930, p. 64).

16. Harrod (1969) reviews all four versions of the equation of exchange, as Keynes did in the *Treatise*, chapter 14.

17. The Quantity Theory of Money is consistent with the logic of neoWalrasian theory.

18. This is the case for Keynesians whose models are imbued with the IS-LM.

19. Andrew (1899).

20. Hicks's description continues: 'this is the point in our story when we come to the Age of Keynes, that new dispensation under which since 1936 we know that we have been living. The lesson that Keynes taught was of the existence of the power that I have just described. It already existed, and Keynes had only to urge that it should be taken up . . . It did already exist when he was writing, but it had not existed for so very long. It is not in the nature of things; it is a consequence of the development of modern banking' (1969, pp. 96–7).

21. In the *Treatise* Keynes defines M_1 and M_2 as Cash Deposits, which he associates with the Transaction Motive. In *The General Theory*, however, M_{2B} of the *Treatise*, as the most liquid form of the *Financial Circulation*, became earmarked as the holdings for the Precautionary Motive.

22. This citation continues: 'This treatment, however, involved a confusion between results due to a change in the rate of interest and those due to a change in the schedule of the marginal efficiency of capital, which I hope I have here avoided.' The word 'confusion' should not be taken literally, although it does require explanation. Such will be provided, as the *Treatise* and *The General Theory* are analysed in depth in Chapters 3 and 4. See also Klein (1966, pp. 15–16).

23. Obviously, given the circumstances contemporary with the publication of *The General Theory*, attention is directed to a situation of less than full employment, but its theory, it is argued, is applicable to any point in the cycle.

3 Keynes's semantic shifts: the shock of *A Treatise on Money*

For all the general attributions of novelty to his ideas, many of which were misplaced (see Appendix), Keynes's proposals in *A Treatise on Money* were 'indeed revolutionary', as Hayek described them in his 1931 *Economica* review (1931, p. 122). There was also the recognition by Robertson that Keynes was contributing 'fertile and penetrating ideas' to 'a field of appalling intellectual difficulty' (1931, p. 395), and further by Hayek that it was 'undeniably in so many ways a magnificent performance' (1931, p. 146). *A Treatise on Money* is definitely as important a work as *The General Theory*. Having said this, the two powerful thinkers, Robertson and Hayek, defined a less than favourable reception for the *Treatise*: one in Cambridge, in the shadow of Pigou the Marshallian, the other at the London School of Economics (LSE), by an icon with a magnetic influence on young scholars. Hayek, perhaps more than any other author of the time, scrutinized the *Treatise*, in two extremely lengthy review articles and yet, unable to identify the Austrian theory within, he was not open to appreciating it from Keynes's perspective.[1] The major difference between Robertson and Keynes lay in Robertson's having been too engrained in the Marshall–Pigou–Fisher school of thought of which Keynes was critical, particularly its conception of money (Chapter 2).

Hayek and Robertson, even as two of its most important reviewers, were unable to see the theoretical aspects of the *Treatise* on its own terms, reading them rather through the lens of traditional monetarist theory. Unable therefore from the start to appreciate its semantic shifts, both reviewers provided a tone of harsh critique and impatience, which created a subsequent, unwarranted inertia of dismissiveness. Among their contemporaries, they succeeded admirably in discrediting the merits of the *Treatise*, and for years after Keynes's death in 1946, Hayek maintained that Keynes had told him that 'he had . . . changed his mind and no longer believed what he had said in that work' (1966; 1995, p. 241). Instead of trying to grasp why Keynes had used causal relationships different from the more conventional, Robertson accused Keynes of a double wrong (1931, p. 405)! Hayek, for his part, demonstrated clear frustration with the incommensurability resulting from Keynes's subtle changes in the meanings of terms: 'There are passages in which the inconsistent use of terms produces a degree of obscurity which, to anyone acquainted with Mr. Keynes's earlier work, is almost unbelievable' (1931; 1995, p. 122); 'I feel altogether helpless in this jungle of differing definitions' (1931; 1995, p. 133).

It seems that the awkward reception of the *Treatise* was rooted in three types of challenges: semantic, methodological, and theoretical. Semantic obstacles and definitions were certainly the main catalyst to the ensuing controversy, and as such, they will be addressed here first. The terms of the *Treatise* presented 'the tools which Mr. Keynes has created for the explanation of dynamic processes, and the trade cycle' (1931; 1995, p. 145), as Hayek called them. Robertson right away detected Keynes's vocabulary shift for the terms 'Incomes', 'Profits', 'Savings', 'Investment', 'P' [Price of Investment-goods], and 'Rate of interest' (1931, pp. 406–7), noting 'I do not think there is any question that this terminology is extremely confusing and will be liable to lead even practiced thinkers into error unless they are continually on their guard' (1931, p. 407). Robertson proceeded in his review of the *Treatise* to wonder with irony:

> How many of those who have taken up the cry that a slump is due to an excess of Savings over Investment, and a boom to be an excess of Investment over Savings, realise that the savings which are so deplorably abundant during a slump consist largely of entrepreneurs' incomes which are not being spent, for the simple reason that they have not been earned? How many of them realise that, in striking the balance during the boom, we must count in Investment all purchases of capital equipment out of the boom profits of entrepreneurs, but must refrain from counting the money so spent on Savings? (1931, p. 407)

When the language of the *Treatise* is both analysed at face value and placed in its intended methodological perspective, it will be shown that most of the criticisms clearly not only had no ground but demonstrate a lack of patience with attempting to grasp Keynes's revolutionary paradigmatic shifts in thought. When Keynes's ideas are distilled and contrasted to those of Hayek's *Prices and Production* (Chapter 4), it will be clear that regardless of whether Keynes's work was without flaw, it was internally consistent and radically different from Classical, neoClassical, and Austrian approaches. Contrary to Hayek's objection that Keynes's theory contained no cycle and no dynamics,[2] Keynes was successful in building a sophisticated theory of the cycle.

3.1   THE CONTROVERSY OVER KEYNES'S *TREATISE*

The controversy following the almost simultaneous publication of Keynes's *Treatise on Money* and Hayek's *Prices and Production* was described by Hicks as 'the thunderstorms of recent years [the early thirties]' (1935; 1982, p. 46). It revealed economists' passion for their divisive views regarding the definition of money and its implications for monetary policy. Hicks struggled for his own perspective on the controversy in two different ways. First, he used it as a springboard for his emerging ideas on money and liquidity. Later, he put the debate into a more historical perspective and traced the major discrepancies on money between Keynes and Hayek back to Thornton and Ricardo, representatives of the Banking and the Currency schools, respectively. One of the merits of Hicks's later exercise is to have shown the disagreement to be far more fundamental to the foundation of economic theory itself than a mere controversy between two strong intellectuals.

The numerous writings about the famous Hayek–Keynes controversy have not grasped what underlies the mutual, harsh, personal criticism between the protagonists and among the others who joined the debate.[3] Nor has its influence on Keynes been appreciated, as his ideas evolved from the *Treatise* to *The General Theory* and as he addressed the haunting realities of his time.[4] The issues as cast by the controversy faded away. Hayek had misunderstood Keynes's *Treatise* and maintained that Keynes had not mastered the more elaborate Austrian production theory; Keynes was not really interested in Hayek's reaction conveyed in his writings and personal letters. The debate was cumbersome, permeated with discussion of terms and definitions, which created additional seeming disagreements about theoretical issues. Rather than focusing on theories over which the camps had *sub rosa* divisions, most commentators since have continued to take rhetorical sides.

The initially hostile reactions to Keynes's *Treatise* by two very intelligent authors, ought not, from a Kuhnian perspective, be perhaps all that surprising, since Hayek, Robertson, and other contemporaries of Keynes were steeped in the thinking of the time. They read it through the lens of neoClassical or Classical models (see Appendix), using a Marshall–Pigou–Fisher monetary perspective (see Chapter 2). The *Treatise* was novel, even revolutionary, and yet largely due to its inherent difficulty, a presentation unconventional to economists, and the few powerful, scathing reviews it received, it failed to acquire the momentum that would have led to its being contemplated by a critical mass of the discipline. To highlight the differences and similarities between Keynes's way of thinking and that of the others, it is necessary (if one might transfer Kuhn's approach to scientific revolutions to social scientific ones) to recognize his vocabulary shifts, his introduction of different causal links, the new insights he drew from a shared historical context, and his new intellectual goals. It might be fair to say bluntly that, whether the *Treatise* or *The General Theory*, Keynes's work has simply not been read over the course of the past 50 years, except piecemeal or through secondary literature or glosses. This was, however, certainly not the case with the publication of the *Treatise* at first; Keynes's very few earliest readers, especially his staunchest critics Hayek and Robertson, and even some others a bit later, read it *in toto*.

To approach Keynes with a detached perspective might well be considered to have been difficult, if not impossible, for his immediate critics. To have had the discipline to rely, however, on their reactions 'à chaud', regardless of increasing distance in time and perspective, and to have made theirs *the* interpretation shows the weaknesses, at least of historians of economic thought and in this case of Keynes scholars specifically, for example, Patinkin and Klein, in analysing sources with full scrutiny.[5] This is of course all the more astonishing in the specific case of the *Treatise*, as economists continued, from time to time, to be challenged by an intransigent Hayek, claiming he had 'succeeded in demolishing his [Keynes's] main theoretical structure' (1963; 1995, p. 59), 'his theoretical scheme, (essentially volume 1)' (1966; 1995, p. 241)! Hayek represented Keynes as struggling to explain his ideas in an understandable way:[6] 'I feared that before I had completed my analysis he would again have changed his mind', wrote Hayek. He claimed that Keynes had earlier told him that between the appearance of the first and the second parts of Hayek's review of the *Treatise*, Keynes had even 'changed his mind and no longer believed what he had said in that work' (1966; 1995, p. 241). Have not historians of economic ideas been the least bit curious to investigate about what 'in that work' Hayek believed Keynes had changed his mind and whether or not he really had?

What is this 'theoretical structure' of Keynes that Hayek claimed he had 'demolished' and had he? Hayek had great difficulty with Keynes's notions of 'profit and income' (1931, pp. 124–8), and 'investment' (1931, pp. 128–31). It is with respect to new investment, the core element to the dynamics of Keynes's trade cycle, which he found most baffling, that Hayek wrote: 'It is certainly no accident that the inconsistencies of terminology, to which I have alluded before, become particularly frequent as soon as investment is referred to' (1931, p. 131); 'I have tried hard to discover what Mr. Keynes means by investment by examining the use he makes of it, but all in vain' (1931, p. 132); 'I understand – I am not sure whether Mr. Keynes really intends to convey the impression – that the total received from these two sources will be equal to the value of the "securities", and there would then be no reason to introduce the latter term' (1931, p. 137).[7]

Keynes was not swayed from his ideas by the early accusations of inconsistency, obscurity, and ambiguity in his use of terminology, but he was disturbed by the distraction they seemed to present to his immediate reviewers.[8] He was very clear throughout his responses to both Hayek[9] and Robertson that he felt that they had got him wrong. In his response to Hayek's review of the *Treatise*, Keynes wrote, 'I think I can show that most of my alleged terminological inconsistencies are either non-existent or irrelevant to my central theme' (1931b, p. 387). Keynes was in fact rather dismissive of that type of criticism, indicating in his rejoinder that it is 'not whether I may have used the word 'investment' in a different sense in one chapter from what I have in another . . . which Dr. Hayek and I ought to debate' (1931b, p. 390).[10]

Most of what has been said about the *Treatise* here thus far stems from the reactions of Hayek and Robertson. Their importance lies in the fact that their assessments were quickly adopted and taken for granted by the next generation of economists, as if they alone defined the work's contribution. First and foremost it is striking with respect to their criticism of his terminology that Robertson's and Hayek's understanding of Keynes's *Treatise* was based almost exclusively on the semantic difficulties raised by that work. Their critiques should, however, be analysed further with regard to the difficulties they also found in his methodology and theory. To do so, it is suggested to take a look first at Books 3 and 4 of the *Treatise*, which both Robertson and Hayek thought were the core of Keynes's main theoretical contribution:

> most of the practical conclusions . . . are based on a part of the work (Books 3 and 4) which is so highly technical and complicated . . . it is this part on which everything else depends. It is here that all the force and all the weakness of the argument are concentrated, and it is here that the really original work is set forth. (Hayek 1931; 1995, p. 122)

Language itself, it would appear, created the impasse that blocked understanding of Keynes's economic theory. The aim here is thus in part to place his critics' evaluations of the *Treatise*, whether opinionated or legitimate, within an analysis and scrutiny of the corpus of his works and their contribution. Some of the critiques were based on Keynes's actual words, found either in the work or here or there in a particular response of his, but these reflections of Keynes cannot circumscribe his contribution overall. Books 3 and 4 of the *Treatise* are thus now to be dissected, and then Robertson's and Hayek's objections, including their unwarranted criticism of the related semantics, will be addressed.

3.2 KEYNES'S DEFINITIONS OF TERMS

Keynes's various commentators focused rather narrowly on specific aspects of the *Treatise*. Hayek, for example, became obsessed with Keynes's unusual use of current terminology. Others were distracted by the so-called mechanical truism of the Fundamental Equations, questioning both their pertinence and their dynamics. In order to be absolutely clear about both Keynes's premises and his theory as a whole, understanding his terms is essential. This can be achieved by analysing patiently Book III of the *Treatise*, chapters 9–14 on the Fundamental Equations[11] and Book IV of the *Treatise*, chapters 15–21 on the dynamics of the price-level.[12] Only then would it be possible to counter Hayek's and Robertson's criticism of the so-called inconsistencies in Keynes's definitions and use of vocabulary.

As will be seen in what follows, despite his critics' accusations, Keynes provided no lack of clarification for his concepts. At the start of Book III of *A Treatise*, 'The Fundamental Equations', Keynes included a whole chapter on certain definitions. First, it must be stressed that his was a new macro perspective in the making, unfamiliar at the time. His concepts were conceived to reflect a totality, an economy as a whole. Which terms were then important for Keynes? How did he define them, and why did he define them the way he did?

1. *Income:* Keynes defined *Income* (**E**, Keynes' own symbol) as '(1) *the community's money income*; (2) *the earnings of the factors of production*; and (3) *the cost of production*' (1930, I, p. 123). Income, from the first perspective (1), as the income of the community in money terms, as a macro-aggregate, includes all revenues or payments, namely, wages, rents, remunerations, pensions, and benefits as well as depreciation on capital. Keynes also defines income as (2) what is earned from producing Consumption-goods (**R**) and Investment-goods (**C**), and (3) what is paid to produce those goods, as can be seen in Keynes's model (Figure 3.2 below).
2. *Profits:* For Keynes, Entrepreneurs's aggregate *Profits* or losses (**Q**) are not included in Income (**E**) (see Figure 3.2). Entrepreneurs' profits and losses are only some of their earnings (as a group). For Keynes, Entrepreneurs play two roles and receive payments from two sources: (1) they are organizers of current production and (2) they are planners of the firms' horizon for long-term production capacity. As organizers, Entrepreneurs receive a salary or 'normal remuneration', an income already included in **E**. Their second task is of a different nature because production planning entails risk, a commitment to investment in capital (which comes in different types: fixed, working, and liquid),

and an understanding of the asymmetrical impact of decisions to expand or to curtail the use of capital. (Entrepreneurs' plans must take into consideration the lags before 'the supply of specialized factors of production can be increased' and the commitments or contracts for a given amount of production when the factors are available (1930, I, p. 126).) At any moment in time, current outputs, made up not only of Consumption goods but also of Investment goods may exceed or fall short of market demands. It is discrepancies between what is available and what is wanted that give rise to windfall profits and losses (**Q**) (see Figure 3.2).[13] Although these profits are abstracted from **E**, as a form of income or earnings for Entrepreneurs – 'traders of all kinds, dealers and as well as producers' – they are either consumed or saved.

3. *Savings: Savings* (**S**) are 'the sum of the differences between the money-incomes of individuals and their money-expenditure on current consumption' (1930, I, p. 126) (see Figure 3.2). Savings, **S**, and profits, **Q**, together form the fund available for investment; 'the aggregate of Savings and Profits' equals 'the value of current investment' (1930, I, p. 126).

4. *Investment:* By *Investment* (**I**)[14] Keynes meant net investment, net of depreciation. It is Investment, or additional increment, that affects the capacity of production. Keynes made a distinction between the physical net addition (reflected in the lower half of Figure 3.2) and the market value of that net addition (its counterpart in the upper half of Figure 3.2). Rate of (physical) investment is 'the net increment during a period of time of the capital of the community' (1930, I, p. 126). The net market value of investment is 'the value of the increment of capital during any period' (1930, I, p. 126).[15]

These four concepts, *Income*, *Profits*, *Savings*, and *Investment*, whose definitions were the main focus for Keynes's critics, are crucial to his theory. Although the vocabulary Keynes chose to use was the same as that of his contemporaries, the way he defined his concepts was highly unusual and unique to his model in the *Treatise*. Semantically and subsequently theoretically, to have separated (windfall) *profits*, **Q** from the *income* of the community, **E**, to have distinguished and adopted two different roles for the Entrepreneurs – managers (who receive a 'normal remuneration' **E**) and risk-taker-shareholders (who reap *profits*, **Q**), to have made *investment*, **I** equal to *savings*, **S** plus *profits* (**I = S + Q**), and finally to have made a distinction between the rate of *investment* and the value of the net *investment* are indeed unusual implications of shifts in meaning in his contemporary vocabulary of economics. In addition to the four central concepts above, there is also a host of other terms which in Keynes's work took on

Total output and stock of real capital

	Flow of use	Flow of goods
Available	**I** Finished *Final goods* [Hoards] Fixed Capital **(FC)** Houses & durable goods Fixed goods	**II** Finished *Final goods* [Hoards] Non-durables: Food & perishables,[a] & other raw materials (redundant or precautionary) Liquid goods and services **(LK)**
Non-available	**III** Unfinished *Goods in progress in process* Surplus stocks **(LK)** Working Capital **(WK)** Raw materials (minimum stocks)	**IV** Finished *Instrumental goods* Fixed Capital **(FC)**

Net Additions

WK + FC + Hoards + Stocks

= FC + WK + LC

Furthermore: **R** goods (Consumption-goods)[b] = Final goods

FC goods (capital goods)[c] = FC + WC_C

C goods (Investment-goods)[d] = Non-available (including WC_R) +
changes in Hoards

Notes:
(a) See 1930, II, p.136 for the distinction between the different categories of final goods.
(b) This corresponds to the goods ready for consumption, namely, part of Boxes I and II.
(c) See 1930, I, p. 130. This corresponds to finished equipment and parts ready to be used to produce more of that equipment, namely, part of Boxes I, III and IV.
(d) See 1930, I, pp. 130–131. This corresponds to all of Boxes III and IV, and to the Hoards of Boxes I and II.

Figure 3.1   Classification of goods

a slight difference in meaning from conventional usage at the time, among them most of the vocabulary related to output, capital, and the production process.

Figure 3.1 has been created to encapsulate some aspects of Keynes's

semantics and perspective on the production of goods. For him, production was an ongoing operation in which at any point there is addition or
subtraction to cumulative past investment. Current output is made of available and non-available,[16] and finished and unfinished[17] goods and services.
A first category, available current output, is comprised of those goods and
services which are 'finished', final goods ready for consumption, and/or
those which are unfinished, namely the surplus stocks, which Keynes called
'other forms of liquid capital' (1930, I, 127).[18] These 'other forms' are raw
materials, held for precautionary purposes. Current output in the form of
non-available goods is also comprised of finished and unfinished goods.[19]
The first are instrumental goods, or fixed capital, and the latter are goods
in progress and raw materials in use that assure the continuation of production. All these categories reflect net additions to the stock of capital.

It is, thus, clear that Keynes was quite succinct about what is produced at
a given point in time, and how much of that is for final consumption (Boxes
I + II) and how much is intermediary goods (Boxes III + IV). Since current
output of all goods and services is conceived as part of a continuum of past
production and what is to come, Figure 3.1 is a snapshot of a flow process in
which some goods coming out of the production flow are consumed at one
point in time (for example, a meal, Box II), while others are enjoyed over a
period of time (for example, a house, Box I). A machine or a tractor comes
out of production at one point in time (Box IV), whereas components,
which lead to the construction of final or instrumental goods, are themselves
produced and used during a period of time (Box III). Not everything that
is produced at one point in time necessarily finds use or demand. 'Stocks' is
the term that Keynes used to mean 'required for efficient business': normal
stocks are 'part of Working Capital and therefore in process, whilst surplus
stocks are to be regarded as liquid' (1930, I, p. 129). He reserves the term
'Hoards' to mean the unsold, current, available, final output or the withdrawal from past, available output when what is demanded is greater than
current production. Therefore, Stocks refer to reserves or stockpiles of
intermediary goods; Hoards, to those of Final goods.

Production is conceived by Keynes as 'flow'; thus, by definition, stocks
and hoards consist of the pluses and the minuses of current output,
added or subtracted to past, accumulated intermediary and final goods.
When current output (depicted in Figure 3.1) is taken together with past
cumulative investment, for an economy as a whole:

> The stock of Real Capital or material wealth existing at any time is embodied
> in one or other of three forms:
> (1) Goods in use, which are only capable of giving up gradually their full
>   yield of use or enjoyment.

(2) Goods in process, i.e., in course of preparation by cultivation or manufacture for use or consumption, or in transport, or with merchants, dealers and retailers, or awaiting the rotation of the seasons.

(3) Goods in stock, which are yielding nothing but are capable of being used or consumed at any time.

We shall call goods in use *Fixed Capital* [FC], goods in process *Working Capital* [WK], and goods in stock *Liquid Capital* [LK]. (1930, I, p. 128)

Keynes's three categories of capital, Fixed, Working, and Liquid, are not necessarily specific to any one box in Figure 3.1. For example, a finished house, whether sold or waiting to be sold, is an item of Fixed Capital in Box I, whereas a machine or equipment is also an element of Fixed Capital, yet it is considered a part of the contents of Box IV. Similarly, Hoards, which consist of consumer final goods (in the warehouse, on shelves, and so on), and/or surplus raw materials held for precautionary motive, both in Box II, as well as surplus stocks in Box III are all referred to as Liquid Capital. Working Capital, on the other hand, is restricted to Box III.

In volume II of *A Treatise*, Keynes devoted a chapter to each of the three categories of capital in which he attempted to give some empirical support to his analysis of their relative importance over the course of the trade cycle. Distinction between these categories of capital is crucial, since individually and collectively, they determine for Keynes the behaviour of the credit cycle, as will be explained in detail in Chapter 4. The chapters in volume II of *A Treatise* give a good indication as to why Keynes chose to define different types of capital, and why he decomposed the process of production the way he did. Briefly, as regards divisions of capital, Keynes's model differs markedly from that of the 'Classical economists' (meaning for Keynes both Classical and neoClassical): 'The Classical Economists emphasized the distinction between fixed capital and what they called "circulating capital". But they did not clearly distinguish my third category of capital "goods in progress" or working capital which is not identical with their "circulating capital"' (1930, II, p. 128).

Now that Keynes's most important terminology and the various categories of capital (which for an impatient Hayek presented a 'jungle of differing definitions') are identified, accounted for, and explained, one can turn to the purpose of Keynes's theory in *A Treatise*. At any point in time what is produced as total output will not necessarily correspond to total demand, but for that total output to have been produced, it will have required payment corresponding to the cost of the factors of production which realized it.

Thus consumption is governed by the amount of the *available* output (*plus* any drafts on hoards), not by that of the *total* output; whereas – so long as the money-rates of remuneration of the factors of production are unchanged – the money-income of the community tends to move with the *total* output. (1930, I, p. 128, original emphasis)

On the whole, for an economy, it is the differences between the when and why payments are received, and the when and how monies received are spent, which give rise to discrepancies between what is available and what is wanted. It is the shortages and excesses in total output that give rise to profits, relative changes in income distribution, and economic fluctuations.

3.3 'WINDFALL' PROFITS: THEIR CHARACTERISTICS AND THEIR IMPACT ON THE THREE CATEGORIES OF CAPITAL, THE SOURCES OF CYCLICAL FLUCTUATION

In an unusual practice in economics, Keynes deliberately isolated windfall profits from total income and made them central to his theory of the credit cycle. In a market economy, the existence of windfall profits and losses is what triggers entrepreneurs to engage in or to curtail additional investments. The trickle-through effect of investment decisions is felt on both the financial and capital sides of the economy. Changes in investment fuel or slow down production. Keynes viewed production as a whole, as a continuous, dynamic process with an overlap of goods produced, goods in use, and goods in progress, some being sold, some intended for absorption in production, and some finding their way in or out of stocks and hoards. In his theory, production takes time and means commitments: monies are spent and machines are put into use. Changing or reversing course in the middle of an operational phase is not always an option.

It is the weighing of the future returns and the costs of carrying the financing for new investment, as well as the current and future performances of the market for the goods and services produced, which together determine whether new investment will take place. Windfall profits are rarely sufficient in themselves to carry the costs of new production; thus even as the catalyst for new investment, they are usually supplemented with large loans from the financial market. For Keynes, profits depend on the efficiency of production, that is, costs in relation to sales of output and ease of raising or obtaining funds in the financial market. He considered profits in the hands of entrepreneurs, dealers, and shareholders to have particular characteristics. Just like income in the hands of individuals, windfall profits can be either consumed or saved. Consumption out of windfall profits obeys, for Keynes, a different logic from consumption out of the money income of individuals:

however much of their profits entrepreneurs spend on consumption, the increment of wealth belonging to entrepreneurs remains the same as before. Thus
profits, as a source of capital increment for entrepreneurs, are a widow's cruse
which remains undepleted however much of them may be devoted to riotous
living. When, on the other hand, entrepreneurs are making losses, and seek to
recoup these losses by curtailing their normal expenditures on consumption i.e.,
by saving more, the cruse becomes the Danaid jar which can never be filled-
up; for the effect of this reduced expenditure is to inflict on the producers of
consumption-goods a loss of an equal amount. Thus the diminution of their
wealth as a class, is as great, in spite of their saving, as it was before. (1930, I,
p. 139)

As will be explained in detail in the next chapter, windfall profits are
additional income, thus, if some of them are put toward consumption,
they create additional strain on current production in the form of added
demand for final goods. If current production cannot satisfy this extra
demand, the goods desired must come from hoards. This in turn imposes
a double economic pressure: on the prices of consumption-goods, R
goods, and on efforts to maintain R-goods stocks, which, as was seen
in Figure 3.1, are part of working capital. With the extra demand for
R goods, output must increase to meet demand and replenish stocks.
Pressure (or contraction) on R-goods prices becomes a source of further
increase in profits (losses) and affects the bullishness (bearishness) of
the market; it is profits (losses) which lead to further additional increment (decrease) in investment, which impacts the various components of
Capital, and so on. What is being alluded to here is a seeming multiplier[20]
effect built into consumption out of profit. It is interesting to note that
in volume II of *A Treatise*, Keynes made a further distinction between
productive and unproductive consumption, which depends on whether
or not the consumption leads to the creation of employment. (This new
distinction will be elaborated in Chapter 6.)

In sum, the deliberate isolation of windfall profits (losses) from the community's income is crucial to Keynes's theory, as windfall profits (losses)
are the central element from which the dynamics of his credit cycle flows.
Before proceeding in the next chapter to the analysis of Keynes's credit
cycle dynamics, it is asked how all the above definitions and components
fit together.

3.4 BOOKS 3 AND 4 OF KEYNES'S *TREATISE ON MONEY*

In an interesting and novel methodological way, Keynes tried in *A
Treatise on Money* to provide an alternative theory relating the general

price-level to money, one appropriate to dynamic analysis. Keynes succeeded in bringing the interest rate implicitly into his theory, in addition to prices and money, and savings and investment. As Robertson and Hayek astutely perceived, all through his Fundamental Equations, Keynes made 'the rate of interest and its relation to saving and investing the central problem of monetary theory' (Hayek, 1931; 1995, p. 121; see also Robertson, 1931, pp. 404–5). Thus far no analyses in the literature[21] (including those of Patinkin and Klein, which have focused exclusively on the mechanical aspects of the Fundamental Equations and the conditions of equilibrium) have systematically gone through Books 3 and 4 of volume I of the *Treatise* and reconstructed how, through the Fundamental Equations, Keynes's theory evolved from a condition of equilibrium into a full-fledged dynamic credit-cycle theory of an open economy. An attempt will thus be made here to do so, in part by distilling Keynes's prose into a diagrammatic representation (Figure 3.2). Keynes's theory of the credit cycle is discussed in full in Chapter 4.

3.4.1   The Model of Keynes's *Treatise on Money*

Windfall profits are defined collectively as the difference between the market value of the total national output – which can be taken as the return from the Gross Domestic Product (GDP) – minus the total Gross National Income (GNI) – which includes every payment, such as pensions and benefits, and the provision for consumption of capital. Obviously, at any one point in time at the end of the line of production, what is produced and what has been paid to the factors of production to produce that total product are by definition equivalent. When, however, that total product actually reaches the market, it is not sure that the market value of what is sold will be equivalent to the totality of what has been earned in producing the total product. It depends on whether the income earned from producing the product will be expended on that product in its entirety or to a greater or lesser degree. In other words, actual sales and purchases are not necessarily equal to expected sales and purchases. There is constant recourse to tapping into stocks and hoards when demand is strong and adding to them when demand is lacking.

Also, as identified in Figure 3.1, in relation to definitions of terms, not everything produced is available for consumption or to be sold (Boxes III and IV). Discrepancy in how much is produced, the decision of entrepreneurs, and how much production is absorbed in the market, the decision of buyers, determines the course of production and employment. Coupled with market speculation and entrepreneurs' strategizing about future earnings, these two decisions, independently meeting different objectives, constantly affect relative prices and demands for goods and services, and in turn shift resource allocation. It is from this dynamic that Keynes's theory of the credit cycle derives. Keynes divided production into two categories, Consumption-goods (**R** goods) and Investment-goods (**C** goods), and made a distinction between the cost-price value of the Investment-goods (**I'**) and the market value of Investment-goods (**I**). The discrepancy between **I** and **I'** is the signal which drives the commitment to or the foregoing of additional investment, which then affects the capacity of production.

3.4.2 Definitions and Causal Relationships

The *Treatise* sets out a macroeconomic model centred on the concept of windfall profits. Figure 3.2 depicts how the macro-relationships of the model in the *Treatise* relate to one another. Macroeconomic windfall profits, given by the difference between the market value and the cost of corresponding total output, are central to Keynes's analysis; their derivation can be expressed algebraically as follows:

$$Q = \prod O - [wL + RE + rK + R + P\&B]^{22} \tag{3.1}$$

Q, or windfall profits (losses) emerge, for Keynes, when the return on total current product $[\prod O]$ is greater (less) than total cost (or income, in terms of wages, remunerations, interest on capital, rent, and pensions and benefits).

Albeit the trigger for increase (decrease) in net investment, windfall profits are one of two components of investment. Keynes defined the value of current investment as 'equal to the aggregate of Savings and Profits'[23] (1930, I, p. 126).

$$I = S + Q$$

Windfall profits can thus also be expressed as:

$$Q = I - S \tag{3.2}$$

Equation 3.1 highlights the relation of profits to market value of output and production cost and equation 3.2, their relation to investment as one of its sources. These are two expressions of profits, articulated in value terms.

Keynes described in detail both the *real* components of the production process, encapsulated graphically in the lower half of Figure 3.2 (Loops I

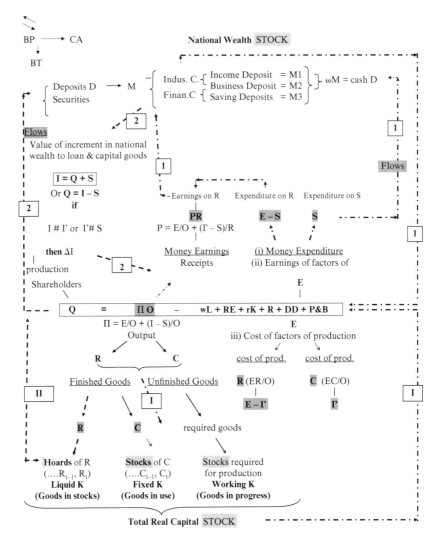

Figure 3.2   Keynes's A Treatise on Money

and II) and the *income and monetary* counterpart, captured in the upper half of Figure 3.2 (Loops 1 and 2). When the market value of the real output and cost of producing that output, or the income received, are identical, (windfall) profits are zero; in Keynes's theory, this describes an economy in a steady state (Loops I and 1). The existence of windfall profits (losses), due to market activity and speculation, which triggers shifts and changes in the monetary aggregate and investment (in the upper half of Figure 3.2), makes the dynamics of the economy more complicated. Finance and speculation enter the analysis, as liquidity shifts affect the market rates of interest, which rates are being continually contrasted by the entrepreneurs to the rates of return from what has been produced. Changes in investment lead to readjustments of the level of production (described in the lower half of Figure 3.2). In terms of the figure, Loops I and 1 become extended by Loops II and 2.

The working of a monetary market economy is determined, on the one hand, by its capacity to produce goods and services and, on the other hand, by its ability to create money to express income and finance investment. The capacity to produce (the *real* side), summarized in the lower half of Figure 3.2, is governed by the state of total real capital. That capital includes the total, past, accumulated investment, namely all quantities of machinery, goods in stock, goods in use, and goods in process, to which there is a constant potential addition of current total output, net of current consumption. This part of Keynes's description is backward looking. In Figure 3.2, the counterpart upper half corresponds to the stock of national wealth, held as assets in various bank deposits and securities. In this half of the diagram, 'traders of all kinds, dealers as well as producers' (Hawtrey, 1931, p. 618) are constantly weighing the market performance of their assets in relation to their expectations of future earnings. Here, the perspective is forward looking.

First, the symbols of Figure 3.2 are examined:

The real or production side of the economy – Figure 3.2, lower half
The economy produces Consumption-goods, **R** goods and Investment-goods, **C** goods, as described in Figure 3.1, 'Classification of goods'. Keynes defined the average unit cost as total cost **E** per unit of output **O**, or **E/O**. The costs of production are divided into the cost of producing **C** goods, **I'**, equivalent to **EC/O**, and the cost of producing **R** goods, **E-I'**, equal to **ER/O**. The sum of the two costs is equal to **E**, defined, using one of Keynes's definitions, as 'the cost of production'.

Of the total output, the final goods or Consumption-goods will in principle be sold, used, and disappear. The Investment-goods, which are made up of goods in use, goods in progress, and goods in stock, are net real investment added to the total real capital stock.

When the economy is in equilibrium, markets clear and **Q** = 0 (Loop I). Consumption-goods supply satisfies market demand. Net real investment is just enough to keep the total capital stock intact. The economy is in a steady state. If, however, there is over or under production and the economy is in disequilibrium, **Q** ≠ 0. As demand is greater or smaller than current production, there is call for drawing on hoards or adding from and to stocks. (Loop II becomes a supplement to Loop I.) The accumulation or depletion of hoards and stocks will correspondingly either require additional investment or allow for depletion of capital. Keynes's model is that of an open economy. There is an inflow and outflow of goods and services (evoked by BT, balance of trade, in Figure 3.2), which complements or draws on the national production and the national stock. Thus the disequilibrium between domestic market demand and actual current supply can be caused either by internal or balance-of-trade discrepancies.

The income side of the economy – Figure 3.2, upper half
The cost of production, **E** above, is also **E**, the earnings of the factors of production, which is also called money expenditure. The earnings are deposited in the bank either as savings, **S**, in a savings deposit, M_3, or as transactional funds, **E-S**, in an income account, M_1 (see Figure 2.3). The **E-S** deposits are used to buy **R** goods and become the total money receipts of the firms. These receipts are deposited by the firms into either business accounts, M_2, to be used to pay for the ongoing costs of production, or savings accounts, M_3, to satisfy the firms' precautionary or speculative motives for liquidity. In addition to the domestic flow of money, there is also the flow of money, which finds its way into the various deposits, resulting from international movement in the balance-of-payment (BP) accounts, in and out of the balance-of-trade (BT) or the capital account (CA, in Figure 3.2).

The holdings of stocks, securities, bonds, Treasury deposits, and so on, and the total deposits in the national banking system, M_1–M_3, constitute the national wealth stock. That stock is in the hands of the public, the banks, and the central bank. It is through the domestic institutions of the Government, the Central Bank, the banking system, and the stock market, and through international foreign exchange that the stock of national wealth shifts in form and location. The supply of money itself (taken in the broadest sense) is the deposits M_1–M_3. The demand for and the supply of money are affected when there is creation of new money by the Government, by international inflows or outflows of capital, and/or by shifts in asset liquidity.

Keynes introduced a division in the bank deposit total between *Industrial Circulation* and *Financial Circulation* (Figure 2.3). *Industrial Circulation* is the money that circulates in the buying of goods and services and in the paying for the ongoing cost of production (Loop 1). *Financial Circulation* is that money used for precautionary or speculative purposes, some of which is funnelled toward new investment, when it is called for (Loop 2). The state of windfall profits shows to what extent the earnings of financial investments are above or below their normal levels, which might induce bullishness and speculation or bearishness and withdrawal from the stock market. When there are windfall profits which end up in the hands of shareholders as dividends, rates of return, and so on, they make their way either into the various bank deposits or back into stocks if there is every indication of the potential for higher future earnings. In this case, money would shift with the buying of stocks and securities from the more liquid assets of the *Industrial Circulation* to the less liquid state of the *Financial Circulation*. This means that more money would become available for new investment, **I**. It is in short the reactions of consumers, firms, speculators, shareholders, and foreign investors that effect transfers of assets from one Circulation form into another. These transfers have an impact on both the market rate of interest and the reallocation of resources to either C-goods or R-goods production.

From Figure 3.2 it can be seen clearly that when the economy is in equilibrium, **Q** = 0, **I** = **S,** and the market value of the total national output (the total receipts of the firms) is equal to the total earnings of the factors of production, $\prod$O = [wL + RE + rK + R + P&B]. In this case in which the economy is in a stationary state, Loop 1 is the flow of money that corresponds to a counterpart flow of the production of goods and services (Loop I). There is no change in either net investment or productive capacity. In this case, and only in this case, the circulation of transactional money equals exactly the flow of goods and services. For Keynes, this is the case of the Classics, in which the Quantity Theory of Money holds (1930, I, pp. 148–50).

Of course what was most important for Keynes were the circumstances of **Q** ≠ 0. For him, a market economy, characterized by fund-raising in the stock exchange to finance a great deal of R- and C-goods production, meant the potential for windfall profits (or losses), **Q**, for the speculators, investors, dealers, and so on. This occurs when the economy is not in a production-demand equilibrium and/or when the market value of the total national output is not equal to the total earnings of the factors of production. If, for example, there is a sudden desire on the part of income earners of the community to save less and consume more, the immediate impact is to increase the price of R goods, which increase in price means positive profits (Loop 2). (Some or all of the demand for increased R goods would be met from hoards, reflected in the counterpart of Loop 2, Loop II.) The profits and accompanying needs to replenish stocks and hoards will stimulate investment, particularly in the C-goods industry. If further profits are forthcoming, expectations can become bullish, although the expansion will not go on forever. Likely, at one point, an overproduction of C goods will depress their prices, and therefore investors' profits, which will lead to an overturn. A more detailed discussion of cases of **Q** ≠ 0 and how windfall profits and losses lead to the credit cycle will be given in Chapter 4.

3.4.3 Fundamental Equations

Keynes's Fundamental Equations have already been introduced in Chapter 2, in relation to the Quantity Theory of Money. Here it will be shown that Keynes's five key concepts – income, profits, savings, investment, and prices – are all encapsulated in his two Fundamental Equations. The 'first' is the overall expression or index of the price of Consumption-goods (1930, I, p. 135). The 'second' is the overall expression or index of the price of the total output (1930, I, p. 137).

Fundamental Equation I: the price of R goods
The price, **P**, of R goods is equal to the unit cost of production, **E/O** plus the difference between the cost of production of new investment goods **I′** and savings **S**, per unit of R good.

$$P = E/O + (I' - S)/R \quad \text{or} \quad P = W_1 + Q_1/R \qquad \text{(FEI 3.3)}$$

The equation can also be formulated as the rate of earnings per output or rate of efficiency earnings, W_1, plus the profit per unit of R good, Q_1.

It should perhaps be noted at this point that Keynes did not devise an equation for **P′**, the price of C goods. He did, however, explain the price formation of **P′** and made clear that it was quite independent of **P**. As seen in equation 3.3, the price of R goods depends on how much income earners are paid for producing goods (whether C or R goods) and how much of their pay they decide to spend on R goods. In the case of C goods, there are no specific buyers who play a role in their price formation. As can be seen in Figure 3.1, C goods or investment goods are goods in use, goods in process, and goods in stock. Some are finished; some, unfinished. Some are available; some, unavailable. As a whole they exist for future use in production or to respond to future demand. **P′** could not, therefore, be determined by a current valuation but depends on a notion of future returns. Entrepreneurs decide independently of the income earners what proportion of their output to dedicate to R and C goods (1930, I, p. 136). Their decisions about any new investment depend on the value of that increment, **I**, relative to the cost of just produced C goods, **I′**. The estimated market value of **I** is determined by expectations of the value of its future yield. These expectations are themselves driven by the bullishness and bearishness of the public (everyone – income earners, speculators, traders, investors) toward liquidity, 'the disposition of the public towards "hoarding" money' (1930, I, p. 144), and therefore the form in which their savings are held.

While Robertson was critical of Keynes for not providing a formula for P', Hayek used Keynes's algebra and derived P' as being equal to the unit cost of production E/O plus the difference between the market value and the cost of producing C goods per unit of C good.

$$P' = E/O + (I - I')/C \quad \text{or} \quad P' = W_1 + Q_2/C \qquad (3.4)$$

Indeed, defining P' in this manner is tantamount to lumping all Keynes's classifications of goods together, save for the final Consumption-goods, and collapsing therefore his liquid, working, and fixed capital into one. This defies Keynes's distinctions (Figure 3.1) and blurs the role each category and each type of capital play in economic fluctuations. While Hayek's P' reflects the current value of all the components of capital, since they are not in the market, existing, as noted above, only for future demand, their valuation depends on the future state of the market. The P' of equation 3.4 is not that of Keynes.

Fundamental Equation I (FEI 3.3) is a price expression of the state of the market in terms of the supply and demand for R goods. Fundamental Equation II (FEII 3.5) is a price equation for the overall output, R goods and C goods together.

Fundamental Equation II: the overall price-level π

$$\Pi = E/O + (I - S)/O \quad \Pi = W_1 + Q/O \qquad (\text{FEII } 3.5)$$

Keynes was aware that the overall price of total output is made up of **P** and **P'**,[24] even though the decisions which determine them are different and independent. It can be seen that the first term of Fundamental Equation II, the cost of production, E/O, is still the same as in Fundamental Equation I (FEI 3.3). The second term is now, however, expressed as the difference between the market value of C goods, **I** and savings, **S**. (Already introduced in Chapter 2, where Fundamental Equation II was related to the Quantity Equation, was its connection to the interest rate.) The overall price depends therefore on the current cost of production, current savings, as well as the estimated market value of **I**, which is determined by expectations of the value of its future yield and the behaviour of the money market.

Further discussion of Fundamental Equation II will be pursued in following chapters, specifically with regard to the dynamics of the overall price level, the discrepancy between investment and savings, and the interest rate.[25] Already, however, it can be noted that unless the Fundamental Equations are considered in the context of their essential definitions, Keynes's classification of goods (Figure 3.1), and the dynamics of *A Treatise* (Figure 3.2), these Equations may well not be understood at all, as was the case with Robertson and Hayek. Others, such as Hicks, simply misunderstood them, for much the same reason of lack of general context. For Hicks's part, although sympathetic, he misread the *Treatise* by taking it piecemeal and thinking thereby that it presented three different theories of money instead of a single, unified one:[26]

> Mr. Keynes's *Treatise*, so far as I have been able to discover, contains at least three theories of money. One of them is the Savings and Investment theory, which, as I hinted, seems to me only a quantity theory much glorified. One of them is a Wicksellian natural rate theory. But the third is altogether much more interesting. It emerges when Mr. Keynes begins to talk about the price-level of Investment-goods; when he shows that this price-level depends upon the relative preference of the investor – to hold bank-deposits or to hold securities. Here at last we have something which to a value theorist looks sensible and interesting! Here at last we have a choice at the margin! And Mr. Keynes goes on to put substance into our *X [marginal utility]*, by his doctrine that the relative preference depends upon the 'bearishness' or 'bullishness' of the public, upon their relative desire for liquidity or profit.
>
> . . . It seems to me that this third theory of Mr. Keynes really contains the most important part of his theoretical contribution: that here, at last, we have something which, on the analogy (the appropriate analogy) of value theory, does begin to offer a chance of making the whole thing easily intelligible; that is from this point, not from velocity of circulation, natural rate of interest, or Saving and Investment, that we ought to start in constructing the theory of money. But in saying this, I am being more Keynesian than Keynes . . . (Hicks 1935b; 1982, pp. 48–9)

From the upper half of Figure 3.2 describing the various monetary flows, it is clear that Keynes did not have three different theories of money, as Hicks interpreted the *Treatise*, but two different situations, as Keynes had indicated: (1) when Q = 0 and (2) when Q ≠ 0. The first is the case when hypothetically an economy is in equilibrium and earnings are equal to the total output produced; windfall profits are zero and the financial markets are neither bullish nor bearish (that is, there are no shifts in liquidity preference that affect the interest rate). Only then does I = S and the Quantity Theory of Money hold. The second is the case when otherwise there is a difference between I and S, and/or the cost of producing capital goods, I′, and their market valuation, I, due to speculation about future earnings; this is when the volatility of the components of investment financing, bullishness and bearishness, (Figure 3.2, Loops 1 and 2) affects decision-making and enters into his model. Therein lies his full-fledged liquidity theory. Hicks was nonetheless insightful in perceiving how, in an original definition of the price-level of Investment-goods, Keynes had introduced a novel way of linking price to expectations and the preferences of investors (and speculators).

Since Hicks, like Hayek, tried to impose Wicksell on Keynes, some clarification about the relation of Keynes's *Treatise* to Wicksell's theory is in order, before addressing the main points of Hayek's criticism of the *Treatise*.

3.5   A NON-SEQUITUR OF WICKSELL

Hayek accuses Keynes of being ignorant of the contributions of Böhm-Bawerk in the treatment of capital, presuming that Keynes could not read German and was thus unaware of the German literature. Keynes, however, acknowledged Spiethoff, Knapp, and mainly Wicksell, whose writings at the time were mostly available in German.[27] There is in fact striking similarity between some of the thoughts expressed by Keynes in *A Treatise* and those in Wicksell's *Interest and Prices* (1936) and *Lectures on Political Economy* (1934 and 1935). On the surface, it might even appear that Keynes so intensively appropriated ideas from Wicksell that some of the so-called novelty of Keynes is already to be found in Wicksell's work (see Appendix as well).[28]

The major, common emphasis in both Keynes and Wicksell is to have brought the interest rate to the forefront in the analysis of prices and to have de-emphasized, even trivialized, the Quantity Theory of Money. As already explained in Chapter 2, both belong to the tradition of the Credit School as opposed to the majority of economists who were steeped in the Currency School. Both used the concepts of a 'natural', 'normal', 'money', or 'bank', 'market', and 'real' rate of interest. Both incorporated 'normal' prices and 'market' prices into their economic picture.

As in Wicksell, for Keynes the root cause of economic fluctuations is to be found in the existence of discrepancies between the real and money rates of interest, and as Wicksell put it:

> for so long as an entrepreneur obtains a larger return on the capital employed in his production than he need pay in interest for borrowed capital – or can himself obtain by lending his own – he will of course, be inclined to increase his employment of capital. Conversely, if the interest on borrowed capital is higher than the return on capital employed in production, or on the last portion employed, then he will, as far as possible, curtail his employment of capital to the most necessary purposes or to the more profitable branches of his production. (1934, I, p. 148)[29]

Furthermore, in Wicksell's 'Note on the Trade Cycle and Crises' in volume II of his *Lectures*,[30] the similarities between his ideas and those of Keynes's later *Treatise*, explaining price movements in prosperity and in depression in relation to the interest rate, go beyond striking:

> Since the demand for new capital in an upward swing of the trade cycle is frequently much too great to be satisfied by contemporary saving even if it is stimulated by a higher rate of interest, and since on the other hand in bad times this demand is practically nil, though saving does not nevertheless entirely cease, the rise in the rate of interest and commodity prices in good times and their fall in bad times would presumably be much more severe than now if it were not that the replenishment and depletion of stocks in all branches of production producing durable goods acted as regulator or parachute. (1935, II, pp. 212–13)

New capital and the resorting to stocks of durable goods as regulator are important themes in Keynes's theory as well. Wicksell's notion of direct correlations between 'additional' profits and losses, rises and falls in the prices of the factors of production, stocks of commodities, money incomes, and 'the normal, natural rate' of interest is also to be found in Keynes's *Treatise*.[31] At times Keynes's text is, with some degree of acknowledgement, almost verbatim Wicksell. Witness Wicksell: 'The loan rate, which is a direct expression of the real rate, we call the normal rate' (1935, II, p. 192) and 'The rate of interest at which *the demand for loan capital and the supply of savings* exactly agree, and which more or less corresponds to the expected yield on the newly created capital, will then be the normal or the natural real rate' (1935, II, p. 193, original emphasis); and Keynes: 'Following Wicksell . . . the natural-rate of interest is the rate at which saving and the value of investment are exactly balanced' (1930, I, pp. 154–5).[32]

The two works can be contrasted in much more detail to find out further common ingredients to their respective theories. Having noted the similarities, there is, however, a fundamental difference in their semantics, in their methodological approach, and in the building of their theoretical dynamics:

1. The Fundamental Equations are unique to Keynes. Wicksell did have a coherent, general theoretical description as to how interest impacts prices, but nowhere in Wicksell can one find a definite expression, similar to Keynes's or otherwise, relating price level to the interest rate, even though it is the core relation of Wicksell's entire theory.

2. The important concept of the capital on which trade cycles are built includes in Wicksell, descriptively, 'all auxiliaries to production . . . the houses and buildings . . . the implements, tools and machinery . . . livestock . . . raw materials . . . the provisions and other commodities

which must be saved up [to support labour]' (1934, I, pp. 144–5). These 'auxiliaries' resemble some of Keynes's categories of capital. Wicksell, however, theoretically, abstracted altogether from them and reduced capital to a single entity: 'all these requisites have only one quality in common, namely that they represent certain quantities of exchange value, so that collectively they may be regarded as a single sum of value' (1934, I, p. 145). He then steeped himself in the marginalist capital theory of Böhm-Bawerk. Wicksell remained a strong proponent of the Austrian marginal productivity theory. For him, *'Capital is saved-up labour and saved-up land. Interest is the difference between the marginal productivity of saved-up labour and land and of current labour and land'* (1934, I, p. 154, original emphasis).

Upon close reading of Wicksell and Keynes, the meaning, incorporation, and causal links around the idea of capital are decidedly different. First, Keynes's different categories of capital, Fixed, Working, and Liquid, which each play a different role in the dynamics of the various phases of the cycle, are not to be found in Wicksell. Second, Wicksell's collapse of all capital into a single unit expressed in terms of saved-up labour and land runs into all the problems of the heterogeneity of physical capital and the controversies related to it.[33] While Wicksell himself raised some of the difficulties, Keynes avoided them altogether. Third and most importantly, while for Wicksell, the real rate of interest is expressed by its marginal productivity, an *ex-post* concept, for Keynes, it is determined by the expectations and anticipation of future returns on investment, *ex-ante* notions. Conceptually and methodologically thus, the two theories of capital and interest are on different plains.

3. While the main cause of fluctuations in Wicksell is due to the introduction of new technology – monetary effects being secondary – which triggers discrepancy between two rates of interest, the money and the real rate, in Keynes, though he admits that technological change might cause discrepancy, the main cause of fluctuation is the state of bullishness and bearishness of the market based on the entrepreneurs' expectations of future earnings or losses. For Wicksell,

> The principle and sufficient cause of cyclical fluctuations should rather be sought in the fact that in its very nature technical or commercial advance cannot maintain the same even progress as does, in our days, the increase in needs – especially owing to the organic phenomenon of increase in population – but is sometimes precipitate, sometimes delayed. (1935, II, p. 211)

Wicksell's perspective is long term, an application of neoClassical production theory, in which capital and labour are factors of production, and the cost of production is made up of Fixed and Circulating (or Liquid) capital, respectively. For Wicksell, since 'new discoveries, inventions, and other improvements nearly always require various kinds of preparatory work for their realization, there occurs the conversion of large masses of liquid into fixed capital which is an inevitable preliminary to every boom' (1935, II, p. 212). Keynes's approach is short term; it is the behaviour of Working Capital that makes his theory original. Fixed and Liquid Capital, defined entirely differently from Wicksell and the Classics, as explained above, do, however, come into play.

In sum, given points (1), (2), and (3), it is clear that Keynes and Wicksell present two entirely different theoretical approaches to describing the economy, even though Wicksell's ideas predate those of Keynes, and Keynes was aware of them. Further, as will be seen in Chapter 6, Section 6.3, in terms of the policy implications of their thought, they also presented two different perspectives. For now, with Keynes's definitions and semantics explained and clarified, the criticism that the *Treatise* generated can be addressed.

3.6   GROUNDLESS CRITICISM OF KEYNES'S SO-CALLED SEMANTIC INCONSISTENCIES

As Hawtrey summed up Keynes's semantics,

> Mr. Keynes has a command of language unsurpassed among contemporary economic writers. But does that justify him in declaring a dictatorship of the vocabulary? Some of his definitions are undoubtedly valuable, and may well form an addition to economic language. But others impose on words of common use, such as Income, Profit, Investment, and Savings new and unfamiliar meanings. (1931, p. 618)

Obvious in the immediate reviews of *A Treatise* was that Keynes's use of terms created uneasiness. While a few of the serious readers of the *Treatise* have made an effort to grasp their meaning, both Hayek and Robertson were carried away and confused, considering semantic differences to be real differences of theory, despite the fact that they agreed from the outset that Keynes's language was difficult and unusual. This cannot be said of Hawtrey, who tried his very best to read Keynes literally, but even he in his interpretation could not help himself from relapsing into use of the words in their 'ordinary sense' (1931, p. 618). It is the criticisms of Keynes's semantics from these early, very powerful thinkers which derailed the focus away from his theory and spilled over into even more criticism over vocabulary – from the less than insightful analysis of Patinkin to the even more frivolous assessment of Klein, whose objections are just bits and pieces picked up and adopted from Hayek and Robertson, and others.

From the impact on the profession as a whole, it is Robertson's criticism to some extent and Hayek's reaction to the *Treatise* to a large extent that set the starting tone. Hayek's very lengthy review was so powerful and dismissive that it became the source to echo by many other critics. Since it is Hayek's review that was the source of the derailment of the *Treatise* and since Hayek, more than any other reviewer of Keynes, dissected the theoretical aspects of the *Treatise*, focusing on that review should be sufficient to clarify where things went astray.

From the reading of Hayek's two-part review of 1931 and 1932 and the description and explanation of Keynes's terminology and semantics (above), it seems that Keynes was right in his response, rejecting the accusations of 'terminological inconsistencies'. If confusion and mixing-up of definitions there was, it was to be found in Hayek's assessment of Keynes and not in Keynes's work itself. Hayek would have obtained a better understanding of the *Treatise* and more dialogue with Keynes had he put his subtle probing of the *Treatise* in the form of questions rather than embarrassing accusations. The puzzle nonetheless is how did Hayek, an extremely intelligent scholar, who read the *Treatise* seriously, fall into such youthful ebullience as to be carried away into error?

The explanation is obvious. Hayek was so steeped in the Austrian theory of capital and the belief in the superiority of that theory that he could not see Keynes's treatment of capital other than through that theory. No wonder he thought that if Keynes had taken another theory of capital, that of Böhm-Bawerk, as given, he would not have run into harm. More will be said about Hayek's own approach to capital theory and the trade cycle in Chapter 4. From what has been examined so far about Keynes's theory, the approach starts from a totally different set of premises and therefore its perspective is quite different from that of the Austrians. It must be read first on its own terms. The theoretical approaches of Keynes and Hayek respectively are so complicated that forcing one into the other *a priori* causes such a confusing intermingling that it is bound to lead to errors of interpretation.

Hayek totally missed the point of a review. In fact he showed that he did not read Keynes to understand him but was instead annoyed that he could not find in either the semantics or the analysis of Keynes's theory what was already well established in the foundations of the Austrian theory of capital, running from Böhm-Bawerk to Wicksell and Mises and beyond.

Mr. Keynes tries to incorporate into his system the ideas of Wicksell. In Wicksell's system, these are necessary outgrowths of the most elaborate theory of capital we possess, that of Böhm Bawerk. It is apriori unlikely that an attempt to utilize the conclusions drawn from a certain theory without accepting that theory itself should be successful. But in the case of an author of Mr. Keynes's intellectual caliber, the attempt produces results which are truly remarkable (1931; 1995, p. 130)

In fact, obliquely critical of the theory, Keynes was clearly not indebted to the Austrian tradition of capital theory.

Hayek's 45-page, two-part review is so dense and terse that if every sentence were to be challenged, it would take another book to do so. There are four difficulties that Hayek had encountered in Keynes's theory which he thought rendered it confused and inconsistent: the concepts of profits, investment, income, and the related notion of dynamics. Hayek tried in the fifth part of his review to make 'an attempt to give a synoptic view of the process as Mr. Keynes depicted it which I hope will give an adequate idea of the essential elements of his exposition' (1931; 1995, p. 133). To highlight the most important points of Hayek's review, it would be quickest to jump directly to his 'Diagrammatic Version' of Keynes's model (1931, p. 283). It is reproduced here as Figure 3.3, in order to pursue analysis of the various points of his criticism.

It is interesting first to note that Hayek refers to his depiction of Keynes's process of production as his 'Theory of the Circulation of Money'. Hayek seems to have understood the importance of money in Keynes's *Treatise*. A contrast between Hayek's representation of Keynes, Figure 3.3, and the diagram of Keynes offered in Figure 3.2, reveals, however, that Hayek's version is a much more simplified picture, which has left out a great degree of essential detail. In Figure 3.2, the whole process is focused on the Profit Equation, which disassociates the aggregate receipts of entrepreneurs, **E-Q**, from the aggregate cost, **E** (which Keynes calls also Community income). In Hayek's representation, Figure 3.3, there is, however, clearly *intended symmetry* between Keynes's income earners, who produce consumption goods and investment goods, and his entrepreneurs, who obtain receipts from those goods.

Hayek created three triangles representing: how Community income is divided into Consumption goods and Savings, how the same Community income results from the Production of consumption and investment goods, and how the income of the entrepreneurs derives from their investment in the Production of consumption and investment goods. As he read the flows of income in his three symmetrical triangles (Figure 3.3), what is paid as income for factors of production, equivalent to the cost of production for entrepreneurs, is also the same thing as what is expended on output. For him, it became evident that Keynes's theory could not handle dynamics. In Hayek's terms: 'income available for the purchase

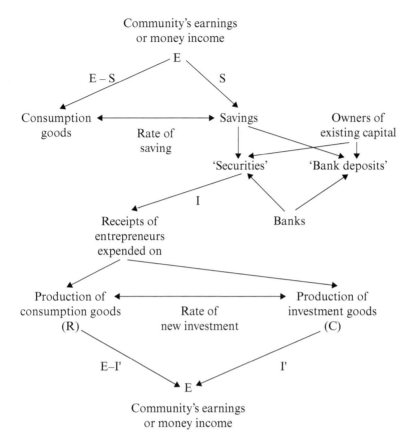

Note: The formulae on which the above diagram is based are as follows:

R + C = O (quantity of total current output)

$$\frac{E}{Q} = W_1 \text{ (rate of efficiency earnings)} = \frac{W}{e} \text{ (rate of earnings per unit of human effort} \div \text{the co-efficient of efficiency)}$$

Q_1 (Profit on consumption goods) = (E − S) − (E − I′) = I′ − S

$$P \text{ (Price level on consumption goods)} = \frac{E}{O} + \frac{I' - S}{R} = W_1 + \frac{Q_1}{R} \qquad (1)$$

Q_2 (Profit on investment goods) = I − I′

$$P' \text{ (Price level of investment goods)} = \frac{E}{O} + \frac{I - I'}{C} = W_1 + \frac{Q}{C}$$

Q (Profit on total output) = (E − S) + I − E = I − S

$$\text{(Price level on total output)} = \frac{E}{O} + \frac{I - S}{O} = W_1 + \frac{Q}{O} \qquad (2)$$

Figure 3.3   Hayek's model of the Treatise

of output and the earnings of the factors of production, will be identical
. . . this could only be true in a stationary state . . . in dynamic society that
assumption does not apply' (1931; 1995, p. 135).

Keynes had attempted to open a breach in the traditional equilibrium
approach, by making windfall profits the trigger of economic fluctuations
and thus change. Hayek, however, in line with his conception of balanced
forces in the market, read the *Treatise* from an equilibrium perspective, in
relation to earning and spending, saving and investing, and the production
of consumption and investment goods. For Hayek, economic change is
part of the market, whose spontaneity makes for equilibrium. For Keynes,
however, change lies in lags, time lapses which define the relationship of
variables to one another: notably profit in relation to income, but also
investment in relation to savings, and production of Investment-goods
in relation to that of Consumption-goods. Hayek had difficulty with
Keynes's methodology and found, for example, that 'the central and most
obscure theme of the book, [is] the description and explanation of investment . . . He does not even explain the conditions of equilibrium at any
given rate of saving, nor the effects of any change in the rate of saving'
(1931; 1995, pp. 128–9).

From his conception of Keynes's *Treatise* model, Hayek had eliminated
the central element in Keynes's theory, profits, **Q**. 'I cannot agree with his
explanation of why profits arise, nor with his implication, that they are the
only source of change'; they are 'simply and solely spontaneous changes
in the quantity and direction of the flow of money' (1931; 1995, p. 124).
Obviously, the two authors had different understandings of profits. From
the outset, Hayek rejected Keynes's separation of profits from income.
Keynes differentiated the ownership of capital from the management
of production, in order to distinguish between the source of financing
(investment) and the creation of added value (production). Keynes's
entrepreneurs wear two hats and receive earnings from both roles. Hayek
objected:

> [it is an] artificial separation of the function of the entrepreneurs as owners of
> capital and their function as entrepreneurs in the narrow sense. But these two
> functions cannot be separated even in the theory, because the essential function
> of the entrepreneurs, that of assuming risks, necessarily implies the ownership
> of capital. (1931; 1995, p. 128)

The existence of profits as defined by Keynes and all the changes in
the monetary aggregate are inconsistent with Hayek's assumption of a
stationary-state analysis, unless in the former money is neutral. This is
certainly not the case for Keynes. (1) 'Money income', (2) the earnings
of the factors of production, Hayek's 'Community earnings', and (3) the

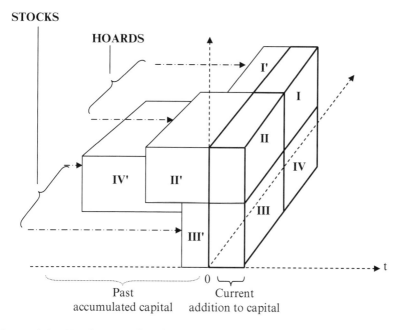

STOCKS

HOARDS

Past
accumulated capital

Current
addition to capital

Figure 3.4   Total accumulated capital

cost of production, again 'Community earnings' in Hayek, are, however, the same quantity for both Keynes and Hayek. They are simply expressed differently: what is received by the factors of production is what the entrepreneurs spend and it is also the cost of what was paid to produce the output from those factors. Production and investment cannot, however, be isolated from monetary factors. Moreover, current production does not necessarily correspond to current demand, as in Hayek's interpretation. Therefore what entrepreneurs receive for their current output can be, but is not necessarily, the same amount as the earnings to the factors of production. It is the unexpected discrepancies between what is produced (current output) and what is sold (available output) that affects stocks and hoards, and gives rise to the potential for windfall profits (losses) which in turn impact investments, and financial borrowing and liquidity shifts.

As mentioned in the definitions above, Keynes made consumption depend on available output, while income depends on total current output. While wealth is financial assets of varying liquidity, it is also physical capital in the form of hoards and stocks and the means of production. This second form is depicted in Figure 3.1, extended now in Figure 3.4, to show both the current addition to capital (Figure 3.1) as well as past accumulated capital.

At any point in time, income for Keynes corresponds to what is received from producing current output (Boxes I through IV). Consumption, however, can draw from current Final Available Goods, Boxes I and II, as well as from past production, the Hoards in Boxes I′ and II′. Boxes I′ and II′ expand or shrink due to whatever current demand happens to be. Changes to them impact Boxes III, III′, IV, and IV′, to curtail or replenish their Hoards. None of these aspects of Keynes's theory made their way into Hayek's interpretation, except as he dwelled on how Keynes's account of net addition to the capital of the community 'is by no means sufficient if only the total or net increment (or decrement) of investment goods in all stages is considered and treated as a whole, and the possibility of fluctuations between these stages is neglected; yet this is just what Mr. Keynes does'[34] (1931, p. 274).

Hayek ignored altogether Keynes's distinctions between the various physical capitals, Fixed, Working and Liquid, and how additions (depletions or decay) to capital make Boxes I′ though IV′ shrink or expand as a reflection of the total capital stock. Hayek does not seem to have been able to move away from the Austrian approach of stages of production, which is not the perspective for Keynes. Hayek twisted Keynes's definition of income back to its ordinary usage and locked his theory into the steady state or equilibrium, by disassociating real from monetary disturbances (their counterparts). Hayek eliminated altogether Keynes's idea of windfall profits (losses) as the prime mover of the shrinkage and expansion of capital and the reason for economic fluctuations, as Keynes described them. Instead Hayek offered a comparative static analysis based on his reduced version of Keynes's theory.

From his truncated interpretation of Keynes, Hayek proposed to analyse independent spontaneous changes in: (1) the rate of savings, (2) the rate of investment, and (3) the money made available to entrepreneurs by the banks from unused savings. Hayek proceeded to show how a change in (1), keeping (2) and (3) constant, will 'never give a rise to total profits, but only to partial profits balanced by equal losses, and only leads to a shift between the production of Consumption-goods and the production of Investment-goods which will go on until profits on both sides disappear' (1931; 1995, p. 141). The same is true when (2) is changed, while (1) and (3) are held constant. Only a change in (3), keeping (1) and (2) constant, will lead to any change, and that change is in the level of Price.

In short, from Hayek's review, Keynes's theory does not allow for discrepancy between I and S. The second term of Keynes's Fundamental Equation thus has no justification. The only change that can effect an increase in current production must come from increased efficiency in production. That is found in the first term of the Fundamental Equation. Those changes are real and not monetary.

The content of Hayek's tortuous detour was not unfamiliar to Keynes. In fact, Hayek's description of equilibrium analysis and its consequences are those described by Keynes himself in the *Treatise* (1930, I, pp. 149–50). Keynes made the observation that his theory could accommodate the Fisherian case, where the Quantity Theory of Money applies, as an extreme case under special hypothetical circumstances, but that it was far from the objective of the *Treatise*. Hayek, however, trapped himself, and Keynes's theory, which he reviewed, in that very hypothetical case, as the only way to define an equilibrium from which one might begin. By redefining Keynes's terms, he established a dichotomy between monetary and real factors and created a case which negates any possible changes of the former on the latter, although he read Keynes to assert that it would not. Since, however, such interrelations are exactly what *A Treatise on Money* is about but in a dynamic system that links precisely money and production, Hayek's challenging criticisms were directed at a theory that does not resemble Keynes's.

NOTES

1. It is from this two-part review that the myth that Keynes was not careful, was inconsistent, and was not well read, especially in the German literature, derived and snowballed thereafter.
2. It is argued here that the trade-cycle theories of Keynes and Hayek had similar features and yet their conceptions of monetary mechanisms and transmissions led to some opposing conclusions. This is contrary to Caldwell's absurd, off-the-cuff assertions in his introduction to *Contra Keynes*, a volume of Hayek's collected works: 'Both purported to be supplying a general theory of the cycle, and in this neither was successful' (1995, pp. 46–7).
3. For example, Pierro Sraffa, Joan Robinson and Richard Kahn.
4. For example, high unemployment, a looming war, and social unrest among intellectuals.
5. Kahn echoed some of the sentiments of Hayek, especially the idea that 'One great problem arises from the ambiguity of the word *investment* . . .' (1984, p. 71, original emphasis). Klein was so bold as to consider the work *and* its reviews as a whole: 'We shall take the *Treatise* and some of the review articles built upon it as the status of Keynesian theory . . .', which derived from 'the confused state of Keynes' ideas at the time' (1966, pp. 15, 16). Patinkin would be another exemplary perpetrator of the mythology: 'The *Treatise*, however, is a book with strange and forbidding formulas, and even stranger concepts' (1976, p. 33).
6. This contributed to the reigning misconception that Keynes's exposition was 'unsystematical' (Klein, 1966, p. 241).
7. Hayek considered 'securities' to mean 'investment in the ordinary sense' (1931, p. 137).
8. Despite Keynes's countering Robertson's and Hayek's accusations, a persisting myth arose from their reviews that Keynes was confused, inconsistent, not careful, and, in addition, not well read.
9. In his response to Hayek's review of *A Treatise*, Keynes dedicated the whole of the last section of his rejoinder, V, to 'Dr. Hayek's criticisms of my use of terms' (1931b, pp. 396–7).

10. Keynes also noted that imprecision of definitions could be found in his reviewers' texts: 'Dr. Hayek and Mr. Robertson both make use of the term "saving" or "voluntary saving". But though they criticise my definition of "saving", I am not aware that they have precisely defined it themselves' (1931b, p. 393).

11. In these chapters of Book III of *A Treatise*, Keynes introduces his Fundamental Equations and their relation to money. He explains the Quantity Theory of Money in the conditions of equilibrium. He presents his perspective on the discrepancies between savings and investment, and the 'modus operandi' of the bank rate. He considers alternative forms of the Fundamental Equations.

12. In these chapters of Book IV of *A Treatise*, Keynes discusses the role of finance in production through his *Industrial Circulation* and *Financial Circulation*. He analyses the various causes of disequilibrium on the purchasing power of money, whether due to monetary factors or investment factors. He studies some aspects of the credit cycle in detail. He finally considers some impacts of international disequilibrium.

13. Keynes chose to call this second type of payment to Entrepreneurs simply *profits and losses* as opposed to 'windfall profits and losses' (1930, p. 125).

14. I is not to be confused with I', which symbol Keynes uses to define the *ex-post* cost of production. I is the *ex-ante* increment of investment.

15. 'the value of current investment . . . will be equal to the aggregate of Savings and Profits' (1930, I, p. 126, see also ibid., p. 130).

16. 'The current output of the community, as distinguished from its money-income, is a flow of goods and services, which consists of two parts – (a) the flow of liquid goods and services which are in a form available for immediate consumption, and (b) the net flow of increments (after allowing for wastage) to capital goods and to loan capital . . . which are not in a form available for consumption. We shall call the former "liquid" or "available" output; the latter "non-available" output' (1930, I, p. 127).

17. 'The goods existing at any time can also be classified into *Finished Goods* and *Unfinished Goods*. The finished goods consist of *Final Goods* which are for the enjoyment of the ultimate consumer, and *Instrumental Goods*, which are for use in process' (1930, I, p. 129).

18. 'The liquid or available output is made up of two streams, namely, (a) the flow of use accruing from fixed consumers' (or final) capital, and (b) the flow of consumers' or final goods emerging from the productive process in a liquid form' (1930, I, p. 127).

19. 'The non-available output is made up of (a) the excess of the flow of increment to unfinished goods in process over the flow of finished goods (whether fixed or liquid) emerging from the productive process, and (b) the excess of the flow of fixed capital goods emerging from the productive process over the current wastage of all fixed capital, together with the net increase in loan capital' (1930, I, p, 127).

20. Keynes did not use the term multiplier in the *Treatise* but the idea was there.

21. Among the supporters of Keynes, Shackle (1938) was perhaps one of the most important in that he actually did study the text word for word.

22. Profits (Q) = Price (Π). Output (O) − [Wagebill, including unemployment benefits (wL) + Normal Remuneration for Entrepreneurs (RE) + Interest on Capital (rK) + Rents (R) + Pension and Benefits (P&B)], net of depreciation.

23. 'We shall mean by Savings the sum of the differences between the money-incomes of individuals and their money-expenditure on current consumption' (1930, I, p.126).

24. See Keynes's simple algebraic manipulation, transforming $OΠ = PR + P'C$ into equation FEII 3.5 (1930, I, p. 137).

25. In terms of the time horizon, it can be seen from Fundamental Equations I and II that the first term is determined in the long run, while the second refers to short-period fluctuations.

26. Hicks did, however, to his credit, indicate which chapters in the *Treatise* were the inspiration of which of the 'three different theories'.

27. Given the depth of Keynes's understanding of Wicksell, is it likely that he would have acquired his knowledge of him through secondary literature?

28. By proponents of the Swedish school, the same is said about Keynes's relationship to their ideas.

29. 'And similarly, in certain cases a great rise in prices, may, in fact be maintained by private credit alone, i.e., by substitution of credit on goods for money transactions. . . . A person who procures goods or services on credit might for one reason or another offer a higher rate of interest without a loss, if the chances of profit have increased. If, however, the seller only demands the usual interest, or, in the case of a short loan, no interest at all, then the buyer might instead offer a higher price for purchased goods' (1935, II, p. 193).

30. Wicksell himself credits some of these ideas to Spiethoff and finds similarities between his own observations and those of Juglar (1935, II, p. 209).

31. 'Entrepreneurs who see their expected additional profits vanishing owing to the rise in price of raw materials and labour will wholly or partly realize these profits, thanks to the rise – which has already taken place – in the prices of the goods they produce, whereas workmen and landlords whose incomes are apparently increased only to a small extent will derive no benefit because the stocks of the commodities in demand are limited. The gains they actually reap correspond *in this case* principally to the positive losses suffered by the other consumers, borrowers, pensioners, and others, whose money income has not been increased at all in the process. On the basis of these new prices the future is judged. Entrepreneurs who until now have been able to offer workmen, owners of raw materials, etc., higher prices simply because they are themselves able to borrow money at cheap rates without expecting more than normal prices for their products, will now, *even if bank rate reverts to the normal natural rate*, on an average be able to offer the same high price, because they have reason to expect the same increased prices for their own products (or rents or freights, etc) in the future. If, therefore, the banks maintain the lower rate of interest, it will act as a tempting extra profit to entrepreneurs and by competition between them they will force up still further the price of labour and materials and indirectly of consumption goods, and so on' (1935, II, p. 196, original emphasis).

32. 'Following Wicksell, it will be convenient to call the rate of interest which would cause the second term of our second Fundamental Equation to be zero the *natural-rate* of interest, and the rate which actually prevails the *market-rate* of interest. Thus the natural-rate of interest is the rate at which saving and the value of investment are exactly balanced, so that the price-level of output as a whole (π) exactly corresponds to the money-rate of the efficiency-earnings of the Factors of Production. Every departure of the market-rate from the natural-rate tends, on the other hand, to set up a disturbance of the price-level by causing the second term of the second Fundamental Equation to depart from zero.

    We have, therefore, something with which the ordinary Quantity Equation does not furnish us, namely, a simple and direct explanation why a rise in the Bank-rate tends, in so far as it modifies the effective rates of interest, to depress price-levels' (1930, I, pp. 154–5).

33. The literature on the capital controversy from Wicksell to Knight to the dispute between the two Cambridges however enormous is well documented and should not concern us here.

34. Furthermore he adds, '[I]nstead of a '"horizontal" division between capital goods . . . Mr Keynes attempts a kind of vertical division, counting that part of the production of capital goods which is necessary for the continuation of the current production of consumption-goods as a part of the process of producing consumption-goods, and only that part of the production of capital goods which *adds* to the existing stock of capital as production of investment-goods. But this procedure involves him, as we shall see, in serious difficulties when he has to determine what is to be considered as additional capital – difficulties which he has not clearly solved' (1931, pp. 278–9, original emphasis).

4   Keynes's theoretical shift: casualty of the criticism of the *Treatise*

It was considered essential in the previous chapter to dwell on the mean-ings of Keynes's terminology in order to understand the premises on which Keynes's theory is built and to counter Hayek's and Robertson's criticism of Keynes for his so-called inconsistencies in definitions and uses of vocabulary. Now that the difficulties with Keynes's semantics, which so distracted Hayek, are clarified, a brief note is added here about Hayek's frustration with Keynes's reaction to his own work. Hayek was, simulta-neously as he was evaluating Keynes's new *Treatise*, defending his own theory presented in *Prices and Production* newly circulating in English in 1931. From Cambridge, both Keynes and Pierro Sraffa harshly rebuked Hayek's work. Leaving aside this time the rhetoric of the exchange, the two theories will be contrasted.

Comparing the almost contemporaneously appearing works of Keynes and Hayek should shed light on the similar and differing aspects of their approaches. Both Keynes and Hayek, like Wicksell, were concerned in their respective models with the causes of economic fluctuations. Both attempted to explain how money, prices or price level, investment, and savings are related and how the interactions of these specific variables impact production, employment, and income or income distribution. Both considered production as a process in which two types of goods are pro-duced,[1] and further like Wicksell, they distinguished them as consumption goods – Hayek's 'consumers' goods' and Keynes's 'consumption-goods' – and capital goods – Hayek's 'producers' goods' and Keynes's 'investment-goods'. For both, fluctuations in the production process at the scale of the economy as a whole come from the constant shifting of resources from producing one type of good into producing the other, depending on where the return is higher.

Identifying the main differences between the thinkers should allow for the more important aim of the comparison to be revealed. It should help to place Keynes's *Treatise* even more accurately in perspective to see how, in their respective models, Keynes and Hayek developed a trade cycle with quite opposite conclusions as to the impact of monetary theory. In short, they started from some different premises. Although both analysed the real economy as having virtually the same structure of production, Hayek saw that process as horizontal; Keynes saw it as vertical.[2] They differed dramatically on what an increase in the money supply would cause. When an economy is about to slide into recession, for example, Keynes prescribed credit expansion as a form of help, while Hayek, quite the opposite, believed that any such intervention would only aggravate a worsening situation.

4.1 STRUCTURE OF THE PRODUCTION PROCESS IN THE MODELS OF KEYNES AND HAYEK

It has already been explained how in Keynes's theory, windfall profits and losses are the leading cause of changes in investment, which, when taken from a macroeconomic perspective, trigger fluctuations. At any time, production requires financing. The sources of funds, for Keynes, come from the Industrial and Financial Circulations. A change in or a shift between the two Circulations affects the money rate of interest. It is the bullish and bearish attitude of the market toward speculation and saving in the Financial Circulation (money sector), together with the state of the supply and demand for **C** and/or **R** goods (real sector) which, depending on relative profits (losses), causes investment to shift in and out of the production of **R** goods and **C** goods.

The inherent cause of the dynamics in Hayek's model of the trade cycle does not reside in the monetary, or financial, sector, but in the real one. Unlike Keynes, for whom one of the fundamental problems of monetary theory was 'to exhibit the causal process by which the price-level is determined' (1930, I, p. 133) and how it is related to fluctuations in the cycle, Hayek did not attribute any importance to general price-levels, averages or macro-aggregates in understanding the influential causes in the business cycle. His approach to prices is entirely from a microeconomic perspective. As he clearly stated at the beginning of *Prices and Production*:

> Neither aggregates nor averages do act upon one another, and it will never be possible to establish necessary connections of cause and effect between them as we can between individual phenomena, individual prices, etc. I would even go so far as to assert that, from the very nature of economic theory, averages can never form a link in its reasoning. (1931, pp. 4–5)

Hayek's model is based on an interactive economy composed of a large number of economic agents in which, as per the Classicals, capital and resources flow where return is higher. The dynamics of the multitude of actions of supply and demand, as well as the movement of capital and resources, is such that relative prices of commodities tend to adjust and lead toward equalization of the rate of return. To explain cyclical fluctuations, Hayek relied, in the Austrian tradition, on an elaborate model of the average process of production. The schematic drawing of simplified inter-temporal processes of production in Figure 4.1 gives a bare-bone representation of the various microeconomic stages of production.

At any point in time t there is a host of producers' goods $(\mathbf{C})^3$ and consumers' goods $(\mathbf{R})$ being produced. Let, thus, total production consist of j output of $\mathbf{C}_{jt}$ and $\mathbf{R}_{jt}$ goods (j = 0, 1, 2, . . ., k) produced at t (t = 0, 1, 2, . . ., i). Every production is a transformation of the sequence of the factors of that production. $\mathbf{C}$ goods, as intermediate resources and products, go through stages or processes of transformation before they are ready to yield $\mathbf{R}$ goods, as final products. Some of the sequences of processes start at $t - $ i and yield $\mathbf{R}$ goods at t. Some start at $t - $ i + 1 and will produce a final output in t + 1, and so on. Each line j in Figure 4.1 could correspond to a triangular figure presented in Hayek's *Prices and Production*, (for example, the one found in 1931, either p. 40 or p. 50). One must keep in mind that in general: (1) not all processes in the real economy have as a whole the same length; (2) the starting and ending points of all the sequences do not necessarily have to be synchronized; and (3) some of the apparently independent processes would be interrelated, either directly or indirectly. As a theoretical point, the average length of the processes of production and, therefore, also the number of successive stages of production, will change as per the relative demand for C goods and R goods. This is to emphasize that the three complicating characteristics of the production process, above, are omitted from Figure 4.1 and from Hayek's figures for the sake of simplicity only.

Hayek characterizes the series of transformations in his vertical process as movement from a range of higher to lower stages of production, over the course of which, for example, wheat is grown, milled into flour, and then made into bread. He assumes that, in the higher stages of production, firms produce non-specific (**NS**) goods. A raw material, such as wood, might begin to be transformed to satisfy many different uses, as a combustible, building material, or paper pulp, for example. As wood moves into the lower stages of the production process, becoming transformed into a table leg, for example, its uses become quite specific. The lower stages of production are seen as more specialized. Hayek assumes that most lower-stage **C** goods are specific (**S**) goods. **C** goods do, however, have lesser and greater levels of specificity. A simple hammer is a relatively **NS** good, in that it can be used in many different stages of production, in both steel-founding, a higher-stage process, and producing bumpers for a specific car model, a lower-stage process. A particular type of metal press, however,

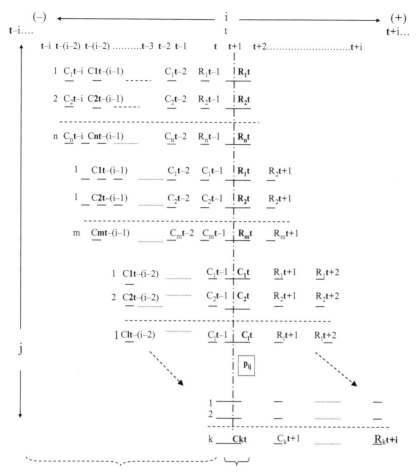

Figure 4.1 contents:

(–) ←——————————— i ——————————→ (+)
t–i....   t   t+i...

t–i t–(i–2) t–(i–2) ....t–3 t–2 t–1   t t+1   t+2...........................t+i

1 C_1t–i C1t–(i–1) C_1t–2 R_1t–1 |R_1t

2 C_2t–i C2t–(i–1) C_2t–2 R_2t–1 |R_2t

n C_nt–i Cnt–(i–1) C_nt–2 R_nt–1 |R_nt

1   C1t–(i–1) C_1t–2 C_1t–1 |R_1t R_2t+1

1   C2t–(i–1) C_2t–2 C_2t–1 |R_2t R_2t+1

m   Cmt–(i–1) C_mt–2 C_mt–1 R_mt R_mt+1

1 C1t–(i–2) C_1t–1 C_1t R_1t+1 R_1t+2

2 C2t–(i–2) C_2t–1 C_2t R_2t+1 R_2t+2

1 C1t–(i–2) C_1t–1 C_1t R_1t+1 R_1t+2

j

P_{ij}

1
2
k ____ Ckt C_kt+1 R_kt+i

Past total cumulated capital   Current output

Notes:
Pij: Price of the ijth C or R good
Vertical perspective i = how the various stages of processes yield final output (Hayek)
Horizontal perspective j = how current output adds or diminishes past total cumulated capital (Keynes)

Figure 4.1   Simple inter-temporal processes of production

designed exclusively for forming bumpers, could be used only in that lower stage of producing a car.

Since he sees the lower stages of production as being those in which specialized goods predominate, Hayek assumes that these stages are more capital intensive. The relative prices (P_{jt}) of the variety of C_{jt} and R_{jt} goods is in relation to their corresponding costs (E_{jt}) at each of the production stages of their output and this determines relative profits, ($r_{C_{jt}}$ and $r_{R_{jt}}$):

$$r_{Cjt} = \frac{P_{jt}C_{jt} - Ec_{jt}}{Ic_{jt}}, j = 1. . .m \qquad r_{Rjt} = \frac{P_{jt}R_{jt} - Er_{jt}}{Ir_{jt}}, j = 1. . .k$$

The factors-of-production prices fall or rise with the prices of **R** goods, whose very output is affected by change in the methods of production. **R** goods prices will fall or rise in greater proportion than those of the factors of production. The average length of the processes of production and, therefore, also the number of successive stages of production, will change as per the relative demand for **C** goods and **R** goods.

Hayek is interested in a vertical perspective of the production processes, in which changes in relative **C** and **R** goods' profits between time t and the time markers of past profit performance constantly redirect the movement of investment to where the returns are higher. Shifts in investment result in a dynamics of the elongating or shrinking of the average period of production. Hayek's approach is both microeconomic and backward-looking, and concerned with a long-run mechanism by which market forces lead to an equilibration of relative prices and rates of profits in every sector.

In comparison, Keynes is not focused on the description of higher and lower stages of production, but only on current goods production. $R_{1t}, R_{2t}, \ldots, R_{mt}$ and $C_{1t}, C_{2t}, \ldots C_{kt}$, is a myriad which, considered in the aggregate, becomes simply **R** and **C** goods at t. The production of **C** goods is, however, sub-categorized into fixed, working, and liquid capitals. Past production is encapsulated in existing current stocks and hoards. It is the expectation, at t, of future earnings, depending on current windfall profits (losses) resulting from both current production and the current state of stocks and hoards of **R** and **C** goods, which determines new investment and whether there will be expansion or contraction in the production of **C** and/or **R** goods. Keynes's approach is both macroeconomic and forward-looking; it is a short-term analysis.[4]

4.2　HAYEK'S MODEL OF *PRICES AND PRODUCTION*[5]

Production equilibrium is Hayek's departure point in *Prices and Production*. He assumes 'all available resources are employed' (1931, p. 32) and then proceeds to explain fluctuations in production and the determination of prices and income by relying on the 'concept of a tendency towards an equilibrium' (1931, p. 31). By production, Hayek means 'all processes necessary to bring goods into the hand of the consumer' (1931, p. 33). Labour and land, he categorizes as '*original means of production*' (1931, p. 33, original emphasis), and together with capital they form the usual '*factors of production*' (1931, p. 34, original emphasis). There are some similarities between Hayek's and Keynes's terminologies. For example, as noted above, in the models of both, there are consumer goods (**R**) and producer goods (**C**). In the case of the latter, all but 'the original means of production', Hayek refers to as '*intermediate products*', meaning '*all* goods which are directly or indirectly used in the production of consumers' goods, *including* therefore the original means of production, as well as instrumental goods and all kinds of unfinished goods' (1931, p. 34, original emphasis).[6]

For Hayek (see Figure 4.2), to the production of each **R** and **C** good must correspond, at any point in time, full payment to the factors which contributed to its production. It is by resorting to the method of 'value added' that Hayek models the covering of the total costs of production, or total expenditure on the factors of production, by the sums received out of the sales of **R** goods. The money earned in producing **R and C** goods is the money income (**E**). Some of the income becomes savings (**S**); some, **E-S**, is used to buy **R** goods. **E−S** expended on **R** thus becomes the Money Earnings of the firms selling the **R**-goods output. Hayek's model, like Keynes's, has a banking system with a variety of forms of deposits. His notion of saving and investment is, however, much simpler. What is saved necessarily becomes investment (**I**); money is not held idle. Both the entrepreneur's earnings and savings become money available to finance the next round of production. Hayek sees no complications in the transformation of savings into investment (**S = I**).

The production cycle in Hayek is a reflection of normal ongoing economic activity, with the multitude of economic actors manifesting, through the demand and supply of goods and services, their preferences for more consumption relative to savings or vice versa. Their economic decisions make resources in the productive process shift from the production of one type of goods into another, namely, from **C** into **R** goods or from **R** into **C** goods. The 'main cause of fluctuation of the output' is the 'changes in the use made of existing resources' (1931, p. 32). In its search for higher return, investment (**I**) flows between capital-intensive (**Sgoods**) processes and stages with relatively lesser specialization (**NSgoods**), resulting in the shrinking or elongating of production. '[I]ncrease of output [is] made possible by transition to more capitalistic methods of production' (1931, p. 32).

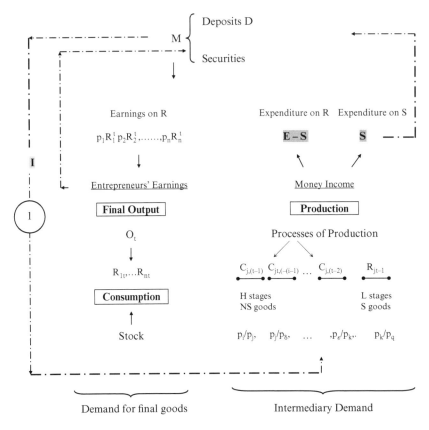

Figure 4.2   Hayek's Prices and Production

Hayek explains the shrinking or elongating of the production process as stemming from changes in the preferences of individuals for consumer goods now or later. Their decisions affect the relative production of **C** and **R** goods. He saw it as 'an essential feature of our modern, "capitalistic", system of production that at any moment a far larger proportion of the available original means of production is employed to provide consumers' goods for some more or less distant future than is used for the satisfaction of immediate needs' (1931, p. 34). For Hayek, deferred consumption was required for capital investment to elongate the structure of production, but the consumer would ultimately reap the benefits of having waited for **R** goods, since 'by lengthening the production process we are able to obtain a greater quantity of consumer's goods . . . provided we are willing to wait long enough for the product' (1931, pp. 34–5).

4.3 THE DYNAMICS OF THE CYCLES OF HAYEK AND KEYNES

The dynamics of the two models are now discussed separately. Given the cumbersomeness of the verbal presentation of each, it will be helpful to reconstruct and compare the two with the aid of two sets of figures. The first is of different 'situations' in Hayek's trade cycle (Figure 4.3). The second represents the sequence of events following, for Keynes, on different 'openings' (Figure 4.4).

4.3.1 The Dynamics of Hayek's Trade Cycle in *Prices and Production*

The trade cycle of Hayek's industrial organization consists in constant movement of resources that creates fluctuations in output resulting from the elongation and shrinking of the structure of production. Among the causes of the shift in resources, for Hayek, the monetary ones are of two kinds: natural, due to individual voluntary saving, or unnatural or forced, due to 'uncalled for' and hence imposed changes in credit. In order to disentangle the impact of these changes, Figure 4.3 presents schematically four different situations Hayek describes, (ii)–(v), set collectively against the backdrop of Situation (i), Equilibrium. Situations (ii) and (iii) represent his descriptions of changes in the economy due to an initial alteration in the quantity of voluntary savings. Situations (iv) and (v) represent the impacts of an infusion of 'uncalled for' credit.

Situation (i): Equilibrium, the starting point for the dynamics of Hayek's cycle In Hayek's mode of reasoning, changes in the trade cycle, and hence the four scenarios to be discussed, can only be understood if analysed against the backdrop of a steady-state equilibrium. If individuals are left to themselves to choose their preferences for current consumption and if future consumption and resources are free to be employed in the stage/s of production where the return is highest, then, Hayek posits, there is inherent tendency in a market economy for the equalization of relative prices and rates of return in each sector, r_n (the dotted line in Figure 4.3), including the money rate of interest, r_m (represented by the dark horizontal line). This is the equilibrium depicted in Figure 4.3 (i), with rate of return and relative price on the vertical axis and the snapshot of the production of **C** and **R** goods on the horizontal axis. For Hayek, 'if we want to explain economic phenomena at all, we have no means available but to build on the foundations given by the concept of a tendency towards an equilibrium' (1931, p. 31). In Hayek's 'stationary society' (1931, p. 37), while all opportunities for relative earnings are exploited, the rates of

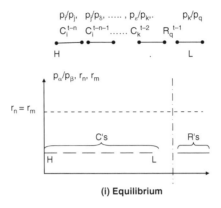

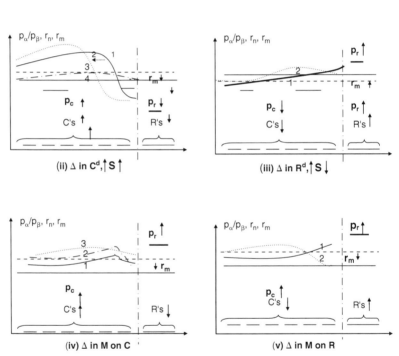

Figure 4.3   Average period of production

return on investment are the same at each stage of the production process of **C** goods, which leads to the production of final goods, **R** goods. This is true whether one considers production at one point in time ($R_{1t} \ldots R_{mt \ldots}$, $C_{1t}, \ldots C_{kt}$) or over time ($C_{jt-i}, C_{jt-i-1}, \ldots C_{jt}, R_{jt}$). Such a stationary state is never fully realized.[7] Hayek recognizes that while there is always tendency toward it, there is as well the potential for fluctuations away from it. One might rightly ask, what impedes the full realization of this equilibrium?

Voluntary saving
Hayek posits two situations of consumers' using a portion of their income of one period voluntarily in a different way from how they used in it a former period, namely, changing the relative amounts of money they spend or save and thereby invest. In either case, consumers will feel the effects of their acts on total real income through their own money income. Hayek assumes that either voluntary activity takes place 'continuously' (1931, p. 46) and that the impact of it on the economy is an immediate translation into correspondingly different processes of production, while '[T]he [total] amount of money in circulation and its velocity of circulation are also supposed to remain unchanged' (1931, p. 47). More (less) money is oriented toward either investment in **C** goods (when **S** increases) or the purchase of **R** goods (when **S** decreases). In both cases, the output of consumers' goods will be sold for a sum different from before (reduced or elevated), since the proportion of the demand for **R** goods, and hence the price of a unit of **R** goods relative to the demand for **C** goods, and the price of a unit of the factors of production, will be changed. While the total spent on **C** goods will increase or decrease because of the addition or subtraction of stages of production, the amount of money spent in the lower stages of production will also change relative to the amount used in the higher stages. Connecting the monetary side of the model with its real side, Hayek reminds the reader that, 'To this change in the distribution of the amounts of money spent in the different stages of production there will correspond a similar change in the distribution of the total amount of goods existing at any moment' (1931, p. 49). Figure 4.3 (ii) and 4.3 (iii) attempt to give a schematic picture of two different impacts of voluntary saving.

Situation (ii): Increase in saving / increase in production of C goods (under full employment) What happens when there is an increase in voluntary saving? Taking the specific example of the situation in which it is supposed that consumers save and invest an amount of money equivalent to a certain portion of their income of one period, the following can be observed. By definition, for Hayek, an increase in voluntary saving means a decrease in the consumption of **R** goods. Hence, the amount of money spent during the period in question on **R** goods themselves and, at the same time, the amount of money received as income in payment for the use of the factors of production to produce those goods decreases. The price of a unit of **R** goods will fall in the greater proportion, but most of the relative prices of the units of the factors of production will also fall, although not in the same proportion overall. Due to the reduced amount of money made available for consumption because of increased saving, the impact of the drop in the prices of **R** goods is felt most strongly in the lowest stage of production, the one 'immediately preceding that in which the final touches are given to consumers' goods' and 'more strongly than the effect of the increase of the funds available for the purchase of producers' goods of all kinds' (1931, p. 70).

A narrowing of the price margin between the last stage of **C** goods production and the actual **R** goods production stage occurs. The last stage of **C** goods' production is less profitable relative to any of the other stages, and 'therefore some of the funds which had been used there will tend to be shifted to the higher stages' (1931, pp. 70–71). If there is less demand for a final product, for example, a table, then immediately there will be less demand for producing table legs and tops. Their prices will drop (Curve 1); in turn there will then be less demand for the wood and planks needed for legs and tops, and in turn their price will drop (Curve 1 will become Curve 2), and so on up the production stages. The amount of money spent in each of the lower stages of production will decrease, while the amount used in the higher stages will increase. The shift, which produces an upward-moving bubble, carrying relatively abundant funds away from the lower stages of production to the higher stages, will subsequently yield new **R** goods of a shorter production process. In addition to use of the new investment to build new processes of production, some of that investment will continue to produce more of the **C** goods that had produced **R** goods before.

> [T]he price margins in the preceding stages [will tend to narrow], and the tendency [is] thus set up towards a cumulative rise of the prices of products of the higher stages . . . the rise of the price of the product of any stage of production will give an extra advantage to the production of the preceding stage, the products of which will not only rise in price because the demand for producers' goods in general has risen, but also because, by the rise of prices in the preceding stages, profits to be obtained in this stage have become comparatively higher than in the lower stages. (1931, p. 71)

In addition to the effect of an increase of savings on the relative prices of the stages of production, the interest rate is also affected. The dotted line, which depicts the industrial production corresponding to a given rate of return in Equilibrium, has embedded in it the impact of the drop in the interest rate (which in part translates into Curves 1, 2, 3, and eventually 4). An increase of savings causes a drop in the interest rate, which represents further lower costs to produce **C** goods and makes returns even greater in

the higher stages of production. This can explain further the encouragement of new processes of production at those stages. Processes of production become more roundabout, that is, the number of successive stages of
production will have been increased or lengthened, and 'the price margins
between the different stages of production will have decreased all around'
(1931, p. 71).

The increase in the production of **C** goods will eventually begin to
impact **C** goods prices negatively: the demand for factors of production
will begin to rise, albeit along with an increase in the earnings of a wider
array of **C** goods and a new demand for **R** goods. The earlier increase in
prices at the higher stages and the decrease at the lower end does not continue forever. Slowly the price of **R** goods will begin to rise, and investment
will start to shift back to producing them. Once the transitional impact
of the new savings is completed, the whole structure of production will
have changed, such that a stretching of the money stream flowing from **R**
goods to the original means of production will have occurred, the initial
tendency towards a fall in the price of **C** goods will have long since been
overcome, and the profits, which had risen in some stages, have become
equalized overall.

Hayek makes two general comments about the impact of a voluntary
increase in savings. First, the effect that results from saving and investing
'is identical with the effect which could have been produced if the savings
were made in kind instead of in money' (1931, p. 49). He is presumably
referring to the initial effect of deferred consumption being analogous
to deferred rewards for labour, for example, as a 'savings made in kind'.
Labour offered today, while earnings are only paid for tomorrow, would
be equivalent to savings made today and only spent tomorrow. Second,
when saving has brought about a change in the structure of production,
Hayek feels 'justified in assuming that the changed distribution of demand
between consumers' goods and producers' goods would remain permanent'
(1931, p. 52). After the changes in the structure of production have been
completed, consumers, who have begun to benefit from an increase in their
real wages, as recipients of 'a greater proportion of the increased total real
income' (1931, p. 52), would have no reason again to increase the proportion of their income spent for consumption (see Curve 4, Figure 4.3 (ii)).[8]

Since, for every one of Hayek's Situations, the working of the model
follows the same logic as has just been laid out above, it should be possible
to describe some aspects of the next three situations more briefly.

*Situation (iii): Decrease in saving / increase in purchase/production of R
goods (under full employment)* Hayek notes 'exactly the reverse of all
changes will take place if the demand for consumers' goods increases

relatively to the demand for producers' goods' (1931, p. 73), that is, if the demand for **R** goods increases but saving does not. Very briefly, the increase in expenditure on **R** goods, equivalent to a decrease in voluntary saving, will increase the money rate of interest. The discrepancy between real and money interest rates will impact investment. The high demand for **R** goods relative to **C** goods will create upward pressure on the prices of **R** goods, however, and downward pressure on **C** goods' prices. The combined impact of the change in the money rate of interest and prices in the two sectors will set a shift of investment from the higher stages of **C** goods' production into the lowest stage, the finishing production of **R** goods (Curve 1, Figure 4.3.(iii)). Due to the higher demand for **R** goods, relative to past demand and hence supply, their prices will rise. Thus, in turn, for more tables, for example, to be produced, there will be a need for more tabletops and legs, and their price will also go up, which will in turn affect the prices of the production of planks and wood for turning legs. Investment in the highest stages will shift toward the stages that are more capital intensive to meet the new demand for **R** goods (Curve 2, Figure 4.3 (iii)).

At the higher stages of production, the impact of an increase in the rate of interest, due to no increase in savings, and the decrease in the prices of **C** goods generally will cause a slow-down, to the point of the extinction of some of the highest processes. The structure of production shrinks toward the lower stages. Increasingly the lowest stage, the sourcing of raw materials, is not undertaken, as no investment is channelled toward doing so. This slowly affects **R** goods production and in turn eases the demand for **R** goods, thus their prices begin to drop. This is the situation in which, in the end, because there is less investment due to less saving, the process of shifting resources is the result of less demand for factors of production at the higher stages and thus less income for them. The dynamics of the equalization of relative rate of profits and prices will eventually settle the economy at a new equilibrium, but at one at a higher level than the old equilibrium (Curve 3, Figure 4.3 (iii)).

If these situations of voluntary saving/spending were seen as parts of an entire trade cycle, Situation (iii) would represent the beginning of the downturn, in which there is little to no new investment and yet **R** goods production is still strong (1931, p. 87). (The start of Situation (ii), with its emphasis on available savings for new investment and deferred spending, could be considered coincident with the start of an upward turn.) Before explaining what could be done to remedy the extremes of the course of the cycle ensuing from Situation (iii), let us consider first the last two Situations posed by Hayek which consider the impact of the infusion of new credit.

Involuntary or forced saving
Hayek defines the source of investment that does not derive from voluntary saving as an 'injection' of 'new money' (1931, p. 52). Whether it is made available for the production of **C** goods or **R** goods (Situations (iv) and (v) to follow) credit is, according to Hayek, not beneficial to the consumer. It leads initially to a 'sacrifice . . . not made by those who will reap the benefit from the new investments' (1931, p. 52), but rather by consumers, who 'get less goods for their money income' (1931, p. 53). In time the impact of either type of initial investment has the same impact on earnings: 'the artificial distribution' it caused will be partly 'reversed'. '[R]eceipts will rise as a consequence of the increase of money in circulation', and yet the voluntary expression of where those receipts will be spent will cause 'the money stream . . . [to] be re-distributed between consumptive and productive uses according to the wish of the individual concerned' (1931, p. 52).

Situation (iv): Increase in production of C goods (through credit; no full employment)   In Situation (iv) Hayek posits the bank's injecting additional money into the economic system by way of investment credit available to producers. For investing in **C** goods, entrepreneurs can use new credit at an attractive rate of interest, which Hayek identifies as a lending rate 'below the equilibrium rate' (1931, p. 76). The line of r_m is now lower than the dotted line corresponding to the rate of return (Figure 4.3 (iv)). Producers will now, he supposes, be most attracted to investing in intermediary **C** goods, which would otherwise have been too expensive, since they are more capital intensive and more costly than the **C** goods of the higher stages. The new money will allow for the 'intermediate product or capital' to be as profitable to purchase, or more so, than 'the original means of production'.[9]

The already produced **R** goods are made available, but as producers invest more in intermediary **C** goods (because of the easy borrowing terms), R_{t-1} will become less abundant, as a result of increases in the costs of the original means of production. Hayek notes that since 'the use of a larger proportion of the original means of production . . . can only be brought about by a retrenchment of consumption', there is what he refers to as 'diminished production'. In point of fact, although the relative use of the means of production for **C** and **R** goods has changed, the total remains the same. The dotted line changes to become first Curve 1 and then Curve 2 (Figure 4.3 (iv)). As a result of the increase in intermediary stages of production, there will be an elongation of the structure of production. An increase in the demand for **R** goods relative to supply causes a rise in the prices of **R** goods; this is how it is that consumers 'get less goods for their money income' (1931, p. 53). While the money income has increased, the production of **R** goods has decreased and the spread between their prices and the prices of **C** goods in the final or lower stages of production has become greater than the price margins in the earlier or higher stages of production.

As the prices of **R** goods are increasing more than the increase in the cost of production, the final stages of production before finished **R** goods are completed continue to be relatively more profitable; they thus attract investment. Hayek notes that it is natural for entrepreneurs to want to produce the lower-stage products, which offer them the prospects, albeit inflationary, of 'extra profits'. 'And, so long as the banks go on progressively increasing their loans, it will, therefore, be possible to continue the prolonged methods of production or perhaps even to extend them still further' (1931, p. 77). He sees consumers and their demand for **R** goods as being in 'competition' with entrepreneurs who are eager to profit more from sustained investment in **C** rather than **R** goods: 'consumers in general because of the increased competition from the entrepreneurs who have received the additional money, are forced to forego part of what they used to consume' (1931, pp. 52–3).

There are major effects on the consumption side of the infusion of uncalled-for credit into the production process: (1) demand is frustrated and (2) savings may be reduced. Demand, Hayek felt, should not be frustrated, as it is when credit is infused into the system for **C** goods production, and thus these are negative effects in two different ways. Voluntary spending can be affected through price inflation. As consumer goods prices rise, '[I]t is highly improbable that individuals should put up' with not buying what they would like to have. While that decision continues to be voluntary, the actual capacity to buy without regard to price is not open to everyone.

Hayek notes that the inflationary price increases change the distribution of **R** goods among consumers. He implies that this is somehow an unfair distorting of the notion of 'voluntary spending'. The second frustration to voluntary spending in an 'artificially' credit-infused production sector is manifest in another form of involuntary reduction in consumption. In this form, society at large is forced to live with pent-up demand by virtue of the fact that in the transition period, due to available credit, there is a disproportionate swing to methods of production of longer duration. At this time, there is no reserve stock of consumer goods available, and 'society as a whole will have to put up with an involuntary reduction of consumption' (1931, p. 79). As noted above, saving is also impacted by credit infusions. It is curtailed, either as consumers, facing 'an unforeseen retrenchment of their real income' make 'an attempt to overcome it by spending more money on consumption' (1931, p. 79), or as those who are no longer employed must weather the storm, and draw on their savings involuntarily.

In due course the money receipts of consumers rises, and all along not having wanted to consume less, they 'immediately attempt to expand consumption to the usual proportion' (1931, p. 53). '[I]f . . . the old proportions are adhered to, then the structure of production too will have to return to the old proportion' (1931, p. 53): Curve 2 becomes Curve 3 (Figure 4.3(iv)). For Hayek, all the effort of injected non-called-for credit is in vain, since its impact is simply to have decreased consumption, only to have it return to the level where it was, with an increase in prices, 'to make profitable the employment of just this sum and no more' (1931, p. 76). Any further intervention by the banks to supply more credit will simply increase **R** goods inflation.

Although 'unnatural', the situation of uncalled-for credit being made available to entrepreneurs gives Hayek the best occasion to demonstrate his general but quite abstract statements, made elsewhere and many years later, about the course of investment:

> The volume of investment is far from moving proportionally to final demand. Not only the rate of interest but also relative prices of the different factors of production and particularly of the different kinds of labour will affect it . . . .. Investment will depend on the volume of the different parts of the stream, whether at one moment total employment of factors of production will be greater or smaller than the effective demand for final products. The immediate determinants directing the tributaries to the main stream will not be final demand but the structure of relative prices of the different factors of production: the different kinds of labour, semi-finished products, raw materials and, of course, rates of interest. ('The Keynes Centenary: The Austrian Critique', 1983; 1995, p. 250)

With credit available, the shift from the use of raw materials to semi-finished products, or from the production of **NS C** goods to goods of the lower stages, will be exacerbated. An initial wide spread in relative profits is, however, temporary for two reasons, each of which poses its own potential difficulties in an environment credit-rich for production processes. First, the initial rise in **R** goods prices is a temporary response to the temporary discrepancy between supply and demand, which will level off somewhat when supply has caught up with demand. Hayek does acknowledge that the moment of acute rise might be a possible window for credit to stabilize the economy:

> if the quantity [of credit] were so regulated as exactly to compensate for the initial, excessive rise of the relative prices of consumers' goods, and if arrangements could be made to withdraw the additional credits as these prices fall

and the proportion between the supply of consumers' goods and the supply of intermediate goods adapts itself to the proportion between the demand for these goods. (1931, p. 86)

He doubts, however, that such fine tuning of credit infusions, to be an effective use of credit, would ever be possible: 'Frankly I do not see how the banks can ever be in a position to keep credit within these limits' (1931, p. 86).

A second impact of widespread relative profits in the elongated production process is that while the number of producers of intermediate **C** goods has grown in the marketplace, the variety of production goods is actually beginning to shrink, due to a concentration of investment in the production of **C** goods of a more specific character. This starts a chain-reaction of the prices of **C** goods dropping relative to one another and to **R** goods, and an ultimate collapse of **C** goods' processes. Such a dramatic shrinkage of the **C** goods sector has many implications. All the higher stages of production will face work stoppages, since **NS** goods and the labour to process them are too high in price, relative to the return from intermediate **C** goods. Shorter, cheaper processes of production, with fewer intermediary goods will be newly devised, but meanwhile virtually all the resources of production (labour, raw materials, and so on) go through a time of being unused. Hayek saw this also as a potential window for credit infusion:

> the existence of unused resources has very often been considered as the only fact which at all justifies an expansion of bank credit . . . so far as the effects of credits granted for productive purposes are concerned. In theory at least it is at least possible that, during the acute stage of the crisis when the capitalist structure of production tends to shrink more than will ultimately prove necessary, an expansion of producers' credits might have a wholesome effect. (1931, pp. 85–6)

Again, however, he backed away from the policy. '[C]redits would do more harm than good if they made roundabout processes seem profitable which, even after the acute crisis had subsided, could not be kept up without additional credits' (1931, pp. 85–6).

Situation (v): Increase in purchase of R goods (through credit; no full employment) If additional credit is used to increase the purchase of **R** goods, the first effect will be to raise the price of **R** goods and immediately 'to make the spread between them and the prices of the goods of the preceding stage . . . greater than the price margins in the higher stages of production' (1931, p. 81). The line identifying relative returns (the dotted line of Figure 4.3(v)) thus takes the shape of Curve 1. The usual shift in production processes transpires: 'the all-around increase of price margins between the stages of production which will follow will cause a widespread transfer of non-specific producers' goods to lower stages' (1931, p. 81). This creates a shrinkage of the structure of production which will eventually undermine the willingness of entrepreneurs 'to make investments suited to this over-shortened process', one which abandons capital-intensive stages for ones which 'produce with relatively little capital and a relatively great quantity of the original means of production' (1931, p. 83). In this situation, credit for capital investment has become so much more expensive relatively that the rise in the rate of interest makes it unprofitable to invest in capital-intensive processes. It must be kept in mind that for Hayek the counterpart to an increase in credit available to consumers (for the purchase of **R** goods) is a lack of saving which can be used for investment.

As a consequence of the shift of resources from the higher and intermediary to the lower stages of production, the production of **R** goods will start to diminish: 'That is to say, production will become less capitalistic, and that part of the new capital which was sunk in equipment adapted only to the more capitalistic processes will be lost' (1931, p. 53). The combination of the decrease in earnings, due to means of production put out of work in the highest and intermediary stages, and the increase of prices in **R** goods, due to increased demand from credit in the hands of consumers, will slowly diminish the purchasing power of consumers. This, in combination with reduced production of **R** goods, due to the entrepreneurs' hesitation to invest in less capitalistic production, will result in a reduced level of production. Curve 2 becomes Curve 3 (Figure 4.3 (v)). '[S]uch a transition to less capitalistic methods of production [will] necessarily take the form of an economic crisis' (1931, p. 53).

In sum, for Hayek there are nefarious consequences of credit infusions into the economy. Hayek is particularly critical of consumer credit expansion, Situation (v), as a means to alleviate the slow-down of an economy. Just as in Situation (iv), he thinks almost any exercise of credit infusion is counterproductive. When infused on the production side, as identified in Situation (iv), since credit artificially props up non-remunerative lower-stage, 'roundabout' production processes – to use Böhm-Bawerk's terminology, as Hayek does – it has a negative impact. With the uncalled-for credit to hand, available resources are being led 'into a wrong direction and a definite and lasting adjustment is again postponed' (1931, p. 87), for 'the banks cannot continue indefinitely to extend credits' (1931, p. 80). Nor, Hayek believed, for inflationary reasons would it be a good idea for them to do so. When, however, banks cease to add to their loans, producers will not have sufficient investment wherewithal, nor experience (1931,

p. 83), to keep pace with, or to respond anew to consumer demand. Hayek concludes,

> The only way permanently to 'mobilise' all available resources is, therefore, not to use artificial stimulants – whether during a crisis or thereafter – but to leave it to time to effect a permanent cure by the slow process of adapting the structure of production to the means available for capital purposes. (1931, p. 87)

4.3.2   The Dynamics of Keynes's Credit Cycle in the *Treatise*

Change, in Keynes, is analysed directly from differences in the values of the components of his Fundamental Equation II, relating price-level (**P**) to the level of money earnings (**E**), the volume of output (**O**) and the difference between investment and saving (**I − S**). He classified the possible initiating causes of economic disturbances as follows: changes due to (1) 'Monetary Factors influencing the effective supply of money for income purposes', (2) 'Investment Factors', and (3) 'Industrial Factors influencing the volume of output and the demand for money for income purposes' (1930, I, pp. 258–9). His analysis of change as cyclic puts the greatest emphasis on monetary factors or credit. Keynes refers throughout to his cycle as a Credit Cycle, which he defined as 'the alternations of excess and defect in the cost of investment over the volume of saving and the accompanying see-saw in the Purchasing Power of Money due to these alternations' (1930, I, p. 277). As can be seen from the definition, the word 'credit' does not explicitly appear, but, as becomes clearer below, credit is essential in allowing Entrepreneurs to decide whether to invest or not. That decision to use all or part of the windfall profits (losses) to expand (curtail) additional investment depends crucially on the availability (lack) of credit. Thus, it is the availability (lack) of credit, which affects interest and prices and therefore profits and losses, that is the catalyst of the movement of resources, which impacts production and employment.

Keynes's types: 'openings' of the cycle
As explained above, Hayek started with the notion of a steady-state equilibrium as the backdrop (Figure 4.3(i)) onto which he superimposed four Situations, representing deviations from equilibrium which over the course of a cycle fall back under the influence of equilibrating forces (the impact of voluntary saving: Figure 4.3(ii-iii); the impact of involuntary saving: Figure 4.3(iv-v)). While Hayek's objective was in part to demonstrate how the infusion of uncalled-for credit creates a distortion from equilibrium, Keynes's goal was to explain how credit, whether called-for (demand-generated) or uncalled-for (supply-driven), is an engrained part

of a monetary production economy that constantly undergoes fluctuations. All of Hayek's Situations seem to have been anticipated by Keynes, particularly in chapter 16, pp. 282–92 of volume I of the *Treatise*, where he describes his Credit Cycle of three phases: (1) the Upward-price Phase, (2) the Secondary Production-stimulus Phase and (3) the Collapse. Focusing his description on the Credit Cycle itself allowed Keynes to compare his 'situations', which he saw rather as four Types of openings to the Cycle, with one another in each phase. Reference to equilibrium is present but not as a specific starting or end point in the sense of Hayek. The economy may or may not be in full employment.

Keynes described the course of the Credit Cycle in reference to four types of 'openings':

(i)   The economy is in full employment and Entrepreneurs decide to increase investment 'by the substitution of the production of capital goods in place of consumption-goods' (1930, I, p. 281).
(ii) The economy is in full employment and 'a drop in saving [is] uncompensated by decreased investment' (1930, I, p. 286).
(iii) There is an increase in investment in capital goods when the economy is not in full employment.
(iv) There is an increase in investment in consumption-goods when the economy is not in full employment.

Each 'opening' represents the situation of an economy whose price-level **P** is moving in an upward direction. Keynes posited the possibility of yet other types of openings to the cycle, which met that criterion, even, for example 'a downward phase, due to Investment falling off whilst Saving keeps up' (1930, I, p. 287). This situation might have been caused by 'some blow to the confidence of entrepreneurs in particular types of enterprise' or by a decreased demand for capital 'which left unaffected the readiness of the public to save' (1930, I, p. 287).

Three of the four types are encapsulated in Figure 4.4 (i), (iii), (iv), representing schematically their course from a specific 'opening' circumstance through the three phases of the cycle. Type (ii), which is described below without diagram, ought to be imagined to be the flip side of Type (i). The same schematic – with rate of return and relative price on the vertical axis and the snapshot of the production of **C** and **R** goods on the horizontal axis – as was used to depict Hayek's Situations is also used here as the reference framework. As before, the dark line represents the money rate of interest, r_m, and the dotted line, the rate of return, r_n. For Keynes, there is a lapse of time between the production of $\mathbf{R}_{t-1}$ and the availability of it as output **R** in the market. Also in a more nuanced way than in Hayek's

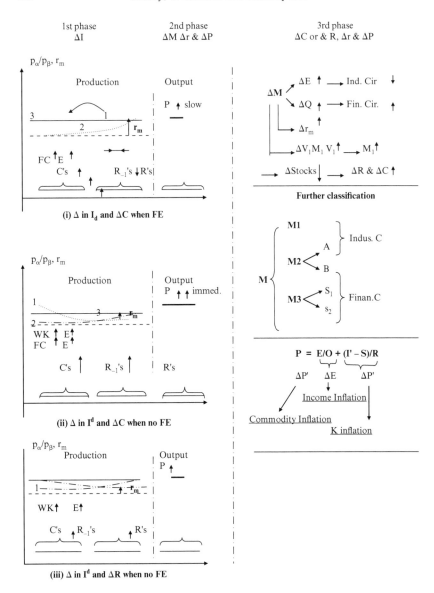

Figure 4.4   Keynes's Credit Cycle

writings, Keynes identifies the production of **C** goods as of different kinds:
Fixed Capital (**FC**), Working Capital (**WC**), and Liquid Capital (**LC**). The
shift of resources to produce more **C** goods has different impacts, depending on the production to which these three kinds of capital investment

are allocated. Earnings, **E**, correspond to the earnings of the factors of production.

As noted above, Keynes meant by 'opening', the point in the cycle in which the price-level of the economy **P** is moving in an upward direction. In such a situation he supposes that entrepreneurs and/or savers 'believe that certain new investments will be profitable' (1930, I, p. 282) and that some entrepreneurs 'see advantageous opportunities for increased activity in particular directions' (1930, I, p. 287). This is a decisive phase in which resources are shifting from one sector to the other, **R** goods or **C** goods production, depending on their relative profits. Noting that to be efficacious the movement of resources 'must either attract factors of production from other employments or employ factors previously unemployed' (1930, I, p. 283), Keynes pictured an economy that, at the start of the Cycle, is not necessarily in full employment. Furthermore, he drew attention to the fact that the first, upward-price phase involves an increase in earnings as well as in profits. Thus, already in the opening phase of the cycle, although not imperative (see the case of Type (i) below), there will usually be a substantial change in the monetary situation which would require the cooperation of the banking authorities.

The second phase of Keynes's cycle begins from 'the characteristic conclusion of the Primary Phase of a Credit Cycle', when **R** goods prices have risen beyond production cost (1930, I, p. 284). The return from this discrepancy, windfall profits, gives stimulus to increased production 'of an all around character and affects all types of goods which are the object of general consumption' (1930, I, p. 288). When the price of **R** goods begins to drop due to saturation of the market, the third phase is announced. The third phase is one of general downward-price movement, 'obliterating in whole or in part the windfall profits which had been ruling previously' (1930, I, p. 289). This does not mean, however, that all investment ceases; some will continue. Some firms will even continue to reap profits.

Type (i): Increase in investment in C goods (under full employment) Type (i) is not the most usual case, in that it posits increased investment in **C** goods not accompanied by an increase in the total volume of production and from the outset, a growth of working capital balanced by additional saving. Increased production of **C** goods is in substitution for the factors of production of **R** goods prior to this 'opening': 'factors previously producing consumption-goods are now turned to producing capital-goods' (1930, I, p. 283) (Curve 1, Table 4.4 (i)). Keynes is working in Type (i) on a similar assumption to that of Hayek's Situation (i),[10] where investment translates into additional factors of production put to work to produce **C** goods or more precisely in Keynes, **FC**. First, it is to be noted that since factors of production engaged in the production of **R** goods 'are not easily turned over' to the production of **C** goods at short notice, 'no effect will be produced on prices until after an interval of time equal in length to the process of production of the consumption-goods which were previously, but are no longer, being made' (1930, I, p. 283). During this early interval 'earnings are as before and the output of available goods is also as before' (1930, I, p. 283). Slowly, however, the quantity of available output of **R** goods will start falling, and its price rising (provided, just like in Hayek's Situation (i), saving is not increasing), since '[T]he change-over from the production of **R** goods to that of **C** goods may have to be achieved with an increase in the cost of production (that is, in earnings)' and the change comes about by 'the new entrepreneurs attracting factors of production to themselves by bidding up the rate of earnings' (1930, I, pp. 283–4). For Keynes, there is increase in the price of **R** goods (Commodity Inflation) and increase in earnings (Income Inflation).

For Keynes, the Type (i) opening to the Credit Cycle entails a succession of implications for the relationship between **R** goods and **C** goods:

1. In the first phase of Type (i), increased production of **C** goods begins and thus the channelling of investment from the production of **R** goods into **C** goods. As more factors of production are used to produce relatively more non-available output (**C** goods in the form of machines and equipment, for example), there will be relatively fewer factors left to produce **R** goods. There will thus be fewer available **R** goods produced. At first, current output of **R** goods is unaltered, but then decreases: '[A]fter the necessary interval of time has elapsed, the available output coming on to the market will be diminished' (1930, I, p. 284). As the supply of **R** diminishes, its price increases. By the secondary phase, increasingly more income is generated in the **C** sector relative to the **R** sector, and all the earlier added **C** goods have been put to work producing **R** goods. This leads to an increase in the volume of **R** goods (Curve 2, Figure 4.4 (i)). It is the convergence of the increasing supply of **R** goods and the response to that increase, a slowing demand, which will create a downward pressure on the price of **R** goods and trigger the overturn in their production. In the last phase, **C** goods production too will reverse itself and begin to diminish, for just like the previous overproduction of **R** goods, too many **C** goods or machines have been produced.
2. In the first phase of the Credit Cycle with a Type (i) opening, **P**′, the price of **C** goods, particularly in the form of **FC**, will tend to increase sooner and faster than **P**, the price of **R** goods. A windfall profit will appear as a result of the difference between the market value (**I**) of **C**

goods and their cost (**I'**), but at the same time, the increase in the production in **C** goods will put pressure on the needed factors of production. '[T]he attempt to increase still further the volume of employment will probably have the effect of stiffening the attitude of the factors of production' (1930, I, p. 288) (Wage Inflation). This will create an upward pressure in their price: 'specialized factors of production will be fully employed, with the result that the emergence of profit will cause entrepreneurs to bid against one another for such supply of these factors as is available, thus raising the rate of remuneration in these particular cases' (1930, I, p. 288). In the first phase, there is an increase in remuneration to the factors of production, thus an increase in the cost of **C** goods, as well as in the price of **R** goods, but since 'the Consumption Price-level must rise more than earnings' (1930, I, p. 284), *in toto*, 'real earnings must fall' (1930, I, p. 284). As a consequence, the price of **R** goods rises relative to that of **C** goods, and the **R** sector becomes more profitable. Entrepreneurs begin to sell some of their stocks of liquid capital, **LC**, 'to reap a windfall profit' (1930, I, p. 287). It is the windfall profits coming from the selling of **R** goods and the depletion of **R** hoards that will induce a shift of resources back to producing **R** goods. Investment is now directed away from **FC** into **WC**, Working Capital. After some time, at the beginning of the second phase, when the production of **R** goods starts to rise again, the price of **R** goods will begin to diminish.

3. From the monetary perspective, the 'Bull' sentiment throughout the economy in the earliest part of a Type (i) investment boom means that the demand of an increased cost of production can be met out of existing savings. 'An expansion – where the volume of liquid goods coming onto the market is diminished because more productive effort has been concentrated on capital goods – can come about with only a slight alteration in monetary factors' (1930, I, p. 286). This 'alteration' could be as simple as an infusion into one part of a firm's portfolio, the *Industrial Circulation*, of monies otherwise stored in another part of a firm's portfolio, the *Financial Circulation*, a shift from M_{2B} to M_{2A}. At some point, presumably at the secondary phase, there would, however, be a need for a further infusion into the *Industrial Circulation* which would have to come from money outside the firm's own savings, namely, from the banks. This spells increased demand for money and a rise in the interest rate (Curve 3, Figure 4.4(i)). As a result of increasing costs (Income Inflation) and profit squeezes (Commodity Deflation), by the end of the secondary phase a 'Bear' mentality develops. A reverse monetary trend thus begins, namely, a reduction in the supply of money available for the *Industrial Circulation* accounts.

With Commodity Deflation and the disappearance of windfall profits, increased liquidity will cease: 'the surplus bank-resources which gave the stimulus to entrepreneurs to extend their activities fade away' (1930, I, p. 288).

Type (ii): Increase in investment in R goods/decrease of saving (under full employment)   Type (ii) represents the situation 'when a Credit Cycle has been initiated by a drop in saving uncompensated by decreased investment' (1930, I, p. 286). Keynes identified only a few characteristics that are specific to Type (ii), an opening similar to Hayek's Situation (ii). Any drop in saving spells an increase in consumption or 'a larger expenditure on the same available consumption goods as before, so that, as in the other cases, prices move upward' (1930, I, p. 287). The price rise, which begins this cycle, is the price of **R** goods, whose increase is due simply to increased demand. This means that initially **R**-goods producers will be able to sell their current output for more that the cost of production and here again, as in Type (i) 'so reap a windfall profit' (1930, I, p. 287).

Since past output too can be sold 'at an unusually satisfactory price' (1930, I, p. 288), wholesalers and retailers alike will be induced to sell their hoards of **R** goods as well, reducing those hoards to a below-normal level. At the same time, if 'a further rise of prices is expected, there may be a tendency to hoard liquid goods' (1930, I, p. 288). Hoarding 'aggravates the excess of investment over saving' and so further precipitates the rise of prices (1930, I, p. 288). As high **R**-goods prices cause the depletion of stocks and hoards, by the secondary phase, in the context of full employment, investment of some kinds is reduced, 'as a partial offset to the excessive investment in other directions' (1930, I, p. 288).

Keynes reminds his readers that '[I]n no case can surplus stocks exist alongside of normal production' (1930, II, p. 145). By the secondary phase, 'the most inevitable result of profits on current output and the visible depletion of stocks' has been 'to encourage manufacturers of consumption goods to strain their efforts to increase their output' (1930, I, p. 288). Due to the length of time required for the push to increase production yet further, 'the falling off in the rate of [other] in-put . . . will cause the rates of employment and earnings to fall off *before* the rate of output declines' (1930, II, p. 146). By the third phase, too many **R** goods will flood a market with too few buyers and Commodity Deflation will strike the entrepreneurs.

Type (iii): Increase in investment in C goods (no full employment)   In Type (iii), factors of production previously unemployed are put to work producing **C** goods (Curve 1, Figure 4.4 (iii)).[11] Keynes is working in this type of model on two assumptions, similar to those of Hayek's Situation (iv): there are no additional savings,[12] and increased investment is translated into additional factors of production put to work to produce **C** goods: 'there is from the outset a growth of working capital not balanced by additional saving' (1930, I, p. 284). While 'the upward-price phase of the Credit Cycle begins immediately' (1930, I, p. 285), this cannot come about without a substantial change in the monetary situation, since it involves an increase in aggregate earnings as well as in profits. For the most part, major monetary issues arise only if and when there is an excess of investment over saving and the demand for investment is high. As in the opening of Type (i), in Type (iii) as well, 'an increased volume of money may be furnished for the Industrial Circulation as the result of a decrease of the Financial Circulation, that is, of the savings-deposits' (1930, I, p. 285). In an emerging 'bull' market, a sustained situation of savings shortfall might materialize, but not in the Primary Phase; in that phase of Type (iii), 'it is particularly likely that in the earliest phases of a boom there will be unanimity of bull sentiment leading to a decrease of the bear position' (1930, I, p. 285) and a willingness thus of entrepreneurs to shift their deposits around. '[I]f the banks have got into the habit of concentrating their attention on the volume of the initial deposits to the exclusion of other factors, the monetary adjustment may come about without arousing their notice' (1930, I, p. 285). Without, however, longer-term consumer deposits, that is, savings, and with greater demand in the *Financial Circulation* of firms, banks are forced into a reduction in available money for investment. This reduction expresses itself as a rise in the interest rate on money (Curve 3, Figure 4.4 (iii)). Should too great a demand be placed on the savings reserve, there might have to be an absolute increase in the money supply, requiring 'the acquiescence of the banking authorities' (1930, I, p. 285), but rather later in the first phase, when symptoms of a weakening return on investment have become obvious. Even then, 'a slight rise in bank-rate . . . may serve to increase monetary facilities sufficiently to look after the increased earnings' (1930, I, p. 285), even if it were 'insufficient to counter-act the tendency towards Commodity Inflation' (1930, I, p. 285). Eventually, banks will reflect their supply of investment funds' falling short of maintaining the volume of the *Industrial Circulation*, even through raised bank rates, and cease being willing to lend at all.[13]

Since the investment is, for Keynes, in **C** goods, 'the increased production . . . additional to the previous factors of production of consumption-goods' (1930, I, p. 284) will cause the earnings of the factors of production to increase. At the outset there will not be any increase in available output, although eventually there will be, '[f]or the increased production of capital-goods is more likely to be additional to, than in substitution for, the previous production of consumption-goods' (1930, I, p. 284). It is, however, due to the lagged increase in output that '[p]rices rise . . . at once relatively to earnings and costs' (1930, I, p. 285). As a last point about Type (iii) in particular, for Keynes, it revealed a new implication for the relationship between **R** goods and **C** goods: **C** goods investment, once well under way, will be accompanied by an increase in the total volume of output; boldly stated, 'increased investment is accompanied by an increase in the total volume of production' (1930, I, p. 284) (Curve 2, Figure 4.4 (iii)).

Type (iv): Increase in investment in R goods (no full employment) In Keynes's Type (iv) opening, 'factors of production previously unemployed are put to work on producing . . . particular categories of consumption goods (1930, I, p. 285) (Curve 1, Figure 4.4 (iv)). In this type, prices rise immediately, as in Type (iii), because the earnings of the new factors rise. Although increased production is in the **R** goods sector, given production lags, '[t]he course of events is exactly as in type (ii) [*sic* Type (iii)] for a period of time equal to the duration of the process of production' (1930, I, p. 285). If the rate of efficiency wages remains unchanged, the newly produced **R** goods output 'coming on to the market is increased by the same amount . . . as total earnings had been increased' in the Primary Phase of the Credit Cycle (1930, I, p. 285). **R** goods, now in sufficient supply to meet demand, will drop back in price to their previous level (1930, I, p. 285).

In all the above Types (i), (ii), (iii), and (iv), changes in investment impact the production of **R** goods and **C** goods relative to one another. For Keynes, the story of investment in production, as was seen in Chapter 3, was not a simple increase or decrease of Capital. It was conceived as a change that would have reverberating and counter-balancing effects within Capital, namely, among its three categories: **FC**, **WC**, and **LC**. For Keynes, the bearing of assertions about the relationship of the different capitals to the Credit Cycle was 'evident' (1930, II, p. 146).

This had, however, not been fully or correctly appreciated by fellow economists up to his writing. On the one hand, he observed that the analysis regarding fluctuations in the volume of **FC** and 'their correlations with the Credit Cycle', long familiar to economists, was incomplete. He attributed the most recent failings in many respects to Tugan-Baranovski, Hull, Spiethoff, and Schumpeter, identifying particularly their emphasis on **FC** to the 'neglect of fluctuations in working capital' (1930, II, p. 99). While they might 'have had a hold of some of the truth', he wrote, in not taking account of **WC** as well as **FC**, they had not perceived that cyclical effects 'due to a growth of Working Capital are at least as "characteristic" as those primarily due to a growth of Fixed Capital' (1930, II, p. 101). On the other hand, Keynes thought that Hawtrey had overemphasized the role of **LC**. Initially, he, like Hawtrey, sought to consider the impact of the actual order of magnitude of changes in **LC** on the theory of the Credit Cycle, thinking 'it possible that some part of the clue to the Credit Cycle might be found in a close study of the fluctuations of the stocks of liquid goods' (1930, II, p. 133). Unlike Hawtrey, Keynes was in the end not persuaded, however, of the capacity of **LC** to 'furnish a balancing factor capable of looking after short-period increases and decreases in the rate of investment in fixed and working capital without any change being required in the rate of total investment' (1930, II, p. 130). Keynes summed up his understanding of the relationship between **LC** and **WC** over the course of the Cycle:

> Just as the improvement in the volume of production can only take place gradually, owing to the time which it takes to build up Working Capital again; so must the falling off in the volume of production take place suddenly, when there is surplus Liquid Capital, owing to the short time within which Liquid Capital must be absorbed. (1930, II, p. 146)

> [T]he theory of Liquid Capital gives us, in relation to the swift downward movement of the slump, the counterpart of what the theory of Working Capital gave us, in relation to the slow upward movement of the boom. (1930, II, p. 145–6)

Investment in **WC** plays a particularly determinant factor in Keynes's Credit Cycle: 'a Credit Cycle will, as we have seen, tend to be associated with an increased investment in working capital – if not in its primary phase, then in its secondary phase' (1930, II, p. 102). Keynes saw in **WC** the key to three aspects of the Credit Cycle: (1) the 'time-element', (2) the varying level of employment of human labour, and (3) the changes in the propensity to consume. First, if 'fluctuations in the amount of revolving fund of working capital . . . are substantial relatively to the time rate at which new investment can be made available to replenish working capital . . . analysis may furnish us with an important clue to the explanation of the time-element in booms and depressions' (1930, II, pp. 102–3). Second, the use of **WC** is directly related to the volume of employment. At the opening of chapter 28 on working capital, Keynes noted the dependence of employment on investment in **WC** in a number of ways, all in the same paragraph (1930, II, p. 102, emphasis added): 'Subject to the necessary conditions . . . *an increase in the volume of employment will usually require a more or less proportionate increase in the volume of working capital*'; '*fluctuations of investment in working capital will be closely correlated with fluctuations in the volume of employment*'; '*it is generally impossible to increase the volume of employment* (even when it is at a level far below the optimum) *unless it is practicable to increase pari passu the volume of investment in* *working capital*. Third, Keynes introduced yet another interesting element into his analysis of investment in **WC**:

> An increase in working capital resulting from an increased volume of production and employment (and not from a lengthening of the production process) also necessitates investment; but in this case *investment does not require any reduction in the level of consumption* below what it would have been if the increase in production had not taken place. (1930, II, p. 124, emphasis added)

As will be seen in *The General Theory*, the marginal propensity to consume, the marginal efficiency of capital and the liquidity preference are the three determinant components of employment. Consumption, in a very peculiar way, is already introduced in the *Treatise* as having a multiplier impact on employment, when investment is applied to working capital rather than fixed or liquid capital.[14] How is it so?

4.4   KEYNES'S PRODUCTIVE AND UNPRODUCTIVE CONSUMPTION AND EMPLOYMENT

Even though the theoretical core of the *Treatise* rests on the Fundamental Equations, namely, on a theory of prices,[15] that theory was not its ultimate goal. As it is by now evident, those Equations were the necessary bridge which permitted Keynes to link monetary aspects of a credit economy[16] to the real economy's setting of production and employment. The Credit Cycle is about an economy's recoveries, booms, slumps, and subsequent recoveries, that is to say, an analysis of what happens, on the supply side, to levels of production, income, and employment and, on the demand side, to income distribution and consumption. It is asserted by Keynes that employment and unemployment are the direct consequences of how investment, whether generated from savings or credit, finds its way into Fixed Capital (**FC**), Working Capital (**WC**) and/or Liquid Capital (**LC**). As explained above, it is the channelling of investment that affects the remuneration of factors of production and thus income redistribution. Keynes thus asserted that investment affects consumption.

Trends in production and consumption, implying decisions by those who contribute to production and by those who consume finished output, both available and non-available, became, for Keynes, key elements in determining the direction of the economy in its Credit Cycle: whether it will move forward on an up- or down-swing. Depending on how investment is applied to FC, WC or LC, because it affects the capital–labour ratio producing **C** goods and **R** goods, when income is redistributed, there are beneficiaries and losers. These changes affect the level of employment and the amount of remuneration of the factors of production, as well as the gains/losses of the entrepreneurs.

> At any time, therefore, the community has two sets of decisions to make – the one as to what proportion of future income shall be available for consumption and what proportion shall consist of fixed capital, the other as to what proportion of present income shall be consumed productively and what proportion shall be consumed unproductively. (1930, II, p. 126)

'The first set of decisions', Keynes wrote, 'is that which is ordinarily in mind when we think of saving and investment'; it concerns the relative investment in the production of one of the two sectors, **R** goods or **C** goods. When, for example, under full employment there is a substitution of production of **C** goods for production of **R** goods, investment is channelled from the production of consumer goods into capital goods, and the necessary payment for the new capital resources comes from saving. As more factors of production are used to produce relatively more non-available output (machines and equipment), or **C** goods, there will be relatively fewer factors left to produce **R** goods. Even though at first the current stream of output of **R** goods is unaltered, the quantity of **R** goods may decrease.

Keynes's analysis of cyclical sector-related production envelops also the role of prices, and hence the redistribution of income. As additional (or lack of) investment is infused, resources are shifted from the production of one type of good into another, such that the more income that is generated in the **C** sector, relative to the **R** sector, the more the increase in the demand for an unaltered supply of **R** goods, and thus an increase in its price. Changes in the volume of production of **R** goods produce changes in the relative purchasing power of the various income earners. Depending on where in the phases of the Cycle the economy stands, shortages or overproduction can cause inflation and deflation. A rise in the price of **R** goods affects the purchasing power of earners differently. The income of the newly employed in the increasing **C** sector competes with those already employed for the same output. Any price rise in **R** goods means a drop in the real wages to all workers, but for those previously and continuously employed it means a diminution of consumption of **R** goods, while for those newly employed a rise in consumption is still possible. In any case it means a 'redistribution of consumption'.

A truly novel contribution of Keynes was, however, to argue that the decisions, which bring about fluctuations in investment in the production of specific goods and hence price changes, regardless of whether they are due to changes in the real or the monetary parts of the economy, may or may not 'require a reduction in the level of current consumption'. To do so, he introduced a distinction between unproductive and productive consumption, distinguishing not when investment is shifted from one sector to another but from one type of capital to another. Increased investment in **FC** goods production was, for Keynes, '**unproductive consumption**', in that it entails reduction in the level of aggregate consumption. Increase in investment applied toward **WC**, Keynes saw, however, as '**productive consumption**', or 'investment which does not require any reduction in the level of consumption below what it would have been if the increase in production had not taken place' (1930, II, p. 124). Determining 'what proportion of present income shall be consumed productively and what proportion shall be consumed unproductively' was the further set of decisions Keynes identified a community has to make, and it is a highly important set, since 'it is on the second set that employment and unemployment depend' (1930, II, p. 126).

In the third phase of the Credit Cycle, the 'collapse' or slump, there is, for example, a characteristic integration of unproductive consumption: 'the slump does not merely result in less production and less consumption, but also in *the substitution of unproductive consumption in place of productive consumption*' (1930, II, p. 133, emphasis added). Not only does production fall off 'much more sharply than consumption', but employment does as well. Keynes noted that '[E]specially is this the case if unemployment relief is maintained at a high level' (1930, II, p. 133). The unproductive consumption takes two forms in the slump phase: investment in **LC** and/ or in **FC**: 'The facts do *not* suggest that this excess-consumption [of LC] is fully balanced by a diminished investment in fixed capital' (emphasis added, 1930, II, p. 133).

It is, however in the first phase of the Credit Cycle, when production and prices are rising, that the decision to invest in productive and unproductive consumption is more possible and more important. **LC** has been exhausted, and thus it is **FC** and **WC** that seem to compete for entrepreneurs' attention. A shift of investment to **WC** – the aggregate of goods in production, including both the raw materials and finished goods needed in the current process and the goods themselves in process whether durable or non-durable – has much in common with a shift in investment to **FC**, which Keynes called 'a change in the demand-schedule for the use or enjoyment of Fixed Capital' (1930, II, p. 97):[17] (1) There is new integration of available unfinished goods[18] and (2) it takes time for **R** goods to be available as finished products. During the initial period of investment, the current **R** goods output will be shared by both those who have been producing **R** goods and **C** goods all along; the new capital investment may cause the price of **R** goods to rise accordingly. There is therefore also an initial 'redistribution of consumption', such that the newly employed now also share the available current output with those who produced that output (1930, II, p. 124). It must be kept in mind, however, as discussed above, that, for Keynes, along with changes in the use of **WC** come changes in the level of employment; they rise and fall proportionally.

The main difference between 'productive consumption' and 'unproductive consumption' turns on employment and whether 'consumption' is or is not being redistributed in a way that affects positively production itself. Understanding these concepts in this way seems to have gone completely unnoticed by the economics profession,[19] and yet, as will be appreciated, they were a totally original contribution. '**Unproductive consumption**' is 'consumption which *could be forgone* by the consumer *without reacting on the amount of his productive effort*' (1930, II, p. 125, emphasis added), while '**productive consumption**' is 'consumption which *could not be forgone*' by the consumer without affecting the amount of his productive effort. Put slightly differently, present income consumed productively is income derived from the productive effort that led to the amount of output available for consumption; that consumption is consummate with production. Present income consumed unproductively is income spent on consumption which does not represent the consumer's own productive effort, but rather that of others which led to the amount of output available for consumption. Productive consumption, the $t+1$ productive effort of those employed, leads to no reduction in the amount of output available for consumption.

With the understanding that all additional investment does not necessarily lead to more employment (and therefore more consumption) – it may or may not – productive consumption is the outcome of additional investment that does generate employment. If increased employment is then the key to increased consumption, Keynes contemplated that

> it may be possible to *redistribute consumption in a way which increases production* . . . Thus whenever available income is transferred from an individual *qua* unproductive or relatively unproductive consumer to an individual *qua* productive or relatively productive consumer, *it follows that the amount of production is increased* and *vice versa*. (1930, II, p. 125, first and third emphases added)

An increase in production derives, however, as has already been seen, not directly from an increase in consumption, but from an increase in investment. The direct source of increased investment is either the savings of the consumers, namely, the earnings they do not spend on **R** goods or those of the entrepreneurs, namely, the profits that they also do not spend on **R** goods. In the case of the savings of consumers, they are either voluntary or involuntary. The rise in the price of **R** goods that ensues upon increased employment amounts to involuntary (or forced) savings or a disincentive to consumption by those continuously employed in the production process. Their buying power is reduced without any reduction in their labour or effort or perhaps desire to consume. A rise in prices redistributes consumption, not only among the workers, but also between workers and employers, in a way which by not stimulating an increase in consumption causes an increase in savings and hence in investment available for production. 'Investment, which requires a redistribution of current consumption but no reduction in its aggregate, may be said to substitute productive consumption for unproductive consumption' (1930, II, p. 125).

Keynes analysed the impact of the increase in employment on prices in relation to consumption in quite a bit of detail in the context of his discussion of the Credit Cycle, since that impact is felt only when the analysis of 'the Cycle does not last for just one, and only one, production period', say a 'week', but is extended forward (1930, I, p. 318). If this is the case, the scenario reminds us of those examined in the 'opening' Types above: 'the new purchasing power will effectively reach the consumer one week late, so that the situations in the first and second weeks are as before: but in each later successive week there will come on the market as purchasing power for finished goods . . . the increased expenditure of the newly employed' (1930, I, p. 318). Due to the rise in prices, consumers have only two options: (1) to 'try to do what it will be impossible for them to accomplish as a body, namely, to maintain their former rate of consumption per unit of output by drawing on their savings' (1930, I, p. 319) or (2) 'to modify the time distribution of their consumption', namely, to postpone the date of consumption by transferring the equivalent to savings-deposits (1930, I, p. 320). The latter choice would have the preferred impact on all, producers and consumers alike, for the consumer would be putting his savings in the bank, gaining 'not only the normal rate of money interest but, in addition, the equivalent of the prospective increase in the value of money calculated as a rate per annum' (1930, I, p. 320), while at the same time allowing producers to use it for investment, 'the outgoings of enterprise may be found either out of thrift or at the expense of the consumption of the average consumer' (1930, I, p. 148).

By linking consumer reduction in spending to increased savings available for investment, Keynes could explain how the consumption of the consumer could be more or less redistributed in a way which increases production. When it came to the employer as consumer, however, as he might have said here, 'it becomes much more complicated'. Recall Keynes's reference to the widow's cruse and the Danaid jar, mentioned in Chapter 3, explaining by symbols how the consumption out of windfall profits by entrepreneurs, dealers, traders, and so on has a different impact on prices from the consumption of others, the wage earners. In the upswing phase of the cycle, the rise in the price of **R** goods, brought about by the increase in demand for such goods by the newly employed created by the infusion of **WC**, produces windfall profits. When any part of these windfall profits is consumed, it creates additional pressure on the demand for **R** goods, which increases further their price, and in turn windfall profits. With yet more profits entrepreneurs can increase their consumption even more, and out of a second increase in windfall profits even more so, and so on. 'Thus profits, as a source of capital increment for entrepreneurs, are a widow's cruse which remains undepleted however much of them may be devoted to riotous living' (1930, I, p. 139). *The interaction between investment in Working Capital and the productive consumption out of windfall profits produces a 'Multiplier Effect'.*

On the other hand, as we have already seen, in the collapse phase of the Credit Cycle, when windfall profits, employment, and earnings are all falling, at first the inertia of output is still present and Liquid Capital increasing; there is, however, no productive consumption. This does not mean that entrepreneurs do not try to survive and some do so by reversing their consumption habits, but to no avail:

> When, on the other hand, entrepreneurs are making losses, and seek to recoup these losses by curtailing their normal expenditure on consumption, *i.e.*, by saving more, the cruse becomes a Danaid jar which can never be filled up; for the effect of this reduced expenditure is to inflict on the producers of consumption-goods a loss of an equal amount. (1930, I, p. 139)

In this case, interaction between the unproductive consumption out of Liquid Capital from falling earnings and the changes in Liquid Capital quantities produces an Accelerator Effect. This explains the shape of the downturn of the economy and the time it takes for recovery. 'As soon as thrift gets ahead of enterprise, it positively discourages the recovery of enterprise and sets up a vicious circle by its adverse effect on profits' (1930, II, pp. 148–9). From these inevitabilities, Keynes established a standard for determining the best way of redistributing consumption, which increases production: it must meet the criterion of diminishing 'the unfavourable reaction on the producer whose consumption is reduced . . . less than the favourable reaction on the producer whose consumption is increased' (1930, II, p. 125).

An important result, almost a by-product of Keynes's thinking about productive consumption was his conceiving already in the *Treatise* both the Multiplier and the Accelerator Effect. A second important conclusion out of the Treatise is that of the *Instability Principle*:

Industry is extra ordinarily sensitive to any excess or deficiency, even a slight one, in the flow of available output ready to be fed back into the production process. If there is a deficiency, full employment is impossible at the existing level of real wages; if there is an excess, equally, though for quite a different reason, full employment is impossible at the existing level of real wages. In the event of a deficiency the means for full employment is lacking; in the event of an excess the incentive is lacking. (1930, II, p. 146)

Although what Keynes is addressing here is how and when to affect the Credit Cycle to buffer against the worst aspects of its downturn and the negative results which would ensue, it seems that the behaviour of consumption, the choices surrounding investment, and the liquidity shifts between *Industrial Circulation* and *Financial Circulation* are already so well developed in the *Treatise* as to be recognizable for what Keynes will call in *The General Theory* the Marginal Propensity to Consume, the Marginal Efficiency of Capital and Liquidity Preference. Much has been repeated about how Keynes's *Treatise* was simply about prices. It is obvious that such a conclusion could derive only from a very superficial reading of Keynes's *Treatise*.

In sum, it can be said from the above detailed if not exhaustive exposition of the essence of Hayek's and Keynes's models that both approaches to dynamic analysis of investment and the role of capital in its diffusion are sophisticated and enlightening. It can also be added that Keynes's theory of capital, with its division into Fixed Capital, Working Capital, and Liquid Capital components, reveals a much more in-depth understanding of the complexity of the market economy than the highly theoretical and stylized theory of Hayek. It is clear that Hayek's insinuation that Keynes would 'have made his task easier if he had not only accepted one of the descendants of Böhm-Bawerk's theory, but had also made himself acquainted with the substance of the theory itself' (1931; 1995, p. 131), is misplaced and unwarranted, and shows that Hayek was not patient nor careful in his reading of *A Treatise*. Furthermore, as far as the inconsistencies attributed to Keynes's use of terms or analysis, none has been discovered, and here again Hayek's reference, to 'passages in which the inconsistent use of terms produces a degree of obscurity which, to anyone acquainted with Mr. Keynes's earlier work, is almost unbelievable' (1931; 1995, p. 122), is unfounded. From the reading of the two works, if inconsistency there is, it is found in Hayek's work rather than Keynes's. For example, Hayek rejects from the outset the usefulness of averages but consciously resorts to their use here and there, whenever convenient. Hayek asserts from the start that 'all resources are fully utilized', yet his analysis of equilibrating equilibrium which never reaches its ultimate convergence ideal reveals that in the shifts of production from one type of good into another, resources are put out of work! His analysis has little to say about these casualties. Leaving aside the interesting Austrian concept of a period of production, Hayek's concept of capital is rather limited compared to that of Keynes. His monetary approach, as simplistic as his theory of saving, does not compare in depth and breadth to that of Keynes. It is nonetheless not the purpose of this book to dwell very much on Hayek's theory, except as was necessary to show that he was wrong in his assessment of Keynes's *Treatise*[20] and remained under that delusion for years without being challenged by generations of Keynes scholars.

No other economist, before or after Keynes, has tackled a monetary theory of production with such a degree of complexity. In the last two sections of this chapter, two essential elements of Keynes's theory have been explored: the monetary components of production as reflected in the Credit Cycle and the most important potential contribution of investment. Keynes's nuanced understanding of both the divisions of the money side of the economy into its various deposits related to *Industrial* and *Financial Circulations* and his pinpointing productive consumption as the primary positive type of investment outcome afforded him far more insight into the workings of the Credit Cycle and how its worst extremes could be mitigated than any of his contemporaries. The policy aspects, which discussion of the Credit Cycle brings to the fore, will be addressed in Chapter 6 on inflation and deflation.

NOTES

1. For Wicksell, these were intermediary and final goods.
2. As Hayek correctly recognized in his review of *A Treatise*: 'Instead of a "horizontal" division between capital goods . . . and consumption goods . . . Mr. Keynes attempts a kind of vertical division' (1931; 1995, p. 129).
3. Using the symbols corresponding to Keynes's model.
4. From Hayek's perspective, Keynes's relation to short-run and long-run analysis is misunderstood: 'The difference between Mr. Keynes's viewpoint and my own here [on what will affect the quantities of money expended on C or R goods] is not . . . due to any neglect on my part of the fact that Mr. Keynes is dealing only with a short-run problem. It is Mr. Keynes rather, with his implied assumption that the real factors are in equilibrium who is unconsciously introducing a long-run view of the subject' (1931; 1995, p. 124, fn. 8).
5. As the analysis continues further, Keynes' notation is still being used.
6. Contrast these definitions with the more nuanced ones in Keynes, Figure 3.1.
7. 'The existence of such unused resources is itself a fact which needs explanation. It is not explained by static analysis and accordingly we are not entitled to take it for granted' (1931, p. 31).
8. 'There would accordingly exist no inherent cause for a return to the old proportions' (1931, p. 52).
9. Hayek also calls these the 'old concerns (as we may conveniently, but not quite

accurately, call the processes of production which were in operation before the new money was injected)' (1931, p. 78).

10. He also introduced another scenario similar to Hayek's. Type (ia), we might call it, represents the situation 'when a Credit Cycle has been initiated by *a drop in saving uncompensated by decreased investment*' (1930, I, p. 286, emphasis added). Any drop in saving spells an increase in consumption or 'a larger expenditure on the same available consumption goods as before, so that, as in the other cases, prices move upward' (1930, I, p. 287).

11. '[F]actors of production are not fully employed at the moment when the Cycle begins its upward course' (1930, I, p. 284).

12. 'No additional savings' means that the savings out of the community's income remains unchanged.

13. Before they cease entirely, the banks will, however, try different tactics to sustain lending: 'increasing the velocities of circulation as a result of the enhanced cost of maintaining balances . . . or . . . attracting gold from abroad' (1930, I, pp. 285–6).

14. Keynes's first discussion of consumption was unfortunately buried in a chapter on working capital in volume II and therefore went virtually unnoticed.

15. This was pointed out by many (for example, Robertson, Hayek, and Hicks), from which the *Treatise* was interpreted as a theory of price that did not deal with employment.

16. Keynes felt Hawtrey had all too enthusiastically focused on these monetary aspects. Drawing attention to statements in Hawtrey's *Trade and Credit* (1928, p. 169), he wrote: 'Mr Hawtrey has gone a good deal farther than I have been prepared to go in arguing that the Credit Cycle is "a purely monetary phenomenon"' (1930, II, p. 131).

17. Keynes did seem to acknowledge that the notion of aggregate investment in FC could pose some problems: 'many so-called new issues merely represent the transfer of existing assets from one party to another' (1930, II, p. 98). In the same discussion, Keynes noted nonetheless examples of such investing: 'the rate of investment in houses' (1930, II, p. 97), 'productive effort' in the direction of 'Land, Buildings, Roads and Railways', to which he also added 'sewers and the like' (1930, II, p. 98), and 'the consumption' of iron and steel (1930, II, p. 99). He seemed also to adopt Spiethoff's reference to 'industrial equipment' as fixed capital (1930, II, p. 100).

18. In order not to entail the tight link between saving and investment in fixed capital in any implied major change in employment, it would seem that Keynes's definition of fixed capital must be very clear (see preceding note). For Keynes the difficulty does not seem to have presented itself explicitly. See the table (1930, II, p. 193) in which he notes in different columns 'Investment in Fixed Capital', 'Net Investment in Working Capital' and 'Aggregate', capturing 'the order of magnitude of the fluctuations in investment in fixed and working capital taken together' in the United States between 1923–24 and 1929–30. Four of the entry years reflect a decrease or no change in working capital during the year, even as fixed capital investment was very sound. In the other three years the spreads between the two types of capital investments range from a high investment in working capital, 14 per cent of the total fixed capital investment, to a low of 4 per cent.

19. The fact that it is discussed in volume II of the *Treatise*, which, in general, is even less read, is a possible explanation of its neglect.

20. A concordance comparing *A Treatise on Money* of Keynes with Hayek's *Prices and Production* is yet to be written.

5 Keynes's causal relations: *The General Theory* derailed

Six years elapsed between the publication of *A Treatise on Money* and *The General Theory*. To try to seize Keynes's thinking during this period, from 1931 to 1936, has been of particular interest, and after the mid-1970s it became somewhat easier. Some new documents of Keynes dating from the early 1930s, which surfaced at that time, have since been gathered and printed in volume XXIX of his *Collected Writings* (Keynes, 1979). They consist mainly of correspondence, preparatory lecture notes, and fragments of drafts of some chapters of *The General Theory*, dated between 1932 and 1936.[1] The contents of volume XXIX alone show just how much ink was spilled on corresponding, explicating, debating, and arguing about how Keynes had spelled out his theory in the *Treatise* but mostly about the way he was trying to carry his ideas forward to formulate *The General Theory*.

The controversy in which Keynes found himself after publication of the *Treatise* was revolving around semantics. Having difficulty conveying the essentials of his theory, Keynes had to resort to redefining terms, introducing new vocabulary, and using alternative symbols. These attempts made it difficult for impatient readers to follow his thinking and gave more ammunition to his critics, like Hayek, to maintain that he was confused and changing his mind. Keynes's re-evaluation of his own writing stems from the complexity of his incredible dissection of the economic world of his time. He had tried initially to capture it fully analytically and over time was simply trying to find alternative ways to convey the same ideas of his unusual analysis, so different from that of the accepted orthodoxy. His new attempts were, however, misunderstood as confusion and a 'change of mind', a criticism that became unjustifiably a myth, which carried on well after *The General Theory*.

It will be shown in this chapter that in the fundamental core of Keynes's theory, regarding the role of money and interest, the interaction of saving and investment, and the importance of the propensity to save (to consume), there is continuity. Keynes did not 'change his mind'. All his essential theoretical elements continued to play an important part in explaining prices and employment. All the basic premises on which the *Treatise* was based found their way into *The General Theory*. What others perceived as a 'change of mind' was simply the new emphasis Keynes chose to place on some particular aspects rather than on others.

This does not mean that there are no differences in perspective between Keynes's two works. Seen from the investigation of the *Treatise*, a great deal of *The General Theory* is about an economy in but one phase of the credit cycle. *The General Theory* presents an in-depth analysis peculiar to that phase, especially given the acute and worsening circumstances in the time between 1929 and 1933, which could not be ignored. Faced with the crisis of unforeseen proportions in personal and institutional casualties, Keynes's approach became more centred on the employment variable of the *Treatise*. Thus, just as in the creation of an image by the photographer who decides to zoom his lens in on a particular part of the macro-picture, although the surroundings seem to disappear, it does not mean that they cease to exist. Analogously, the same is true for the narrower *General Theory* and its larger reference framework, the *Treatise*.

There was in fact a major change in focus between the two works. The *Treatise* was more general in scope and, given that it was oriented toward explaining the complex environment of production with its heterogeneities and interdependencies, its focus was the directions in which an economy fluctuates. In *The General Theory*, although the same relationships among the core macroeconomic variables remained, their meanings were somehow simplified to aid in the specific search for quantifying how the use of resources translates into employment. Establishing commensurability thus became a main objective for Keynes in this work. Its conclusions, as a result, lent themselves more easily to translation into applicable economic policies.

Unfortunately most of Keynes's challenging ideas, whether before or within *The General Theory*, still remain in the dark, despite industrious efforts to interpret and implement his contribution by generations of economists, from the most faithful post-Keynesians to the more neoClassical Keynesians. It will be shown here how, from the very start of its reception, *The General Theory* was derailed by Sir John Hicks in his two reviews of the work. The damage wrought was comparable to, if not more serious than, that of Robertson and Hayek in relation to the *Treatise*. Hicks's impact was even more profound than Hayek's because, while seeming to have control of the content of *The General Theory* and to be in full accordance with it, in a very non-confrontational way, he nonetheless subtly twisted the lines of Keynes's theoretical argument, placing the focus on the simple and irrelevant parts. Identifying Keynes's fit within the general teaching in the contemporary economics and assessing Keynes's novelties as minor differences, Hicks trivialized Keynes's contribution. The point here is that Hicks's would-be simplification of Keynes's theory into the accessible LL-IS framework (later the IS-LM) was so elegant, powerful, and pedagogically appealing that it instantly became, in the profession, the reference point from which it was thought Keynes must have begun and without which since, no stripe of Keynesian or anti-Keynesian can do. Like Hayek's and Robertson's distortion of the *Treatise*, Hicks's contortion of *The General Theory* has to date never been seriously challenged, despite Hicks's later increasingly frequent cautionary but couched warnings.[2]

The objectives in this chapter are thus threefold: (1) to show that there is a straight line of development in Keynes's theoretical analysis from *A Treatise* to *The General Theory*, (2) to demonstrate where Hicks's conception went astray and why his assessment of Keynes is at best simply a misrepresentation and at worst an offence to the truth, and (3) to argue that the concluding chapters of *The General Theory* hark back to *A Treatise*. In short, in this chapter it will be shown that the two books, *A Treatise* and *The General Theory*, are intimately connected. To do so the following will be undertaken:

- Clarification of the initial definitions and concepts that created controversy, such as income, profits, savings, and investment – these have first to be clarified in order to contrast Hicks's interpretation of Keynes to the words of Keynes. Their meanings, as they are found in the drafts of *The General Theory* (Keynes, 1979) and in the work once published are discussed in contrast to how they were understood in the *Treatise*.
- Explanation of how Hicks constructed his Keynesian model of Keynes (the most influential of many others).
- Discussion of why *The General Theory* fits neither Hicks's nor any of the other models in the IS-LM family.
- Interpretation of chapters 22 and 24 of *The General Theory* – although very brief in their exposition, these chapters do place *The General Theory* back into the more general trade cycle of the *Treatise*.

5.1 DEFINITIONS AND CONCEPTS

In order to show how Hicks's schematic rendition of *The General Theory* and the ensuing Keynesianisms, which have relied on that apparatus, represent an approach antithetical to *The General Theory*, it is necessary to turn again to elucidating the semantics and the premises from which Keynes's theory was built. Keynes, more than any other economist of his time, was almost obsessive in his concern for definitions. He cannot be accused of not having defined his terminology enough. If anything, it is the reverse; he perhaps stressed definitions overly much. His command of the language gave him an edge in carefully introducing each term and explaining meticulously its *raison d'être*.

Keynes tailored the definitions of his vocabulary and concepts to the needs of his theory. The main methodological difficulty of Keynes's treatment in *The General Theory*, which led to controversy, derived from the fact that he had attempted to build a basic macroeconomic theory just as he understood the business world to work. Keynes devised an unusual approach to separating the components of the economic environment, different from that of the well-established orthodox economics, whether Classical or neoClassical. Keynes gave technical meanings to some terms that are not usually understood except in the ordinary sense even by the majority of his fellow colleagues. In addition to its semantic complications, Keynes's theory revealed itself to be too unorthodox to digest. Facing continual resistance and reluctance, Keynes persevered and tried re-defining from different perspectives the same concepts and ideas found in his earlier work, introducing different symbols, which required even more patience to grasp.

Keynes had become aware, since the writing of the *Treatise*, that his explanation there of the directions in which macroeconomic variables change was simply not complete. In *A Treatise* he had wanted to lay down the monetary foundation of the credit cycle from which the general *direction* in which the economy would fluctuate could be explained, according to whether it is subjected to inflations or deflations and how these pressures impact employment and wealth. Keynes became, however, convinced that a theory ought to be able to go further and that striving toward some form of quantification, even if approximate, might allow it to do so. In *The General Theory*, his interest was thus turned toward finding measurements, specifically for employment and wealth.

> The three perplexities which most impeded my progress in writing this book, so that I could not express myself conveniently until I had found some solution for them, are: firstly, the choice of unit of quantity appropriate to the problems of the economic system as a whole; secondly, the part played by expectation in economic analysis; and thirdly, the definition of income. (1936; 1970, p. 37)

Keynes constantly juggled between the theoretical level for developing his macroeconomic relationships and the level of empirical evidence to support his theory, which led him to point out difficulties in the units of quantity 'in terms of which economists commonly work' (1936; 1970, p. 37). As has been stressed throughout the discussions of previous chapters, the profits of the entrepreneurs are central in Keynes's analysis and constitute his point of departure. As a macroeconomic variable in *The General Theory*, they are expressed as the difference between the 'total proceeds' and the earnings of the factors of production. The total proceeds from the volume of total output, measured by the National Dividend, are to be expressed as money income. Keynes objected to Marshall's and Pigou's resorting to the use of net, real income, as he saw it raising insurmountable difficulties at the empirical level: 'the community's output of goods and services is a non-homogenous complex which cannot be measured, strictly speaking . . . The difficulty is even greater when in order to calculate net output, we try to measure the net addition to capital equipment' (1936; 1970, p. 38).

A further difficulty Keynes identified was one related to the 'vagueness' of economic quantity concepts, for example, that of the general price-level. To avoid the problems of the use of a vague price-level as well as measurement incommensurability, Keynes chose wage units as the value in terms of which to express income. At the theoretical level, he thought the use of the concept of the wage-unit could do for developing the logic of his macroeconomic relationships. At the level of seeking empirical evidence to support his theory, where statistics and measurement are required, Keynes admitted, however, that his measure of the price-level could only be viewed as an approximation:

> we limit ourselves strictly to the two units, money and labour, when we are dealing with the behaviour of the economic system as a whole; reserving the use of units of particular outputs and equipments to the occasions when we are analysing the output of individual firms or industries in isolation; and the use of vague concepts, such as the quantity of output as a whole, the quantity of capital equipment as a whole and the general level of prices, to the occasions when we are attempting some historical comparison which is within certain (perhaps fairly wide) limits avowedly imprecise and approximate. (1936; 1970 p. 43)

As said above, Keynes's definitions and redefinitions were specifically tailored to his theory. His definitions of money have already been discussed in Chapter 2, and more will be said about them later, but what now about the wage unit? Keynes's choice of the wage-unit can only be understood as a useful quantifier in the context of his definitions of money and with respect to his definitions of profits and income, which underwent slight changes from *A Treatise* to *The General Theory*. The evolution of their changes is traced in relation to the following three sets of variables:

1. Recall from Chapters 3 and 4 on the *Treatise* that the central macro-economic variable from which Keynes's theory starts is **profits (Q)**. He

termed them there windfall profits (losses) and expressed them as the difference between the values of the total output (National Dividend, in the terminology of *The General Theory*)[3] and the total earnings:

$$Q = \prod O - [wL + RE + rK + R + DD + P\&B] \qquad (3.1)$$

Q is also expressed as the value of current investment minus the aggregate of Savings:

$$Q = I - S \qquad (3.2)$$

Keynes pursued his analysis of windfall profits into his Fundamental Equation II:

$$\prod = E/O + (I - S)/O \quad \prod = W_1 + Q/O \qquad (\text{FEII } 3.5)$$

2. After much reconsideration, in a chapter entitled 'Certain Fundamental Equations' in a 1933 draft of *The General Theory* (1933; 1979, pp. 68–73), Keynes relabelled windfall profits (Q), **Quasi rents (Q)**. He also restricted the earnings of the community (**E**) to the earnings of a single factor of production, labour. Further, Keynes identified total aggregate income ($\prod O$) as **PO** or **Y** (in the terminology of *The General Theory*, National Dividend) and introduced aggregate Disbursement (**D**) as the sum of (aggregate) Consumption-expenditure (**C**) and Investment (**I**). So, in comparison with the symbols of the *Treatise*, the 1933 draft model was:

$$Q = Y - E \qquad (5.1)$$

Q is also expressed, as before, as the value of current investment minus the aggregate Savings, which is now represented as **S′**:

$$Q = I - S' \qquad (5.2)$$

From Equations 5.1 and 5.2 combined, $Y = E + Q = PO = wN + Q$, where **wN** is the wage bill (**N** is labour and **w** is money wage), it follows that:

$$P = wN/O + (I - S')/O \qquad (\text{FEII } 5.3)$$

Equation FEII 5.3 is Fundamental Equation II redefined, or a slightly altered version of Fundamental Equation II in the *Treatise*. As Keynes put it, it is 'substantially the same as the fundamental price equation in my Treatise on Money' (1933; 1979, p. 73).

3. The passage from the draft of 1933 to the printed content of *The General Theory* is rather straightforward, but again with Keynes's making some modifications to terminology. In his chapter on 'The Definition of Income, Saving and Investment' (1936; 1970, p. 52ff), Keynes began by defining 'the *income* of the entrepreneur as being the excess of the value of his finished output sold during the period over his prime cost' (1936; 1970, p. 53, original emphasis). For the economy as a whole, where **A** is the total output, and **U** the user cost, 'aggregate income is equal to A – U' (1936; 1970, p. 54), or the net addition to wealth or the change in investment. Aggregate income minus the aggregate factor cost, **F** equals aggregate profits, **Q**, that is, Q = A – U – F. Total net output, A – U is **Y** in the notation of 1933, and the 'income of the rest of the community [E] is equal to the entrepreneur's factor cost' [**F**] (1936; 1970, p. 54), thus, as above:

Income of the	=	Aggregate	–	Income of
Enterpreneurs		Income		Community
Q	=	Y	–	E	(5.1')

Implicitly in symbols (although explicitly in text),[4] if aggregate consumption (**C**) is added and subtracted from Equation 5.1', then Q = (Y – C) – (E – C). The first term is the aggregate savings out of aggregate income; it corresponds to the symbol for savings, **S** in the notation of the 1933 draft of *The General Theory*. The second term is the aggregate savings out of the income of the community, which corresponds to **S'** in the 1933 draft notation. Therefore Q = S – S'. For Keynes, this **S** is always equal to **I**. Thus:

$$Q = I - S' \qquad (5.2')$$

Furthermore, from Equation 5.1', Q = Y – E = PO – wN, and here again, when combined with Equation 5.2', it follows that

$$P = wN/O + (I - S')/O \qquad (FEII\ 5.3')$$

Before discussion turns to the full model of The General Theory, *it should be crystal clear from what has been shown above that for Keynes both in the* Treatise *and in* The General Theory: (1) *it is the entrepreneurs who determine the fate of the economy;* (2) *it is the entrepreneurs' earnings, whether they are called windfalls, quasi rents or simply profits, which are the central macroeconomic variable from which his analysis begins and from which everything else ensues; (3) the basic structure of Keynes's theoretical model is the same; and (4) Fundamental Equation II is present and essential to both works.*

Throughout the drafts of *The General Theory* and in its final version, Keynes stressed at every stage, in order to make his theory more understandable and acceptable after the *Treatise*, where and why some clarifications and redefinitions had to be made and where and why certain simplifications had to be undertaken. Should this be taken to mean that the models of the *Treatise* and *The General Theory* are the same? If not, what are their differences? Pursuing the analysis of changes above, Keynes's other key concepts are now considered in relation to his notion of profits:

Income and *Profits*: the concept of income in the *Treatise*, meaning the earnings of the factors of production, included 'some normal remuneration' for entrepreneurs, which was to be understood to be different from the entrepreneurs' windfall profits. This distinction provoked much criticism, and in *The General Theory* Keynes subsequently redefined income.[5] *The General Theory*'s Equation 5.1' separates the different categories of income in a much simpler manner.

Saving and *Investment*: Equations 3.2 and 5.2' relating profits to Investment and Savings are virtually the same in both the *Treatise* and *The General Theory*. S in Equation 3.2 is the same as S' in Equation 5.2'. The S which Keynes used in Fundamental Equation II of the *Treatise* is the same as the S' of *The General Theory*.[6] As explained above, S, or aggregate savings, which is the difference between total income and aggregate consumption ($Y - C$, in *The General Theory*), corresponds to what entrepreneurs choose to invest. In the sense that the amount of investment causes the amount of saving (1933; 1979, p. 108), investment and savings are always equal, $I = S$. S' ($E - C$ in *The General Theory*) is the savings out of the earnings of the community or voluntary savings (ibid.). $S - S'$ is involuntary saving. This distinction is crucial to understanding Keynes's productive and unproductive consumption, discussed in Chapter 4. There is no inconsistency between Keynes's assertions in the *Treatise* and *The General Theory* that $I = S$ always (that investment is always equal to profits and the savings of the community, or S, total savings) and that I is not necessarily equal to S (that investment is not necessarily equal to the saving of the community, S or S'). Notwithstanding use of different symbols the two concepts, the identity and the equality, are both consistent features of both the *Treatise* and *The General Theory*.

Price-level and *Wage-unit*: the *Treatise* was concerned with fluctuations caused by the discrepancies between savings and investment in the phases of the credit cycle. The behaviour of the price-level is determined by the two terms in Fundamental Equation II (Equation FEII 3.5). The second term corresponds to short-term fluctuations in profits. The first term corresponds to the cost of production, which can be interpreted as a long-term component. This means that if the second-term fluctuations cancel themselves out, prices will converge to their cost of production in the Classical sense.

In *The General Theory*, Keynes concentrated his attention on a given short period at the ebb of the credit cycle and attempted to show how the level of employment is determined then, and otherwise. To separate the remuneration of labour from that of capital, he distinguished 'two kinds of production period' (1933; 1979, p. 74), an accounting or employment period and a production or investment period, and two types of entrepreneurs:

> the producer or manufacturer and the investor or capitalist respectively. It is the former who employs labour; he produces goods for sale either to the consumer or the investor; his goods are for sale as soon as they are finished; and his forecast relates to the period which elapses between his decision to employ labour and the sale of his output. The latter does not employ labour but must be conceived as hiring out his capital goods to a producer from one accounting period to the next. (1933; 1979, p. 75)

The accounting period is the shorter of the two periods during which, Keynes assumed, labour was the sole factor of production (1936; 1970, p. 213) and capital entered in as a rented service. The investment period corresponds to the life of the entrepreneurs' rented fixed capital and extends through successive short periods. Thus, while labour receives wages for its productive services, '[I]t is much preferable to speak of capital as having a yield over the course of its life in excess of its original cost, than as being *productive*' (1936; 1970, p. 213, original emphasis).

The costs of employed labour and fixed capital translate, in the above equations of the Price-level, FEII 5.3 and FEII 5.3', into the first and second terms. The first term is the cost of labour determined by the short-term expectations of the entrepreneur as to how much (he expects) to sell at the end of the accounting period and how much (he expects therefore) to produce. The second term depends on the yield of his fixed capital, which he tries to forecast according to his long-term expectations. It is employment during the accounting period that is the subject of investigation in *The General Theory*. As the unit of value for this analysis, Keynes preferred to use a Wage-unit, specifically the wage per unit of output

(W/O, where **W** stands for **w**N), rather than the price-level because of the vagueness of the latter, already noted.

Before turning to Hicks's interpretation of Keynes's theory, one more general comment about the terms in the equations of the price-level could be made in relation to the time horizon contemplated. The first term of Fundamental Equation II, which was a long-term concept in the *Treatise*, became a short-term concept in *The General Theory*; the second term, which was referent to the long term in the *Treatise*, became a short-term variable in *The General Theory*. This is not a reversal of mind, but an outcome dictated by the different time perspectives: the former required by the analysis of cyclical fluctuation; the latter stemming from the perspective of equilibrium during a particular period. All these observations further reinforce the assertion that for Keynes, *A Treatise* was the backbone of *The General Theory* and the theory from which his generalized General Theory derived.

5.2 HICKS'S MR KEYNES'S *GENERAL THEORY OF EMPLOYMENT* RECONSIDERED

From the appearance of Keynes's *General Theory* in 1936, Hicks commented on, or related and compared Keynes's ideas to his own, in almost all of his writings. Specifically Hicks produced two reviews of *The General Theory* of particular interest here: 'Mr Keynes's Theory of Employment' (1936; 1982), and 'Mr Keynes and the "Classics"' (1937; 1982), which he called his 'most convenient summary of the Keynesian theory' (1950, p. 137). It is in this second review that he suggested the IS-LL device as a simplification of Keynes's special general theory. Hicks did not accept Keynes's theory without reservation. 'On some, at least, of his empirical assumptions, and on the policy prescriptions that he held to follow from them, I already had some reservation' (1979; 1989, p. 210). While he admired Keynes and was influenced by him, in his own mind he never thought of himself as Keynes's disciple.

Hicks did not deny that he shared some ideas with Keynes and even at moments counted himself as a Keynesian in relation to some specifics: 'I counted myself a Keynesian, it was an *IS-LM* Keynesian that I meant. I was contending that Keynes's model, though an extreme case of the *general IL-LM* model, is an extreme case that is outstandingly important' (1979; 1989, p. 210). Hicks became increasingly unhappy, however, about the way his apparatus had come to supplant any reading of Keynes. He wrote both *The Crisis of Keynesian Economics* (1974) and '*IS-LM* – an explanation' (1980; 1982) as a reassessment of his two reviews of *The*

General Theory, provoked in part by his sense that Keynesians were reading too much into his interpretation. Despite his dissatisfaction with the way the profession had let his reading and apparatus dictate the interpretation of Keynes, when he went back to introducing the reprinting of the early reviews in 1982, he nevertheless stood firmly by them.

From the start, Hicks eyed Keynes with a 'Walrasian monocle' and attempted to graft onto him his own 'general' theory of expectations and stock-flow analysis: 'I find that there are some things to be said about that, which are rather interesting. And they may perhaps point to ways by which one could possibly push on further' (1979; 1989, pp. 2–3). Indeed, Hicks did push forward with some of what he thought were Keynes's ideas. The purpose here is not to examine Hicks's transformation of his Keynesian IS-LL into its standard IS-LM form and all the ensuing discussion of the apparatus – the literature on those developments is enormous and still growing under the multiplier effect. Instead, it is to ask how in Hicks's interpretation, Keynes's claim to have produced a general theory, encompassing the Classical theory as a special case, became an assertion in Hicks's writing that *The General Theory* was itself a special case of the Classical theory and also of Hicks's own general model.

5.2.1 Hicks's Models of General Theories

The key to understanding Hicks's interpretation of *The General Theory* is to examine what he took specific passages of Keynes to mean. From the outset of *The General Theory*, in the chapter 'The Principle of Effective Demand' (1936; 1970, pp. 23ff), Keynes enunciated his objective: 'the volume of employment in equilibrium depends on (i) the aggregate supply function, Φ, (ii) the propensity to consume, χ, and (iii) the volume of investment, D_2. This is the essence of the General Theory of Employment' (1936; 1970, p. 29).

In his review 'Mr Keynes and the Classics', Hicks interpreted this passage as follows:

> it is now the rate of interest, not income, which is determined by the quantity of money. The rate of interest set against the schedule of the marginal efficiency of capital determines the value of investment; that determines income by the multiplier. Then the volume of employment (at given wage-rates) is determined by the value of investment and of income which is not saved but spent upon consumption goods. (1937; 1982, p. 107)

Hicks immediately found it useful to express his prose interpretation of the passage in question in the form of the apparatus of the IS-LL, which rapidly became the surrogate of *The General Theory* and the standard

Keynesian interpretation of Keynes. Although a quick and general glance at the above passage and at Hicks's first two reviews of *The General Theory* leaves the impression that Hicks understood Keynes's ideas, this is not the case at all.

Closer scrutiny reveals Hicks to have been insensitive to the enormous complexities that Keynes had attempted to embrace within his theory from as early as the *Treatise*. Just as Hayek was steeped in the Austrian theory of capital, Hicks for his part was so immersed in marginalism and a preoccupation with the rediscovery of Walrasian economics (see, for example, his 'Bread' paper of 1935, where 'bread' is numeraire, 'Wages and Interest: the Dynamic Problem' (1935a; 1982)) that it was difficult for him not to read Walras into Keynes and draw parallels in his reviews of Keynes. Hicks began his 1937 assessment of *The General Theory* by setting up a very simple and crude Classical model: two goods, investment x and consumption y, are produced, respectively, by Nx and by Ny labour, at a given money wage w, determined by the respective marginal productivity of each sector. The earnings from each sector, Ix and Iy, together constitute total income I. 'Ix is therefore a given function of Nx, I of Nx and Ny. Once I and Ix are determined, Nx and Ny can be determined' (1937; 1982, p. 103).

In his second review, Hicks set out to encapsulate Keynes's key concepts in three different equations, respectively:

1. the liquidity preference, in a money equation
2. the marginal efficiency of capital, in an investment equation, and
3. the propensity to consume, in the usual saving-investment equality.

Hicks then made each equation depend on the interest rate i or income I or both, to show how his three equations compare to those of others. His four models are:

(i)   a typical 'classical' model, as, he says, 'built on an earlier and cruder model than Professor Pigou's' (1937; 1982, p. 102)
(ii)   the 'Treasury View'
(iii) Keynes's *General Theory*, and
(iv)   Hicks's own Generalized *General Theory* model.

In the case of Keynes's model, (iii), Hicks left 'out of account all secondary complications which do not bear closely upon this special question' of the relation between money wages and employment (1937; 1982, p. 103). He assumed 'a short period in which the quantity of physical equipment of all kinds available can be taken as fixed' and 'homogenous labour'. He considered that both 'depreciation can be neglected, so that the output of investment goods corresponds to new investment' and 'the important issues raised by Mr Keynes in his chapter on user cost are irrelevant'.

With each set of simple equations comprising three unknowns (I, Ix and i), Hicks found comparison of the three rival models to the one he built for Keynes quite straightforward, especially given the assumptions he had made for Keynes's model (1937; 1982, pp. 102–3). Several things became clear to Hicks from the comparison he had created.

1. From equation (1), it could be seen that Keynes's liquidity theory was not all that novel, since the concept was already to be found in the 'Treasury View' model (Figure 5.1). Also, Hicks himself had already developed an aspect of liquidity theory in his 'simplifying the theory of money' paper (1935b; 1982).
2. To Hicks's mind, as he would develop it in the more general Walrasian framework of *Value and Capital*, and as he had already conceived it in his 'Bread' model (1935a; 1982), whether the interest rate is determined in the money market (as in Keynes's theory) or through savings and investment (as in the Loanable Fund theory), the outcome of these basic models is the same.
3. In an ingenious way, Hicks managed to combine Keynes's three equations and to reduce them diagrammatically into the IS-LL curves that depict the interest rate in terms of income (Figure 5.1).
4. To reflect his reading of Keynes, that a change in the inducement to invest does not affect the interest rate, that an increase in effective demand will yield an increase in employment while leaving the interest rate unchanged, and also that the interest rate cannot drop below zero, the shape of his LL curve was flat in its lower part (Figure 5.1, diagram b). Hicks thus concluded that Keynes's theory could only hold in the flat part of the LL curve. Any shift of the IS curve in that flat part, 'either because of a strong inducement to invest or a strong propensity to consume' (1937; 1982, p. 109), will leave the interest rate unchanged, even while increasing income and employment in turn. Keynes's *General Theory* model became thus a 'special form' of the model of the Classical theory.
5. Finally, by making Keynes's so-called Saving and Investment function dependent on both income and interest rate, Hicks also believed that he had derived Keynes's 'Generalized General Theory': 'When generalized in this way, Mr Keynes's theory begins to look very like Wicksell's; this is, of course, hardly surprising. There is indeed one special case where it fits Wicksell's construction absolutely' (1937; 1982, p 114). Hicks was, however, well aware that the 'skeleton apparatus' that he had created, based on the simplifications that he

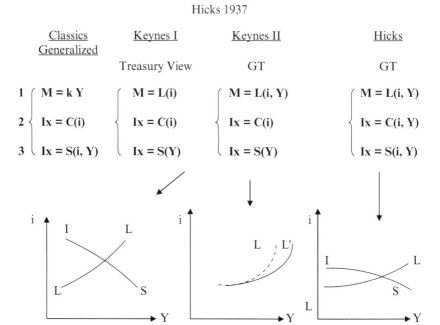

Figure 5.1   Mr Keynes and the Classics

had made in order to be able to construct his Keynesian model, was quite a stretch removed from Keynes's original ideas: 'These, then, are a few of the things we can get out of our skeleton apparatus. But even if it may claim to be a slight extension of Mr Keynes's similar skeleton, it remains a terribly rough and ready sort of affair' (1937; 1982, p. 115). Hicks acknowledged any number of additional, potentially distortive elements: 'the concept of "Income" is worked monstrously hard: most of our curves are not really determinate unless something is said about the distribution of Income as well as its magnitude. . . . all sorts of questions about depreciation have been neglected; and all sorts of questions about the timing of the processes under consideration' (1937; 1982, p. 115). Indeed Hicks had depleted Keynes's *General Theory* of its essence.

Hicks, in fact, provided a model for Keynes's theory that has all the attributes of the Classical theory, which Keynes had tried to rebuke or at least to counter. In Keynes, income distribution is determinant; the concepts of income, savings, investment, depreciation, and user cost all have different meanings from those Hicks attributed to them; and lags and timing are elements crucial to the theory. When these points are taken into consideration and the distortions in the definitions of income, savings, and investment, not to mention profits, are identified, they show a very different picture of *The General Theory* from that of Hicks's Keynesianism. Before showing, however, where Hicks's interpretation of Keynes went astray, an exposition of Keynes's model in *The General Theory*, read in light of what has been explained so far, will be presented.

5.3 KEYNES'S *GENERAL THEORY OF EMPLOYMENT* RECONSIDERED

It is revealing that chapter 2 of Book I of *The General Theory* starts with Keynes's discussion of specific aspects of Classical economics, followed by the presentation of his own principle of effective demand in chapter 3. In these second and third chapters of the Introduction, Keynes attempted to explain his differences from the Classics and to announce his own theory of employment. Keynes discussed first what he called the two Classical postulates. He acknowledged acceptance of the universality of the first postulate of the Classics: 'The wage is equal to the marginal product of labour' (1936; 1970, p. 5). At issue for Keynes was, however, his reservations regarding the implications of his second Classical postulate.

5.3.1 The Classical Postulates

The assertion, 'The utility of the wage when a given volume of labour is employed is equal to the marginal disutility of that amount of employment' (1936; 1970, p. 5), is understood by the Classics to define all equilibrium points and to describe a situation of full employment for any equilibrium in a market free of institutional constraints. For the Classics, this postulate excludes the existence of involuntary unemployment: anyone without work is in the position voluntarily (rather than involuntarily) to accept employment or not. Employers know that no one will accept, unless by force, to work for a real wage below his/her marginal disutility of labour. Hence, the real wage is by definition always at or above the reservation wage of the workforce. When the two Classical postulates are combined, the Classics' definition of full employment becomes that level of employment that corresponds to the point where the real wage equals the marginal disutility of labour and the marginal product of labour, as depicted in Figure 5.2.

In Figure 5.2, the horizontal axis represents employment 'in the

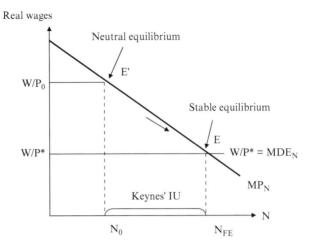

Figure 5.2　Marginal product vs marginal disutility of labour

wage-goods industry', **N**; the vertical axis, the real-wage, **W/P**. Let the downward sloping dark line **MP$_N$** be the diminishing marginal product of labour, and let the point **E** on the curve at the level of employment **N$_{FE}$** correspond to the real-wage **(W/P)***, equal to the marginal product and also to marginal disutility of labour **MDE$_N$**. The intersection of the horizontal line at **(W/P)*** and the marginal product line determines the level of full employment. For Keynes, that intersection is a stable equilibrium because were **N** on the right side, it would '*exceed* the value which reduces the real wage to equality with the marginal disutility of labour' (1936; 1970, p. 29, original emphasis), and hence no one would work. For any real wage greater than **(W/P)***, that is, were **N** on the left side of this intersection point (for example, **E$'$** which he calls a neutral equilibrium), the marginal utility of work would be greater than the marginal disutility of employment (in other words, the marginal utility of leisure), and everyone would choose to work.

It seems that the forces are at work in such a way that the economy will always find itself at the intersection point **E** (Figure 5.2), hence at a stable equilibrium. For the Classics, any level of employment **N** below **N$_{FE}$** is possible, only if the wages are set forcibly above the market wage. Therefore it came to be thought that collective bargaining was the cause of unemployment. For Keynes, however, the issue of involuntary unemployment had nothing to do with wage rigidity (even though, he agreed, as Pigou had demonstrated, this might be a logical conclusion to draw (1936; 1970, p. 278)). An economy can find itself at a level **N** of employment below **N$_{FE}$**, even if there are no rigidities of any kind.

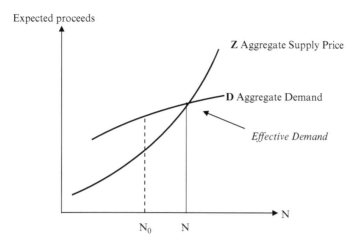

Figure 5.3 Keynes's effective demand

5.3.2 Effective Demand

For Keynes, 'the volume of employment is not determined by the marginal disutility of labour measured in terms of real wages, except in so far as the supply of labour available at a given real wage sets a *maximum* level to employment' (1936; 1970, p. 30, original emphasis). Thus, the Classical theory applies only in the special case of full employment. At any other level of employment, its second postulate does not hold: hiring decisions are solely those of the firm, regardless of whether wages are higher than the marginal disutility of labour. Entrepreneurs' decision to offer employment depends, for Keynes, entirely on the comparison they make between their expectation of proceeds, or their aggregate income,[7] in return for hiring 'a given amount of employment' (1936; 1970, p. 24) and their expectation of proceeds for selling the output of that employment. The first is called the aggregate supply price, **Z**; the second, the aggregate demand, **D**.

In Figure 5.3, two curves, that of the Aggregate Supply Price, **Z** and that of the Aggregate Demand, **D**, are depicted. Both aggregate costs and aggregate prices rise, as production increases. Thus, as shown in the figure, by the profit-maximizing entrepreneurs, consideration is taken of both how much the cost will be to hire n men and how much of that cost, which will become income to those n men employed, will become in turn proceeds to the entrepreneurs-employers, if the employees purchase the output they themselves produced. In Figure 5.3, both curves **Z** and **D** increase as employment increases, the first more steeply than the second.

Z slopes upward at an increasing rate, because as expected proceeds from future sales increase, both the volume of output and the price increase. The expected proceeds from different levels of employment **D** also increase, but at a decreasing rate because of diminishing returns.

In Figure 5.3, at any point left of employment level **N**, the return from investment in labour is greater than the expected proceeds from output. It would thus be worthwhile to increase employment, and, vice-versa, on the right side of **N**. There is only one point where **Z** and **D** are equal, their intersection, which Keynes called the *effective demand* (1936; 1970, p. 25). It is a stable equilibrium, since at this point the forces are such that what is expected to be able to be realized in terms of production or output from a certain level of employment is equal to what is expected to be realized in terms of the proceeds from the demand of that output. It is assumed by Keynes that for the Classics this equality is always the case, because they start with the premise that what is expected is (will be) always realized (see 1936; 1970, appendix to chapter 19, p. 272). Therefore, whatever the level of **N**, there is/will always be a corresponding intersection where **Z** = **D**: 'The classical theory assumes, in other words, that the aggregate demand price (or proceeds) always accommodates itself to the aggregate supply price; so that, whatever the value of N may be, the proceeds **D** assume a value equal to the aggregate supply price **Z**, which corresponds to N' (1936; 1970, p. 26).

Figure 5.4 brings the previous two figures together. Assume again that the level of employment is established at N_0 (in Figure 5.4, upper half), such that the real wage corresponding to MP_N at **E'** is

$$(W/P)_0 > (W/P)^* \tag{5.4}$$

and

$$(W/P)^* = (MDE)_N \tag{5.5}$$

Assume also that the level N_0 corresponds to expected proceeds EP_0 (in Figure 5.4, lower half), such that Z = D. For the Classics, the point EP_0 in Figure 5.4 corresponds to **E'** (upper half), although in a neutral equilibrium, in Keynes's sense, that is:

$$Z = D \text{ and } (W/P)_0 = (MP)N_0 \tag{5.6}$$

This equilibrium is not a stable equilibrium, in the sense that the real wage is higher than the reservation wage (equation 5.4).

Unless there is some wage rigidity at **E'**, there will be movement in

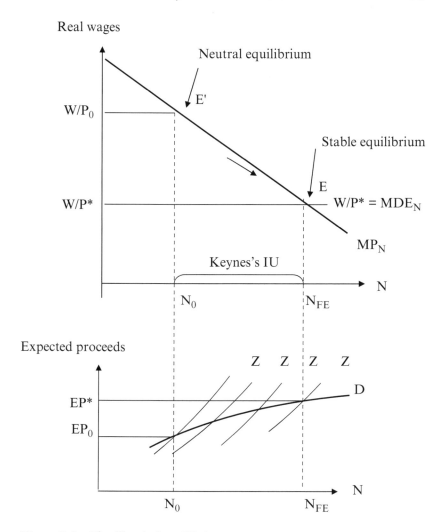

Figure 5.4   The Classical equilibrium

Figure 5.4 from **E'** to **E** (upper half) and from **EP$_0$** to **EP*** (lower half), such that as long as the real wage is greater than the marginal disutility of employment, there will always be workers who would prefer to work even at a lower real wage, as long as the condition of equation 5.4 prevails. This means that there will be continual movement from **E'** to **E**, since the marginal productivity of the additional units of labour is decreasing and with it, real wages. A diminishing real wage means diminishing cost per unit of factor of production, which shifts Curve **Z** slowly to the right as **Z** slides on the aggregate demand curve up to the point of intersection **Z** = **D** corresponding to the stable equilibrium **E** (upper half).

In other words, for Keynes, the Classics assume that if there are no wage rigidities, the reservation wage, represented by equation 5.5, will determine a level of employment that is always Full Employment. For Keynes, however, even in the absence of rigidities, it is not the reservation wage, but the combination of '[T]he propensity to consume and the rate of new investment [which] determine between them the volume of employment, and the volume of employment is uniquely related to a given level of real wages – not the other way around' (1936; 1970, p. 30).

In order to understand the way in which Keynes distinguished himself from the Classics, one cannot follow Hicks's route, described above. Hicks's interpretation of Keynes got him embroiled in the differences between the two of them in terms of real wages and money wages, with his starting from the following perspective, one which Hicks later called the *wage theorem*: 'When there is a general (proportional) rise in money wages, says the theorem, the normal effect is that all prices rise in the same proportion – provided that the money supply is increased in the same proportion (whence the rate of interest will be unchanged)' (1974, pp. 59–60).

To have assumed the 'wage theorem' as a premise of *The General Theory* was an erroneous starting point for Hicks, since it means that nominal wages and prices change together in the same direction and that whatever the nominal wage, the prevailing real wage corresponds to where the supply of labour equals the demand for labour, or the point where the real wage equals the marginal disutility of labour. This was tantamount to denying Keynes's rejection of the second postulate. Even though Hicks was well aware that his approach was simplistic, his caveats cannot cover his construal of the role of wages and labour in *The General Theory* in a way that is not completely distortive of Keynes's theory. More will be said below about why Hicks's approach is too inadequate to be claimed as an interpretation of Keynes.

5.3.3   Prospective Yield or Marginal Efficiency of Capital

The starting point of the analysis in Keynes's *General Theory* is neither the labour market nor any presuppositions about wages, but rather it is 'capital' which set the stage for what was to follow. Keynes's causal theory unfolds from the concept of capital and its impact on production and employment. By capital, Keynes meant in fact 'additions to capital', that is, net investment, which he also referred to as capital-assets (1936; 1970,

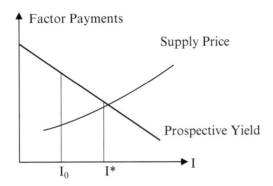

Figure 5.5   Prospective yield of a typical investment

pp. 135ff *passim*). Recall from above that it is assumed in *The General Theory* that labour is the sole factor of production and that capital is factored in only as a rented service. Thus, for Keynes, when an entrepreneur contemplates an investment, that is, 'buying a capital-asset', it means that the entrepreneur 'purchases the right to the series of prospective returns, which he expects to obtain from selling its output, after deducting the running expenses of obtaining that output, during the life of the asset. This series of annuities Q_1, Q_2 . . . Q_n it is convenient to call the *prospective yield* of the investment' (1936; 1970, p.135, original emphasis).

Against the prospective gains from capital, there are its corresponding costs, which Keynes refers to as the *supply price* or *replacement cost*. The gain and the cost relationship for a typical investment is depicted in Figure 5.5.

Let the horizontal axis of Figure 5.5 be investment, and the vertical axis, the costs and the prospective yield corresponding to that investment. As in Marshall, Keynes incorporated diminishing marginal returns, which means 'the prospective yield will fall as the supply of that type of capital is increased' (1936; 1970, p. 136). The cost of capital, its *'supply price'* or *'replacement cost'*, is noted by Keynes as meaning 'not the market-price at which an asset of the type in question can actually be purchased in the market, but the price which would just induce a manufacturer newly to produce an additional unit of such assets' (1936; 1970, p. 135).

In the representation in Figure 5.6, further separation is made in the cost of capital, between the capital assets' 'net cost' (comprising the costs of amortization, depreciation, and so on) and their 'gross cost' (which includes the interest rate). Suppose that the entrepreneurs have decided to invest I_0 dollars. For that volume of investment, as can be seen in the figure, the Prospective Yield (Curve I_0) is greater than the Supply Price

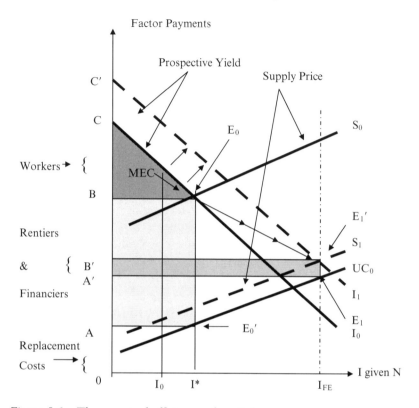

Figure 5.6   The marginal efficiency of capital

(Curve S_0). It is therefore worthwhile for the entrepreneur to keep investing up to the point where the Prospective Yield is just equal to the Supply
Price. This point corresponding to **I*** constitutes the market equilibrium,
which is a short-term equilibrium.

The intersection of the Supply Price and the Prospective Yield curves,
at **I*** in Figure 5.6, shows the point at which, at the margin, the gain from
an additional unit of investment is just equal to its cost. It is based on a
calculation of investing just up to that point where the difference between
the prospective yield of their capital and its supply price reaches zero.
Entrepreneurs in a free-market economy pursue their goal of maximiz-
ing the prospective yield of their capital, *such that it is their decision about
expected future returns that determines how much they are prepared to
invest, and thus the corresponding amount of how much to produce and to
employ.* The equilibrium point where the intersection is realized may or
may not correspond to full employment. The entrepreneurs' cost–benefit

assessment of the prospective yield and the supply price of an investment determine, for Keynes, the marginal efficiency of capital (MEC): '[T]he relation between the prospective yield of one more unit of that type of capital and the cost of producing that unit, furnishes us with the marginal efficiency of capital of that type' (1936; 1970, p. 135). *The marginal efficiency of capital was considered by Keynes to be* the *guiding criterion as to whether an entrepreneur would or would not undertake an investment.*

> Thus for each type of capital we can build up a schedule, showing by how much investment in it will have to increase within the period, in order that its marginal efficiency should fall to any given figure. We can then aggregate these schedules for all the different types of capital, so as to provide a schedule relating the rate of aggregate investment to the corresponding marginal efficiency of capital in general which that rate of investment will establish. We shall call this the investment demand-schedule; or alternatively, the schedule of the marginal efficiency of capital. (1936; 1970, p. 136)

In Keynes, a macroeconomic schedule of the marginal efficiency of capital is derived from the aggregation of all the various investments undertaken by all the entrepreneurs in the economy. This schedule became the cornerstone of Keynes's theory of employment. It is to this aggregate concept of the marginal efficiency of capital that reference is made throughout this book.

As can be seen in Figure 5.7, the equilibrium E_0 corresponds to the level of investment I_0 for a given employment N_0. That intersection E_0 for the Prospective Yield and the Supply Price determines the level of investment that will be undertaken at the macroeconomic level. It corresponds exactly to the intersection of the aggregate demand D_0 and the aggregate supply Z_0, consistent with the level of employment N_0 (Figure 5.7, upper half).

5.3.4 Income Distribution

The intersection E'_0, a unique point, is referred to by Keynes as the *effective demand.* Keynes's notion of Effective Demand is not to be understood as the usual Hicksian market Aggregate Demand but rather as that demand as perceived by entrepreneurs. This is to say that Keynes's Effective Demand is the entrepreneurs' expectation of the demand for the product they intend to produce and sell, at the price determined by the amount they would invest on producing a given volume of output with a given employment, technology, and prices. Different levels of investment yield different equilibrium outcomes (Figure 5.7, lower half) and different corresponding Effective Demands (Figure 5.7, upper half). It still remains to be explained how an economy moves from one level of investment, production, and employment to another or in other words, what makes the

Money, investment and consumption

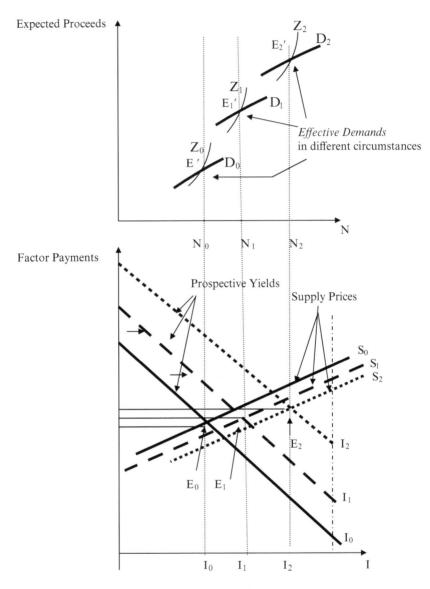

Figure 5.7   Investment–employment correlations

Prospective Yield and Supply Price curves shift, from E_0 to E_1 to E_2 (Figure 5.7, lower half) and from E'_0 to E'_1 to E'_2 (Figure 5.7, upper half). There are causes for shift of the intersection E_0 to the right. It can occur, for example, if the Prospective Yield schedule shifts upward, as from I_0, I_1, I_2, . . . and/or if the Supply-Price schedule shifts to the right, as from S_0, S_1, S_2, . . . (Figure 5.7, lower half). Keynes identified several causal reasons that could effect a change singly, doubly, or multiply. (1) Upward shift of the Prospective-Yield schedule can occur as a result of one or more of the following three changes: (a) an improvement in technology, whereby the same amount of investment will produce more product and more income, (b) an increase in the price-level, whereby the value of a sale is greater, or (c) a decrease in taxes, which would mean that the net earnings of entrepreneurs are higher. (2) Rightward shift of the Supply-Price schedule can occur as the result of one or both of two changes: (a) lower costs of replacement capital and/or (b) a lower interest rate.

Two implications can now be drawn from Figures 5.6 and 5.7. First, the shares of income for each factor of production can be read directly from both figures. Given that the horizontal axis represents investment (for a specific level of employment), the rectangle OBE_0I^* represents the 'gross' earnings of capital, considered *in toto*, and the triangle BCE_0 corresponds to the earnings of labour. If the user cost of capital, U, can be separated from the 'gross' earnings of capital, it can be seen further that the share of capital is made up of two payments (rectangles in Figure 5.6): (1) the user cost of capital, rectangle OAE'_0I^* and (2) the remuneration to the investors, whom Keynes also calls the 'speculators' (1936; 1970, p. 316) (which includes the interest rate), rectangle $ABE_0E'_0$. Keynes's 'user cost' comprised all costs associated with 'the sacrifice of value involved in the production' (1936; 1970, p. 53), including the costs of amortization, sinking funds, and depreciation, net any interest.

The second implication is that Figures 5.6 and 5.7 offer a window on the dynamics of Keynes's distribution of income. It can be seen from Figure 5.6 that an increase in capital would shift the Supply Price to the right and induce more investment. Further, this same increase in capital is revealed in Figure 5.7 to mean a higher effective demand and thus a higher level of employment. Making capital abundant through a low interest rate policy would thus stimulate employment. As seen in Figure 5.6, it would also cause a general increase in wealth.

It became clear to Keynes that if it were possible to make capital abundant, the return from it to interest earnings would diminish and income would be redistributed from the rentiers to labour. As has just been noted, the area OCE_0I^* (Figure 5.6) represents the 'gross' earnings of capital and can therefore be taken to correspond to the earnings value of the total product of using a volume **I*** of capital. As introduced still earlier, the prospective yield at $\mathbf{E_0}$ determines the share of capital (**OBE$_0$I***). As seen in Figure 5.6, since the triangle designated as the income share of labour, the area **BCE$_0$**, is residual, as the rectangle of capital's share becomes smaller, the triangle of labour's share becomes larger. This shift represents therefore an improvement in income distribution in favour of labour, provided that the upward shift of the Prospective Yield curve is less than the rightward shift of the Supply Price curve.

One of the long-term implications of Keynes's theory in *The General Theory* was that through appropriate fiscal and monetary policies, it would be possible to move an economy from $\mathbf{E_0}$ to $\mathbf{E_1}$. It can now be understood how Keynes could feel so

> sure that the demand for capital is strictly limited in the sense that it would not be difficult to increase the stock of capital up to a point where its marginal efficiency had fallen to a very low figure. This would not mean that the use of capital instruments would cost almost nothing, but only that the return from them would have to cover little more than their exhaustion by wastage and obsolescence together with some margin to cover risk and the exercise of skill and judgment. In short, the aggregate return from durable goods in the course of their life would, as in the case of short-lived goods, just cover their labour-costs of production *plus* an allowance for risk and the costs of skill and supervision. (1936; 1970, p. 375, original emphasis)

More will be said about Keynes's vision of the long-term implications of *The General Theory* in Chapter 6. Now, a general explanation of the working of his theory of employment is to be presented. If all the figures developed above were brought together, it might become clearer that Keynes provided enough ingredients to build an overall model. It is cast here as the appropriate alternative to the IS-LM framework.

5.3.5   Keynes's EC-SP Model

All of Keynes's variables and correlations will now be brought together within a single diagrammatic representation, Figure 5.8, labelled the EC-SP model. To put both the EC-SP and the IS-LL models in perspective, it is imperative to recognize within Keynes's account which are his dependent and which his independent variables. As he summed it up himself, near the end of his *General Theory*:

> Our independent variables are, in the first instance, the propensity to consume, the schedule of the marginal efficiency of capital and the rate of interest . . . Our dependent variables are the volume of employment and the national income (or national dividend) measured in wage-units. . . .

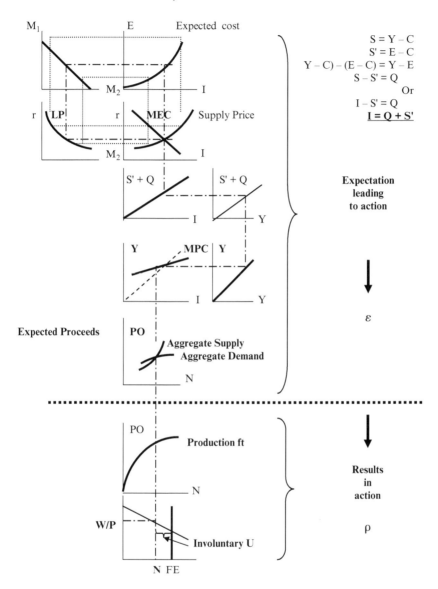

Figure 5.8   The EC-SP model

. . . the given factors allow us to infer what level of national income measured in terms of the wage-unit will correspond to any level of employment; so that, within the economic framework which we take as given, the national income depends on the volume of employment, *i.e.*, on the quantity of effort currently devoted to production, in the sense that there is a unique correlation between the two. (1936; 1970, pp. 245–6)

The new EC-SP model is the crux of this entire study of Keynes. As its name reflects, it culminates in the relationship of the EC (Efficiency of Capital) curve, which represents the Prospective Yield, and the SP (Supply Price) curve.

Explanation of the various components of the model will follow, but the general layout of Figure 5.8 should first be introduced. The lower half of the figure is identified as *Results in action* (ρ), by which is meant that, from a macroeconomic perspective, once the collective decisions of the entrepreneurs to undertake investments are made, they are translated into certain results, among them the determination of employment. The upper half of the figure, identified as *Expectations leading to actions* (ε), represents the expectations side of the economy, most notably the investment decisions which depend on the entrepreneurs' expectations of its returns. ρ (Results) is predetermined by ε (Expectations). The entrepreneurs' expectations about the Marginal Efficiency of Capital, **MEC**, the Liquidity Preference, **LP**, and the Marginal Propensity to Consume, **MPC** *simultaneously* determine the Aggregate Demand *and* the Aggregate Supply, which together determine the Expected Proceeds, or the national income, for which a certain level of employment (**N**) is required. This level of employment may or may not be that of full employment; if it is not full employment, then the second Classical postulate does not hold, and the resulting unemployment is involuntary employment (**ie**).

From the component graphs of Figure 5.8, it should be obvious that when a whole chain of expectation decisions has been realized and a level of employment is established in a context of a certain technology and the usual production function, then – and only then, namely, when ε causes ρ – do the total value of output, **PO** and the real wages, **W/P** become known. The Supply Price curve is composed of the expected costs of the factors of production: on the one hand, the cost of labour, which rises as its volume increases, and on the other hand, the cost of capital, which in *The General Theory* Keynes considered a cost to the entrepreneurs in terms of services rented from the investors, which is a decreasing function. The interest the investors receive is also depicted here in the Liquidity Preference curve, also as a decreasing function. In the economy as a whole, the total income, which is the total money received to produce total output, is also the total amount that has to be paid to the factors of production to produce that level of output. For any given level of money available in an economy, aggregate payment is made up of the wage bill, M_1 and interest cost, M_2. Thus, given an intersection of the Supply Price and the **MEC** curves, the level of investment is determined. That level of investment corresponds to total savings, $S' + Q$. Total saving is an increasing function of total income. From the expenditure side, total income corresponds to expected total output (consumption and investment goods), which would be produced by the level of employment N. For Keynes, Effective Demand or the intersection of Aggregate Supply and Aggregate Demand, is that expected level of employment which would present to the entrepreneur a wage bill just equal to the return expected by the entrepreneur from the sales of the goods which that employment would produce. N is thus that level of employment that corresponds to Expected Proceeds.

While thus it can be seen from Figure 5.8 how the triad of **LP**, **MEC**, and **MPC** leads to the level of employment N, the investment-saving relation in Keynes's *General Theory* seems still a bit trickier to draw in. As has been observed repeatedly, for Keynes too there is equality between investment and total saving. Even as entrepreneurs and savers are two different classes of individuals and even as it is the entrepreneurs who decide in their projections of future expectations how much they are willing to invest, the equality of their actions stands, in the sense that a quantity of investment brings about an equal quantity of savings (not the other way around). Recall, from above, that Keynes made a distinction between total savings, S, which he defined as the difference between total income and total consumption, that is, $Y - C$, and savings out of the earnings of the community, S', or the difference between the earnings of the factors of production minus total consumption, that is, $E - C$. It is S, not S', which is always in equilibrium with I. Thus, in the upper right corner of Figure 5.8, it can be seen how the difference between S and S' corresponds to Q, the profits of the entrepreneurs. This is also another way of saying $I = Q + S'$ or that the quantity of investment is the result of both profits and savings, which is what lends volatility to Liquidity Preference.

From this presentation of the EC-SP model, it can now be reaffirmed that for Keynes the level of employment in an economy depends directly on the investment decisions of the entrepreneurs. As has been seen, various factors (technology, prices, taxes, costs, rate of interest, and so on), which impact the intersection of the **MEC** and the Supply Price curves, can shift either one or both curves. It is the fact that the movements of these curves will result in many different levels of employment that rendered Keynes's theory capable of explaining any and all such levels. It should be apparent now that his theory can explain, not just, as Hicks claimed about the account in *The General Theory*, the special case of an economy in a slump, but also, as another obvious example, the special case of the Classics, the situation where the intersection of **MEC** and the Supply Price will produce a level of employment N compatible with full employment.

Like the instance of the slump, pertinent for the historical circumstances surrounding the writing of *The General Theory*, the full employment case was also important, as Keynes was building a general *General Theory*. It is only at this point, where the real wages are equal to the marginal disutility of labour, that the second Classical postulate holds; it is only in the special case of the Classics that no involuntary unemployment occurs.

5.4   HICKS'S MISINTERPRETATION OF *THE GENERAL THEORY*: THE IS-LM

Recall that in the three equations of his model, Hicks thought he had captured the essential of Keynes's Liquidity Preference, Marginal Efficiency of Capital and Marginal Propensity to Consume. He had, however, so distorted and misrepresented Keynes's own notions that the resulting model of the IS-LL can hardly be said to resemble the ideas of Keynes. Hicks depleted *The General Theory* of all the substance of its novelty, and steeped in Walras, inadvertently rendered Keynes's model but a special case of the Classical theory. The iconic diagrammatic presentation of Hicks's model, the IS-LM, will now be contrasted to the EC-SP model.

The first misrepresentation of Keynes by Hicks pertains to the definition of income, which had already created much fuss even before the appearance of *The General Theory*. For Keynes, total income is equal to the community's earnings, or the wage bill, and the earnings of the investor as profits, thus $Y = E + Q$. Hicks defined, however, Keynes's total income as solely the labour earnings in the consumer and investment goods sectors. There were two noteworthy consequences of Hicks's leaving profits completely out of his Keynesian equations, just as Hayek had done. First, Hicks had eliminated the major component from which Keynes's theory flows and by extension had done away with the role of the investor on which Keynes dwelt so much. Second, with profits omitted from the model, Keynes's definition of investment is flipped back to the meaning it had for the Classics: Keynes's $I = Q + S$ is reduced to the traditional equality $I = S$. As a result, Keynes's emphasis on the bearishness-bullishness of investors toward the market, which captures the volatility related to the financial market and is filtered by him into the model through profits in the investment equation, has disappeared.

A second misrepresentation of Keynes by Hicks turns on Hicks's idea of generalizing the three equations of his Keynesian model. Making them each and all depend on both the interest rate and income allowed him to conclude first that Keynes's model, comprised of only the three equations, had only the two unknowns, **r** and **Y**. He could claim that Keynes's simple system of equations was over-determined: one equation was redundant, since any two equations out of the three could determine the interest rate (see Figure 5.1). Therefore, from a Walrasian perspective, which Hicks was in the process of discovering, the exercise of understanding Keynes's theory was to his mind one of choosing a set of equivalents to determine **r**: the equality between savings and investment or the supply and demand for money. According to Hicks, Keynes had chosen the latter; Wicksell, the former.

Hicks's generalization of the three equations of the model and the presumed redundancy of one was nothing but an obliteration of Keynes's monetary theory. Hicks reduced Keynes's notion of money to a unit of account or a *numeraire*, rendering it neutral in its role as a medium of exchange. There is no need to repeat here, what has already been said in Chapter 2 about the importance and the special characteristics of money for Keynes. Credit creation due to liquidity shifts in the financial market, filtering into the model through Keynes's Liquidity Preference, is not compatible with the neutrality of money. Even if there are no changes in money supply, liquidity shifts do disturb the availability of finance and thus the interest rate.

Hicks was in fact ascribing to Keynes's model what Keynes himself had called that of the barter-like 'cooperative economy', not the fully monetary 'entrepreneurial economy' (1933; 1979, p. 77). To emphasize the different roles these two variables play in the minds of the entrepreneurs when they assess the future returns from spending on capital-assets, Keynes had deliberately made savings a function of income, not of the interest rate, and investment a function of the interest rate, not of income. Since all variables are expressed in value terms, the price-level (approximated by the wage-unit) is lingering in the background; it is not fixed nor given and is therefore an unknown to be determined. These are characteristics of an entrepreneurial economy, which the loanable-fund theory of Hicks does not have. The three equations of Hicks, if they truly represent Keynes's ideas, cannot be reduced to two, as his simplification would have it.

The unique characteristic of money that, for Keynes, makes profits volatile and impacts investment to cause economic fluctuations, is transformed into the unit of account of the Walrasian world. Supplies and demands are the result of a symmetrical balance between the wants and desires of the consumers, on the one side, and the profit maximization for given endowments of the institution of the firms, on the other. Demands and supplies are, for Hicks, 'determined by these tastes, resources and anticipations, and [for] prices as determined by demands and supplies, once the missing element – anticipations – is added, equilibrium analysis can be used' (1936; 1982, p. 86). By 'anticipation', Hicks really meant calculation, not expectations in Keynes's sense; thus for Hicks even in a changing economy, supplies and demands are equal. They are equal so long as we define supply as that amount of a commodity which sellers are willing to offer at a particular date in the market conditions of that date; unsold stocks being unsold because sellers prefer selling them later to selling them at a lower price now. These stocks being reckoned as part of future supply, not current supply, it follows that current supply and current demand must be equal – just because every transaction has two sides. (1936; 1982, pp. 85–6)

It is clear from this quotation that there are major differences in Hicks's and Keynes's semantics, even if there is use of the same notions ('a changing economy', 'unsold stocks', 'future supply').

Hicks's assessment of Keynes's *General Theory*, which led to the classic IS-LM model, depicted in Figure 5.9, will now be contrasted to Keynes's EC-SP model. The IS-LM model, the textbook rendering of Hicks's Keynesianism, is sufficiently well-known that it does not need to be explained here in detail; a general overall presentation of its structure should suffice to make the necessary points. In the figure, a dark dotted line delineates the variables that determine, on the one hand, the Aggregate Demand from those that determine, on the other hand, the Aggregate Supply. The ingenuity of Hicks consisted in his reducing his three equations, for the Liquidity Preference (money side) and the Marginal Efficiency of Capital and Marginal Propensity to Save (expenditure side), into the two curves of the IS (Investment and Savings) and LM (Liquidity and Money) graph, which relate the interest rate, r, to output, Y, and from which derives the Aggregate Demand. The Aggregate Supply is, however, determined by completely different sets of variables, namely, those related to production and the labour market. If, in addition, it is assumed that the level of price affects both the supply and the demand for labour in the same proportion, then there is a complete dichotomy between the forces that determine the Aggregate Demand and those that determine the Aggregate Supply, regardless of whether the supply and the demand for labour are expressed in real or money wages.

A quick glance at both models, the IS-LM and Keynes's EC-SP, reveals that that they have distinctive diagrammatic profiles. This is an attribute that is quite striking for models that derive ostensibly from the same theory. Aside from Hicks's truncation of profits from the definition of income, his misspecification of Keynes's investment-saving relation, and his reduction of Keynes's monetary setting into that of the world of neutral money, it should also be noted that Aggregate Supply and Aggregate Demand relate, in Keynes, the expected proceeds (or total aggregate expected income) to the level of employment and not, as in the IS-LM, the level of price to the level of output. Further, in the upper half of Figure 5.9 of the IS-LM, one can see diagrammatically that Hicks

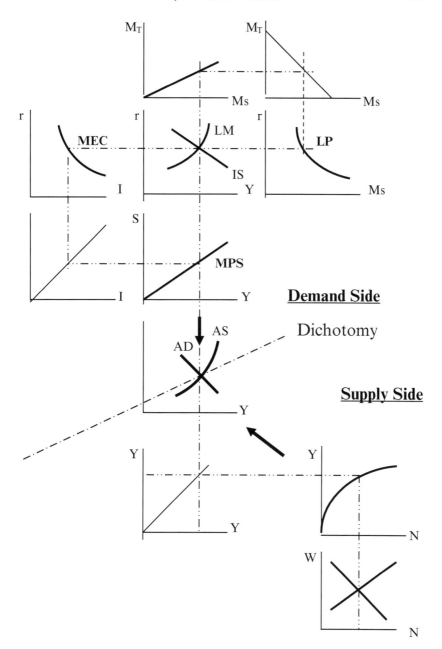

Figure 5.9 The IS-LM model

used Keynes's MEC, LP, MPS, his three determinant elements of Income and employment, as the main variables to determine solely the Aggregate Demand, leaving the Aggregate Supply to be determined by forces in the labour market and the production function. Contrast this to Keynes's EC-SP model, where the three concepts determine simultaneously the Aggregate Supply *and* Aggregate Demand and all the variables are defined by Keynes as expectations perceived by the entrepreneurs.

More importantly, in Hicks's model, the Aggregate Supply is determined by what happens in the labour market. The labour market becomes thus determinant of Income rather than determined by MEC, LP, and MPS. By construction, for Hicks, every point on the Aggregate Supply curve corresponds to a point on the production function curve, and every point on the production function curve corresponds to an intersection of the demand for and the supply of labour. Whether expressed in real or in money terms, this intersection is exactly the condition where the marginal product of labour equals the marginal disutility of labour or again in Keynes's words already quoted above, it is when '[*T*]*he utility of the wage when a given volume of labour is employed is equal to the marginal disutility of that amount of employment*' (1936; 1970, p. 5, original emphasis). This is the second Classical postulate that Keynes had tried to overthrow, largely to explain the rationale for the existence of involuntary unemployment: 'We need to throw over the second postulate of the classical doctrine and to work out the behaviour of a system in which involuntary unemployment in the strict sense is possible' (1936; 1970, pp. 16–17).

The second classical postulate had thus crept back into the IS-LM, making the apparatus classical and antithetical to Keynes. This has held true no matter what cosmetic modifications have been made to the model, in its transformations by generations of Keynesians, whether in the hands of Hansen or Malinvaud or more recently Stiglitz, Blanchard, Mankiw, and many, many others. As has been seen in Figure 5.8, the Classical situation is a limiting case of Keynes's theory. Hicks's analysis of Keynes resulting from the IS-LM had confined *The General Theory* to the status of a special case. The attempt here, however, has been to show that Keynes's theory is applicable to any case of employment or income distribution, whether encountered in a severe, extreme depression, or a mild recession, or even in circumstances closely approaching full employment.

NOTES

1. Volume XXIX has become the subject of many studies of how Keynes moved from the *Treatise* to *The General Theory*.

2. Hicks himself became slowly aware that his simplification of Keynes was misleading. The inertia was, however, already too wide and strong for him to be able to reverse the course. He never, however, came fully to terms with the impact of his interpretation.
3. See 1936; 1970, pp. 37–38.
4. See 1936; 1970, ch. 6.
5. '[I]n my *Treatise on Money* I defined income in a special sense. . . I am afraid that this use of the terms [components of income] has caused considerable confusion, especially in the case of the correlative use of saving; since conclusions, (relating, in particular, to the excess of saving over investment) which were only valid if the terms employed were interpreted in my special sense, have been frequently adopted in popular discussion as through the terms were being employed in their more familiar sense' (1936; 1970, pp. 60–61).
6. To arrive at $I = S$ in *The General Theory*, Keynes used an S or saving that derived from the total income, not simply what he called in the drafts S', the savings out of the earnings of the community's income. S in the *Treatise* derived exclusively from savings out of the community's income. In the *Treatise*, it is both profits, Q and savings out of the community's income, S which are the total aggregate savings, which are in turn equal to I. See the above note concerning the conditions under which $I = S$ always and I is not necessarily equal to S' in the terminology of Keynes. Since this is one of the issues on which economists consider Keynes to have been the most confused, it is obvious he was not being read in his own terms.
7. '[A]ggregate income (that is, factor cost *plus* profit)' (1936; 1970, p. 24, original emphasis).

6 Inflation/deflation and the policy of the general *General Theory*

In terms of its immediate reception, one of the most devastating and damaging impacts of Hicks's interpretation of Keynes's *General Theory* had been to make of Keynes's 1936 work a story (not a theory) of Depression. Hicks's reading of *The General Theory* was centred on the issue of wages as determinant of employment in circumstances where prices are irrelevant, since he thought Keynes assumed them fixed. Without challenging scrutiny, this interpretation became that of the profession, to which it immediately responded almost by open consensus. Hicks's reworking of *The General Theory* was coupled with the easy acceptance of Hayek's and Robertson's attacks on the *Treatise*, making that contribution of Keynes even less read than *The General Theory* and quickly dismissed and forgotten by most. The combination gave the impression that Keynes had little to say about, among other things, inflation and deflation. It is not surprising thus to read that Tibor Scitovsky at the Keynes's Centenary Conference in 1983, a gathering which was designed to assess the general contribution of Keynes, stated bluntly, 'Inflation was not a problem Keynes gave much thought to' (Worswick and Trevithick, 1983, p. 223). John M. Fleming, his discussant, rightly responded, 'This is an extraordinary proposition to make', but Fleming, himself, under the influence of the Hicksian tradition of Keynesianism, went on to characterize the argument of *The General Theory* as centred around wages as cause rather than effect (Worswick and Trevithick, 1983, p. 223).

It is ironic that Hubert Henderson in June 1936, just after the publication of *The General Theory*, was under the illusion, just like Scitovsky, although more subtly stated, that Keynes's advocacy for increasing the money supply to keep the interest rate down was tantamount to his story's being unconcerned with inflation. At the time Keynes replied:

> The ultimate emergence of what I call 'true inflation' is a recurrent theme in my book. When all the resources are employed which are sufficiently efficient for the purpose to bring in a return not less than the marginal disutility of labour, a further fall in the rate of interest can do no good and will merely lead to a true inflation of prices. (1933; 1979, p. 227; letter in response to Henderson)

Fleming's comments are pertinent as a starting point to grasp Keynes's concerns regarding inflation and deflation, particularly his suggestion that Keynes addressed unemployment as a cyclical rather than a structural problem,[1] but that is not enough. Above all, if one is to make sense of *The General Theory*, it is imperative to *get out* of thinking in the mould of the IS-LM, the mode of the Classicals's reasoning, antithetical to Keynes, and reassess the work in terms of the EC-SP model. Keynes's contribution on inflation and deflation concerns the determinations of income distribution and employment through a general *General Theory* in which unemployment in the slump phase of the cycle is but one facet, albeit a critical one. Thus, as clearly stated in the first paragraph of the concluding section of his work, 'Short Notes Suggested By The General Theory': 'Since we claim to have shown in the preceding chapters *what determines the volume of employment at any time*, it follows, if we are right, that our theory must be capable of explaining the phenomena of the Trade Cycle' (1936; 1970, p. 313, emphasis added).

It is now time to consider Keynes's contribution to the analysis of inflation and deflation, which is to be read, from now on, from the perspective of a generalized General Theory, deriving from the combination of his ideas in the *Treatise* and its sequel, *The General Theory*, including, in particular, its concluding chapters 22–24, one on the trade cycle, one on thrift, and one on the role of the rentier. It is true that discussion of inflation is found in much more detail in the *Treatise* than in the first four books of *The General Theory*, but Keynes's earlier work is taken as their backbone and chapter 21, its distillate. It has been demonstrated throughout this book that the Fundamental Equations crucial to the *Treatise* are also critical to *The General Theory*. Recall, from Chapter 4 above, that analysis of inflation and deflation stems from Fundamental Equation II, the Price Equation of the *Treatise*, in which decomposition of the price level leads to changes in profits, income, wages, and the price of capital. It has been shown further, in Chapter 5, that that Fundamental Equation extended its use into *The General Theory*, with a slight modification in formulation but with components comprising the same type of variables. It is the components of Fundamental Equation II which, in light of the EC-SP model, can now be analysed in terms of inflation and deflation in the dynamics of Keynes's credit cycle, all found in chapters 22 and 24 of *The General Theory*.

Thus, once the belief, unwarrantedly initiated by Hicks, that the theory of *The General Theory* is one of depression is recognized as the myth it is, comprehension of the generality of Keynes's theory, as far more than analysis of just a particular period in the slump, can come to light. When placed in its more general context, as was Keynes's intention, it is easier to see that the goal of *The General Theory* turned on much more than finding an economy's way out of the slump; it was also to provide the preventative theoretical tools for checking an economy's falling into one. This chapter starts with a discussion of the general implications of *The General Theory*'s main theory, one of employment. This is followed by a discussion of the Trade Cycle of *The General Theory*, which is intimately connected to the Credit Cycle of the *Treatise*. Although Keynes's policy recommendations to sustain an economy in the boom phase of the trade cycle, a policy which might come as a surprise to many, will become the end focus of the chapter, this discussion offers the opportunity to show first why the idea that Keynes's theory of interest is very close to the theory of Wicksell is not the case. Although even before the appearance of *The General Theory* Hicks had perpetrated this idea, there is a gulf of difference between Wicksell, on the one hand, representing the tradition of the loanable fund and advocating currency stabilization, and Keynes, on the other hand, who was not concerned with stabilizing the purchasing power of money at all. His approach was instead to sustain or stabilize the marginal efficiency of capital by having the monetary authority provide more finances to investors. Keynes's policy of low interest, to sustain booms, was also one which would, in providing an abundance of disposable funds, in itself diminish the scarcity of capital and, through competition, make the margin of gain, and hence the distribution of returns to the rentier, ever smaller.

6.1   KEYNES'S THEORY OF EMPLOYMENT

For Keynes, the discussion of inflation and deflation in *The General Theory* turns on how each of the components of Fundamental Equation II interacts with the others and how together they affect the marginal efficiency of capital, which in turn impacts employment. Already in the *Treatise*, Keynes devoted an entire book, Book 4, 'The Dynamics of the Price-Level', to analysing inflationary and deflationary pressures in the course of the cycle. He developed a sophisticated analysis of the price-level by revealing the impact on it deriving from each of the elements of Fundamental Equation II. He saw cyclical inflationary and deflationary pressures as caused by the values affecting both the cost as well as the proceeds side. His decomposition included, on the proceeds side, Commodity Inflation/Deflation, Capital Inflation/Deflation, and Profit Inflation/Deflation, and on the cost side, Income Inflation/Deflation (understood to be decomposable into Wage Inflation/Deflation and Inflation/Deflation of the other factor costs). Perception of each one as independent was to give clearer indication as to the relation between profit-maximization and a correspondingly appropriate level of employment.

It should be remembered from the analysis of the previous chapter that in Keynes's theory, a shift of resources always implies a redistribution of earnings, which changes relative prices and therefore the relative purchasing power of individuals. Assume that a raw-materials inflation or a profit inflation develops which impacts prices. It is then possible for a situation to build up whereby there is, for example, the redistribution of the consumption of an unchanging volume of final output goods. This could be the case if some sectoral earnings are increasing (although not keeping pace with profits), while other earnings are experiencing decreasing purchasing power. This is Keynes's famous case of the Daniad jar where entrepreneurs' consumption out of their profits creates additional profits for them which induces additional consumption by them, and so on. Such a scenario would be one of stagflation. It is a situation where the relationship between the preference for liquidity, and the marginal of efficiency of capital schedule and the propensity to consume are compatible with constant output. Employment is below the level of full employment but consistent with both Profit and Commodity Inflation.

In Figure 6.1 (a), (b), and (c), the interactions between the preference for liquidity, which is imbedded in the supply price curve, and the marginal of efficiency of capital schedule and the propensity to consume, which are implied in the aggregate demand curve, are depicted to yield three scenarios of outcomes corresponding to three different levels of employment. Figure 6.1(a) illustrates the case of Keynes that is most known and accepted as his by the profession. It is the one that corresponds to the collapse of the marginal efficiency of capital and with it the entrepreneurs' profit. It represents a period of a high level of involuntary unemployment. The other two cases are so far unfamiliar to the profession, at least as they are presented here.

Figure 6.1(b) is that of a stagflation period which might arise somewhere in the middle of the rising phase of the cycle. The third, Figure 6.1(c), is the Classical case of full employment, representing what Keynes considered the picture of true inflation.[2] Keynes regarded this as the case of the Classics, the only situation in which his second Classical postulate holds. It is the case when all resources, particularly labour, are fully exhausted and only then might labour be in the position of choosing not to work. It is only then when the real wage equals the marginal disutility of labour. For Keynes, as in the Classics, market forces tend to stabilize the labour market, and when the demand for and supply of labour are equal, real wages equal the marginal disutility of labour.

For Keynes, unlike for the Classics, the economy as a whole is quite

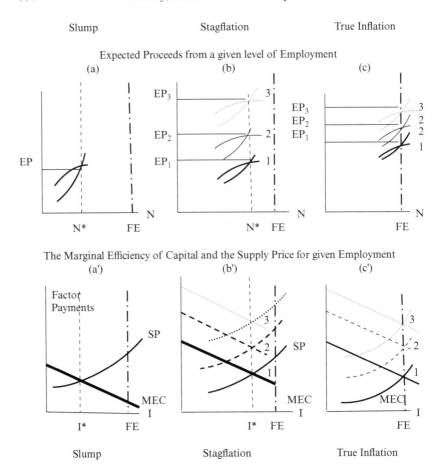

Figure 6.1   Three scenarios in various phases of the cycle

unstable and hence suffers both inflation and deflation. Entrepreneurs' decisions to invest rest largely on their expectations of unknowable future earnings. Industry is extremely sensitive to both deficiencies and excesses in the production of goods and services. If and when labour pressure presents itself, cost factors change. The economy is constantly in a state of flux, and however cyclical, the changes are asymmetrical.

There is, perhaps, something a little perplexing in the apparent asymmetry between Inflation and Deflation. For whilst a deflation of effective demand below the level required for full employment will diminish employment as well as prices, an inflation of it above this level will merely affect prices. This asymmetry is, however, merely a reflection of the fact that, whilst labour is always in a position to refuse to work on a scale involving a real wage which is less than the marginal disutility of that amount of employment, it is not in a position to insist on being offered work on a scale involving a real wage which is not greater than the marginal disutility of that amount of employment. (1936; 1970, p. 291)

6.2 THE TRADE CYCLE OF *THE GENERAL THEORY*

Instability and volatility in economic activity are inevitable. Entrepreneurs' profits are what make for the investment, which sustains or derails an economy's course. For Keynes, these two statements were both simply facts about the market economy, where individual initiative determines the bulk of the actions with which economists have to deal. The economy's cyclical fluctuations are studied from the perspective of their resulting from individual actions, with all their advantages and disruptions. Having said this, there are regularities in the economy, which allow for understanding and prediction to some extent. This was the object of chapter 22 of *The General Theory*.

Keynes had the instability of the Credit Cycle of the *Treatise* in mind,[3] when writing chapter 22 of *The General Theory*, 'Notes on the Trade Cycle'. Just as his analysis of the cycle in the *Treatise* began from the recovery phase, with signs of rising prices, in *The General Theory* he also focused his attention first and foremost on a particular part of the cycle, a period of the slump phase, when prices have completely collapsed. He dedicated most of the work to building a robust general theory applicable to that particular period, but in chapter 22 Keynes then placed that single aspect of the slump phase back into the trade cycle as a whole. His definition of 'cycle' in the *Treatise*, as 'fluctuations in the relative discrepancies of "the cost of investment over the volume of saving"' (1930: I, 277), is slightly shifted to one 'being occasioned by a cyclical change in the marginal efficiency of capital', where emphasis is placed on the regularity of the 'time-sequence' and the 'duration' of its fluctuations (1936; 1970, p. 313). It is nonetheless still a cycle of fluctuating investment, as earlier described.

In the context of discussion of the trade cycle in *The General Theory*, Keynes extended his analysis to the question of how to prevent slumps by curbing booms. To do so, he began by seeking (1) to identify the signs of an impending crisis and (2) to ascertain its mechanism. Further he attempted (3) to find out if regularity characterizes investment in Fixed Capital, Working Capital, and Liquid Capital. These steps were (4) to establish finally the full 'pathology' of a pending crisis. It is these findings which allowed Keynes (5) to devise policy recommendations.

1. For Keynes, the opportunity to observe the signs of pending changes in the course of the trade cycle was provided by the causal chain that leads to investment. Remembering that 'current expectation as to the future yield of capital-goods' was, along with 'the existing abundance or scarcity of capital-goods and the current cost of production of capital-goods', one of the three main determinants of the marginal efficiency of capital, it is not surprising that such expectations should be a bellwether of the future state of the economy. Entrepreneurs determine the amount of their investment, particularly in Fixed Capital, based on an expected future return deriving from it. Thus, if they are optimistic about the future, they will invest more than if they are pessimistic. As Keynes put it, 'In the case of durable assets it is, therefore, natural and reasonable that expectations of the future should play a dominant part in determining the scale on which new investment is deemed advisable' (1936; 1970, p. 315).

To read the course of the economy, Keynes was particular interested in signs of over-optimism and over-pessimism, each of which he linked with excessive over- or under-investment respectively. What he observed as a 'normal characteristic' of the boom phase of the cycle was that as it progressed, optimism turned into overly optimistic expectations and over-investment (1936; 1970, p. 320). The sign of expectations being overly optimistic regarding the future yield of capital goods was that they induce over-investment. These expectations are 'sufficiently strong as to offset their growing abundance and their rising costs of production and, probably, a rise in the rate of interest also' (1936; 1970, p. 315). They bring about over-investment, or 'investments which are destined to disappoint the expectations which prompted them' (1936; 1970, p. 320). Keynes attributed the wave of optimism in the later stage of the boom less to the expectations of entrepreneurs than to those of investors, 'speculators who are more concerned with forecasting the next shift of market sentiment than with a reasonable estimate of the future yield of capital-assets', but he noted, it is their decisions which will determine the continuing investment, due to 'the nature of organised investment markets' (1936; 1970, pp. 315–16). Along with sustained strong over-investment, Keynes was alert to the sign of over-consumption, sustained interest by 'purchasers largely ignorant of what they are buying', a combination which under the slightest downturn in optimism would lead to a fall in the market 'with sudden and even catastrophic force', a crisis (1936; 1970, p. 316).

2. While the course of the economy leading up to the crisis has its character, the crisis itself also had to Keynes's mind a specific nature and an
internal mechanism of chain reactions. It is the nature of 'the phenomenon of the crisis' or 'the substitution of a downward for an upward
tendency' that it usually occurs 'suddenly and violently' (1936; 1970,
p. 314). Its mechanistic effects are thus also marked: 'a collapse in the
marginal efficiency of capital naturally precipitates a sharp increase in
liquidity-preference' (1936; 1970, p. 316) and a sharp decrease in the
propensity to consume (1936; 1970, p. 319). The increase in liquidity
preference would normally cause a rise in the rate of interest. The
change in the propensity to consume would, Keynes wrote, 'of course,
result in a fluctuation in employment' (1936; 1970, p. 314). These
mechanistic effects leading to a severe drop in employment are also
for Keynes accompanied by the psychological ones for all, of 'dismay
and uncertainty as to the future'. Even more potentially devastating, however, to recovery from the crisis period was, for Keynes, the
troubling less-than-rational tendency of the banking system to raise
the rate of interest with the shift in liquidity preference, which might
'seriously aggravate the decline in investment' (1936; 1970, p. 316).

3. It is important to remember, however, that, while particularly atten-
tive to the gravity of the effects of a crisis, Keynes's concern was with
the whole cycle and where and why such a drop in prosperity fits into
the sequence of its changes. He placed the crisis or collapse within
'a *cyclical* movement' which provides not only distinctive signs that
changes are imminent but also 'some recognisable degree of regularity in the time-sequence and duration of the upward and downward
movements' (1936; 1970, pp. 313–14, original emphasis). Keynes saw
the regular duration of the phases of the cycle as deriving from aspects
of the three different types of investment capital: Fixed, Liquid, and
Working. In the case of Fixed or durable Capital, 'average durability
of capital in a given epoch' was a 'somewhat stable function' dependent on 'use, decay and obsolescence' (1936; 1970, p. 318). A rather pre-
dictable interval of time has to elapse before Fixed Capital is rendered
enough in short supply that its 'sufficiently obvious scarcity . . . [will]
increase the marginal efficiency' (1936; 1970, p. 318). Thus at periods
quite regularly set apart investment in Fixed Capital will be required
for its replacement:

> capital-assets are of various ages, wear out with time, and are not all very
> long-lived; so that if the rate of investment falls below a certain minimum
> level, it is merely a question of time (failing large fluctuations in other
> factors) before the marginal efficiency of capital rises sufficiently to bring
> about a recovery of investment above this minimum. (1936; 1970, p. 253)

Liquid and Working Capital, it seemed to Keynes, manifest cyclical regularity more in terms of time-sequence than in terms of duration, although the expense of carrying costs does impose a duration regularity on Liquid Capital, similar to that of Fixed Capital. Following the different steps into and through the phase of a 'typical' slump revealed to Keynes that both Liquid and Working Capital undergo a specific regular sequence of changes: (a) in the earliest part of the slump phase, Liquid Capital is increased while Working Capital is sustained (Working Capital is producing stocks, not goods for sale); (b) in the next and worst phase of the slump, there will likely be 'a short period of disinvestment' in both Liquid and Working Capital (1936; 1970, pp. 318–19), ('stocks of materials are for the time being redundant and working-capital is being reduced' (1936; 1970, p. 320)); (c) since there is 'as a rule, no such sharp turning-point when an upward is substituted for a downward tendency' (1936; 1970, p. 314), in the regular sequence of events, reinvestment in Working Capital partially offset by 'further disinvestment in stocks' or Liquid Capital is the indication that the bottom of the slump is passed; and (d) finally, once the economy is in its recovery phase, both Liquid and Working Capital will be the object of investment (1936; 1970, pp. 318–19). Liquid Capital for its part does also lend an aspect of duration regularity to the trade cycle which could be particularly crucial to its dynamics in the slump: 'The second stable time-factor is due to the carrying costs of surplus stocks which force their absorption within a certain period, neither very short nor very long' (1936; 1970, p. 318).

4. While Keynes observed a certain normalcy and regularity to the phases of the cycle, he did not consider the extremes of its booms and slumps to be healthy for an economy to suffer. He actually perceived them both as pathological phases. In the depths of the slump, 'the schedule of the marginal efficiency of capital may fall so low that it can scarcely be corrected' (1936; 1970, p. 320). In the height of the boom, 'illusions' of high returns cause 'particular types of capital-assets to be produced in such excessive abundance that some part of the output is, on any criterion, a waste of resources . . . or misdirected investment' (1936; 1970, p. 321). '[C]ontemporary booms are apt to be associated with a momentary condition of full investment or over-investment in the strict sense', by which Keynes meant 'an aggregate gross yield in excess of replacement cost [that] could no longer be expected on a reasonable calculation from a further increment of durable goods of any type whatever' (1936; 1970, p. 324).[4]

5. Keynes endeavoured to devise a remedy for the nefarious extremes of the cycle. In order to do so, having analysed its entirety, he determined

that monetary policy targeted at investment was the key and that even with the most flexible monetary instrument, the interest rate, it would be easier to curb the excesses of the boom than those of the slump. The famous concept of the 'liquidity trap', attributed to Keynes, derives from his despairing that an interest rate policy could bring an economy out of the downward phase: 'the schedule of the marginal efficiency of capital may fall so low that it can scarcely be corrected, so as to secure a satisfactory rate of new investment, by any practicable reduction in the rate of interest' (1936; 1970, pp. 319–20). His idea thus became to use interest rate policy to prevent the boom from being destined to end in a slump, or in fact to end at all. 'The right remedy for the trade cycle is not to be found in abolishing booms and thus keeping us permanently in a semi-slump; but in abolishing slumps and thus keeping us permanently in a quasi-boom' (1936; 1970, p. 322).

Keynes's recommendations entailed an interest rate policy contrary to contemporary approach. Despite the increase in liquidity preference in an upswing, 'remedy would not lie in clapping on a high rate of interest' (1936; 1970, p. 321); interest rates ought to be kept low rather than be allowed to rise. His reasons were numerous. Since a boom was for Keynes, by definition, 'a situation in which over-optimism triumphs over a rate of interest which, in a cooler light, would be seen to be excessive', so long as investors are in 'a misguided state of expectation' even an exorbitant rate of interest is prevented from being a deterrent to the course of a boom's over-investment trend (1936; 1970, p. 322). By the same token, high interest rates 'would probably deter some *useful* investments' (1936; 1970, p. 321, emphasis added). It is true that high rates might 'diminish the propensity to consume', while lower rates might 'stimulate the propensity to consume', 'by redistributing incomes or otherwise' (1936; 1970, p. 321), but with lower interest rates, 'a given level of employment would require a smaller volume of current investment to support it' (1936; 1970, p. 324). In short, 'the remedy for the boom is not a higher rate of interest but a lower rate of interest! For that may enable the so-called boom to last' (1936; 1970, p. 322).

Keynes's position on adopting a low interest rate policy to sustain investment required further a policy of financing. Changes in the realm of banking credit, as the result of assets shifting from a less liquid to a more liquid form or vice versa, had, in Keynes's theory, direct implications. For him, there was a direct link between the size and the distribution of the existing money supply over its possible liquidity range and the mode in which new investment comes to be financed. Keynes was particularly concerned about the inflationary or deflationary effects of fluctuations in the cycle, since, as has been seen above, he saw the extremes of both phenomena as potentially nefarious. The necessary financial arrangements for effective monetary policy, namely, any required changes in the quantity of the money supply, should, he thought, be provided for by the national government relayed through the banking institutions. Since, for Keynes, the absolute money supply can expand as a result of either credit or the new creation of money by the monetary authority, for him, as will be discussed below, appropriate national policies should be adopted to implement measures to meet liquidity needs in the boom or the slump.

One might still wonder why Keynes was so concerned with inflation and deflation. The multi-dimensional discussion of the causes and effects of inflationary and deflationary pressures – in terms of the welfare of a nation, its losses in wealth creation, the redistribution of income domestically and/or internationally, the volatility and disruption of economic activity, or the weakening of an economy – has been and continues to be a major preoccupation of economists. Many have seen a correlation between interest rates and the health of the economy. Hicks thought there were strong parallels between Wicksell and Keynes in terms of their theories about cyclical fluctuations and the interest rate. One focus for both was indeed the interest rate as they tried to determine how and by what mechanisms inflationary and deflationary pressures come to affect the activity of an economy. It is thus of interest here to inquire whether there is in fact a parallel between their models.

6.3 WICKSELL: STABILIZATION OF THE PURCHASING POWER

Wicksell saw both inflation and deflation as serious problems with welfare implications, not only for working and non-working men and women, but also for those engaged in production or investment. As he originally stated in his 'Framtidens myntproblem', *Ekonomisk Tidskrift*, in 1904, deflation specifically 'entails an unmerited advantage for those who for one reason or another have money to pay, and equally undeserved suffering for those who have money to claim, whether as wages, pensions or interest on money loaned' (1999, II, p. 17).

Having determined inflation and deflation to be serious problems, Wicksell then asked how one should deal with them. While he did provide a theoretical foundation that others would use to analyse inflation and deflation, Wicksell himself saw great limitations in theorizing, difficulties in establishing causality, and practical constraints on policy rectifications, and this despite the simplicity of his own prescriptions. Wicksell's own focus was on money and how its value is determined, and less on business or trade cycles, theoretical or real. It is nonetheless out of this central concern that other considerations, which included cyclical fluctuations, the gold standard, taxation and social programmes, and the banking system, would grow to preoccupy much of his writing.

To alleviate the distributive distortions Wicksell noted as ensuing from inflation and deflation, price stability became his prime objective. His concern with the value of money was thus really simply a preamble to his principal goal, maintaining the constancy of the purchasing power of money. He investigated different theories under various forms of money: coinage under the gold standard, a mix of coinage and banknotes, paper money alone, and, in the most theoretical and advanced of scenarios, pure credit. He felt he had to understand the notion of money itself as a prerequisite before turning to policy prescriptions. To him, the major troubling aspect was 'valuation': '. . . we mean by the value of money exactly the same thing as the exchange value of money, its purchasing power as against goods and services' (1935, II, p. 129). The direct link thus between money and its purchasing power was for him the level of price. 'To us, therefore, the value of money and the price level are synonymous, or, more correctly correlative ideas.' (ibid.).

The questions Wicksell posed were, what are the causes of price fluctuations? and, if that can be established, what then are the mechanisms required to stabilize the price level? From the outset, Wicksell rejected the tenets of the Quantity Theory, which make the proportionality between money and prices almost an independent relationship grafted through the medium of exchange or *numeraire* into the real sector. Instead he made both the money rate of interest and the natural, or real, interest rate the link between the monetary and the real sectors of the economy. The interaction and the discrepancies between these two rates became central to Wicksell's entire theory. In his *Ekonomisk Tidskrift* of 1909, Wicksell posited that 'a rise in productivity that is not accompanied by a corresponding rise in the loan rate of interest . . . would *always* bring in its train a *continuous rise in commodity prices*' (1999, II, p. 40, emphasis added/in original). Such a rise in productivity would engender a rise in the real rate of interest. In such a situation, it is always profitable to borrow at a lower money rate and invest in economic activity for which the return is higher. As long as the discrepancy persists, borrowing will continue.

It was thus not difficult for Wicksell to assert the following: 'the immediate precondition of and reason for every change of price, of any kind whatsoever and no matter what its ultimate causes might be, is always a disproportion that has come into being between the money rate of interest and the natural or real rate of interest on capital' (1999, II, 35). Having established this causal relation, Wicksell's prescription for remedy was simple: '*If prices rise, the rate of interest is to be raised; and if prices fall, the rate of interest is to be lowered; and the rate of interest is henceforth to be maintained at its new level until a further movement of prices calls for a further change in one direction or the other*' (1936, p. 189, original emphasis). His position was that if a policy could be devised to achieve such a goal, then keeping the purchasing power of money constant would be feasible and the desirable social welfare objective would be achievable. Wicksell believed that the banking system could *in principle* exercise such a simple mechanism to regulate the money rate of interest so as to keep it in pace with the natural rate. With a degree of confidence that it is actually feasible, modern central banks have taken something like Wicksell's ideas to be the guidelines for what ought to be monetary practice in an industrialized economy. It is in fact in this neo-Wicksellian guise that Wicksell's original theory has become known and considered attractive and fashionable.

The apparent simplicity of Wicksell's monetary theory and policy rules masks enormous theoretical as well as practical difficulties, of which Wicksell was mostly well aware. Several of these which Wicksell identified himself are addressed here below. It is noted right away that on the theoretical side, before discussing the discrepancy between his two key rates of interest, one would have to explain what the factors are which determine each rate and whether the two rates are independent of one another. In addition and more important are the real and practical puzzles that remain as to how to maintain constancy of value for money. When and according to which criteria ought the bank/s to intervene? Should and could the banking system place social interest before their own in the requisite way?

1. It is not always easy to determine 'when the time has come to make a reasonable change in the interest rates' (1999, II, p. 37). The lag between inflationary build-ups and deflationary slow-downs usually has to be well under way before they become noticeable socially. For instance, it is certainly possible that by the time banks begin to raise the money rate of interest to slow down inflation, the economy may already have reached its peak and prices may have begun to drop. In this case, the application of a policy of increasing interest will, due to the lag, actually make the situation worse by accelerating deflation and thus creating a crisis. Nonetheless, '[I]n the authors who have treated the history of crises in the greatest detail, the reflection constantly recurs that the outbreak of these various crises could have been

prevented or substantially mitigated if the leading banks had raised their interest rates *in time*' (1999, II, p. 36, original emphasis).

2. Furthermore, it is difficult to establish 'according to which criteria it shall be determined that this time [for bank intervention] has come' (1999, II, p. 37). Here, by 'criteria', Wicksell is referring to the types of possible, reliable indicators suitable as sensible measures of discrepancy between the two interest rates.

3. Wicksell had mistrust of the banking system regarding its acting in the best interests of the public, for any number of reasons: its own profit motive, its private rather than social role, and its narrow view of the national economy. On the one hand, he underlined that banks themselves are private enterprises. Their actions, to adhere to the rule of keeping rate discrepancies narrow, might well at times not be to the advantage of their profit margin. For instance, '[A] fall in rates of interest may diminish the banks' margin of profit more than it is likely to increase the extent of their business' (1936, p. 190). On the other hand, he was also aware that banks are concerned with macro or international economic policy only from their business perspective and their perception of their own market is only a subset of that of the whole economy. It would therefore not be expected that they would have any broader social goal.

4. In Wicksell's opinion, 'the main cause of the instability of prices resides in the inability or failure of the banks to follow this rule: *if prices rise, the rate of interest is to be raised; and if prices fall, the rate of interest is to be lowered*' (1936, p. 189, original emphasis). It was thus lastly and most importantly an issue of Wicksell's scepticism, as expressed in 1909, whether policies, even the main one he suggested, could be implemented in practice: 'the difficulty here lies . . . in the question as to whether there is any possibility at all of the banks being able to implement such an interest rate policy in present conditions' (1999: II, p. 37). His reservations stem again from numerous reasons. On the one hand, the banks in general deal only with a particular kind of credit and lending, the one that presents relatively little risk. There are therefore a great number of cases where potential borrowers exist but are without sufficient security to satisfy bank lenders. Such borrowers 'instead fall into the hands of a usurer', an extremely high-interest-rate lender (1999, II, p. 9).These volumes of monies loaned as well as the determination of the non-bank interest rates remain thus outside the control of the banking system; yet they are part of the overall economy and may impact the money rate of interest. On the other hand, to achieve his policy of a stable purchasing power of money in an open economy, presented a difficult task that only a national bank

alone could achieve. Wicksell wrote, 'It must be achieved rather by common measures on the part of all countries and more particularly on the part of their central banks' (1935, II, p. 222).

If and only if the world were organized in such a way that the banks play their social role, being open to establishing 'a line of business, the aim of which, quite openly, should be to lend money against inadequate security, but at a correspondingly higher interest rate' (1999, II, p. 9) and to intervening in the economy when the time is right, or alternatively, that a monetary authority existed which was sufficiently alert to be able to anticipate changes in the economy, and central banks coordinated their policies as to the respective differences of countries' productivity and exchange rates, then Wicksell believed that truly 'the stabilisation of the value of money would constitute a means of precluding *crises*' (1999, II, p. 36, original emphasis).

6.4 KEYNES: STABILIZATION OF THE MARGINAL EFFICIENCY OF CAPITAL

Having established, with regard to inflation and deflation, Wicksell's understanding of a constant purchasing power of money and the disparity between the money rate and the natural or real rate of interest as the pre-condition for him of any change in the value of money or level of prices, it is now asked where Keynes's theory stands in relation to that of Wicksell. To the theoretical differences already discussed in Chapter 3, section 3.5 'A non-sequitur of Wicksell', there are further fundamental dissimilarities between Keynes and Wicksell as to their respective understandings of how to tackle issues of inflation/deflation in relation to the trade cycle. Unlike Wicksell, whose prime objective was the stabilization of the value of money and whose theory of the trade cycle was grafted on only as an illustration to show the interactive disparity of his two rates of interest, the trade cycle was Keynes's prime concern. He was, however, not only well aware of but actually stimulated, with reservation, by Wicksell's analysis,[5] witness his comments in the *Treatise*:

> Whilst Wicksell's expressions cannot be justified as they stand and must seem unconvincing . . . without further development, they can be interpreted in close accordance with the Fundamental Equation of this Treatise. For if we define Wicksell's natural-rate of interest as the rate at which Saving and the value of Investment are in equilibrium . . ., then it is true that, so long as the money-rate of interest is held at such a level that the value of Investment exceeds Saving, there will be a rise in the price-level of output as a whole above its cost of production, which in turn will stimulate entrepreneurs to bid up the rate of earnings

above their previous level, and this upward tendency will continue indefinitely so long as the supply of money continues to be such as to enable the money-rate to be held below the natural-rate as thus defined. (1930, I, pp. 197–8)

It is clear from the quotation that Keynes twisted (to say the least) Wicksell's concepts of interest as well as his causal mechanism to fit the Fundamental Equations. The natural rate of interest Keynes referred to in the quotation is not that of Wicksell.

Keynes was clearly influenced but not persuaded by Wicksell's analysis. Inspired by Wicksell's notion of cumulative process, Keynes did put causal emphasis on disparities, rather than equalities, in his case, between Savings and Investment. In Keynes's and Wicksell's theories, money and the real rate of interest are both important, but determined by quite different forces: by the loanable fund in Wicksell versus the money market in Keynes, and the real rate of interest by the marginal product of capital in Wicksell versus the marginal efficiency of capital in Keynes. A very significant difference between them, however, is that not only did Keynes not see stabilization of the value of money as a crucial issue, he actually used Price Inflation/Deflation as a means of explaining the existence of the cycle and its pressures as a means of rectifying the cyclical extremes.

Further, as noted in the earlier discussion, Keynes and Wicksell differed in their conceptions of the cycle. Keynes's theory saw the cycle as made up in fact of two cycles: a real business cycle, related to fluctuations in production and employment, and an interwoven credit cycle.[6] While, he thought, there might not be inherent necessity for the real cycle to be subject to major booms and slumps – with the existence of stocks as a buffer – the credit cycle transferred the impact of vagaries in the uses of money and the unstable shifting of expectations into the real sector to form the root of its deflationary and inflationary episodes. It is in this sense that Keynes's cycle was a monetary business cycle. In contrast, he found in Wicksell, that 'the money rate of interest depends upon the supply of and demand for *real capital*, or, as Adam Smith, and later Ricardo, expressed it, that the rate of interest is regulated by the profits from the employment of capital itself and not by the number or quality of the pieces of metal which facilitate the turnover of its products' (1935, p. 190, original emphasis).

What then was Keynes's explanation for how the credit cycle could be controlled to avoid the inflationary highs and the deflationary lows of the monetary sphere, which otherwise would be mirrored as ups and downs in the production cycle? Two situations present themselves in which, according to Keynes, the banking system could manage the money supply so successfully that booms and slumps would not occur at all. The central bank would, however, have to behave according to the principle of fixing and maintaining the effective bank rate so 'as to keep Saving and Investment at an appropriate equality throughout' (1930, I, p. 291). One situation, the deflationary one, is when the money supply, M_1–M_3, is large enough to provide the economy with funding for investment. This situation is troubling because there is no demand for money. The bank's strategy must in this instance be to make credit desirable (by lending below prime, for example).

The other situation in which credit intervention could be managed effectively is when the size of the existing money supply cannot meet the demand for investment funds. This is when there is not enough available money to fill, in Keynes's theory, the needs of Industrial Circulation, the buying of **C** goods and services, and the paying for the ongoing cost of production.[7] Keynes correlates this situation with a phase of the production cycle, the one in which windfall profits have begun to reduce because production has sent to the market enough **R** goods to meet demand. In this phase, as a result of the fall in consumer-goods prices, net Investment in Working Capital is beginning to diminish and the production of **C** goods is being impacted. There is risk of a savings–investment disequilibrium coming into play.

The sophisticated banking system of Keynes had to be responsive to the 'bear'–'bull' liquidity preferences of consumers, firms, speculators, shareholders, and foreign investors. Whether in the *Treatise on Money* (1930) or in *The General Theory* (1936), in a market economy Keynes saw the volume of production and economic activity, and thus the level of employment, as entirely in the hands of the investors whose decisions effect the transfer of assets from one Circulation form into another. As has already been seen, their actions depend primarily on their expected future prospects for earnings, whether they are 'bullish' and demanding of funds to bring about new investment or 'bearish' and, with negative expectations for future returns, shrink from investment. Keynes insisted that the banking system had itself to be prepared for the impact of investors' liquidity transfers, since, for example, as noted above, if the lending-for-investment market were to begin to shrink suddenly and rapidly in a bearish market and hence to starve willing investment, normally a crisis would develop. Keynes suggested it assume responsibility for responding to any monetary disequilibrium between savings and investment by either changing the size of the money supply or the money rate of interest or both.

For Keynes, the bank's money market had constantly to be adjusted such that the Marginal Efficiency of Capital is always kept at a level adequate to induce new investment. '[O]ften the predominant explanation of the crisis is not primarily a rise in the rate of interest, but a sudden collapse in the marginal efficiency of capital' (1936; 1970, p. 315). Keynes thus recommended that the Marginal Efficiency of Capital (MEC) of *The General Theory*, or simply 'profits', or rate of return, in the *Treatise*, was the main variable to target for the stabilization of cyclical fluctuations. In order to prevent economies' drifting into slumps from booms, MEC was the most preoccupying variable for Keynes. Without adequate MEC, there would be no new investment which in turn would affect production and employment and again in turn income distribution. Thus for example, when an economy is heading toward a slump, because of the collapse of MEC, the monetary authority should intervene and lower the market rate in such a way as to make the discrepancy between the money and real rates of interest just inducing enough for investment to resume.

The challenge set by Keynes was thus how to keep new investment in pace with a certain rate of growth just adequate to a near full-employment economy. He thought that investment was vulnerable to volatility, since the market economy generates, through competition, increases in efficiencies in the uses of labour and technology. Being neither always present nor constant, these changes in efficiency, when they occur, fuel the expectations of the speculators who provide the finances for such investment. It is these changes which, when translated into increases and decreases in expected future returns, alter the values of stocks and create the speculative volatility which yields new profits and distorts market values from the cost of producing the previous goods. Keynes believed that the impact of investment could get out of hand and, if unchecked, could easily produce either inflationary booms or deflationary slumps, both with social welfare implications. Although he accepted all this as being in the nature of the market economy, he also thought that in the interests of public well-being, policies ought to be devised to alleviate harmful extremes.

Obviously, changes in the monetary aggregate and in the interest rates do impact the price level and the purchasing power of money. Thus, as explained above in the case of Wicksell, they impact the redistribution of income among the various economic agents (savers/investors, lenders/borrowers, buyers/sellers). For Keynes, the inconveniences of the changes in prices due to short-term income redistribution were outweighed by the gains of keeping employment strong as well as of sustaining growth. Keynes devoted the entire Book 4 of his *Treatise*, 'The Dynamics of the Price-Level', to discussing inflationary and deflationary pressures in the course of the cycle. He developed there a sophisticated analysis of the price level by revealing the impact on it deriving from each of the elements of the Fundamental Equations.

Unlike Wicksell, Keynes actually sought to rely on inflationary and deflationary price changes as a means of tempering the business cycle to

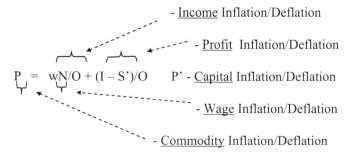

Figure 6.2 Inflations and deflations

guarantee a high level of employment. Keynes's decomposition of cyclical inflations and deflations encompassed values on both the cost and the proceeds sides of the economy: on the proceeds side, Commodity Inflation/Deflation, Capital Inflation/Deflation, and Profit Inflation/Deflation and on the cost side, Income Inflation/Deflation (understood to be decomposable into Wage Inflation/Deflation and the Inflation/Deflation of other factor costs). Keynes's discussion of inflation and deflation turned thus around how each of these components interacts with the others and affects the Marginal Efficiency of Capital, which, when compared to the money-rate, determines where the economy stands in relation to the phases of the cycle. While these various concepts of inflation/deflation derive directly from the Fundamental Equations of Keynes's *Treatise*, they can also be inferred from *The General Theory*,[8] through Equation FEII 5.3′ from Chapter 5 (See Figure 6.2).

Keynes believed that it was only by understanding the intricacy of the dynamic interactions between the various inflations and deflations which are responsible for the cyclical changes in costs and benefits that countermeasures could be devised and applied to rectify socially undesired deviations. Largely because his theory of the level of price was much more sophisticated than that of Wicksell, it can be seen that keeping the value of money constant did not make sense to Keynes:

> For my part I am somewhat inclined to think, without having reached a final conclusion, that it is more important to have a system which avoids, so far as possible, the necessity for induced changes, than it is to attempt to stabilize the price-level according to any precise principle, provided always that the rate of change in the price-level is kept within narrow limits. (1930, I, p. 170)

Keynes, however, also proposed policies of a stabilizing nature, depending on the state of the economy. He discussed the general interaction of the various inflationary and deflationary pressures over the cycle. In *The General Theory*, Keynes paid particular attention to the specific case of the collapse, where the Marginal Efficiency of Capital is so low that monetary policy has no correcting effect (the so-called 'liquidity trap', noted above).

Once he had identified the various sources of inflations and deflations within the price equation, Keynes sought to disentangle them, as ongoing changes over the course of a typical credit cycle. He described its phases, starting from an upswing in the course of the cycle, as follows:

> First, a Capital Inflation leading to an increase of Investment, leading to Commodity Inflation; second, still more Capital Inflation and Commodity Inflation for approximately one production period of consumption-goods; third, a reaction in the degree of the Commodity and Capital Inflations at the end of this period; fourth, a collapse of the Capital Inflation; and finally, a decrease of Investment below normal, leading to Commodity Deflation. (1930, I, p. 304)

When Keynes broke the 'normal' Credit Cycle down further into three types, he identified yet more distinctive inflationary and deflationary components. The Credit Cycle 'may also be complicated by the presence of some measure both of Income Inflation (*i.e.*, of rising costs of production) and of Capital Inflation (*i.e.*, a rise of the price-level of new investment-goods relatively to their cost of production)' (1930, I, p. 282). The existence of either Commodity Inflation or Capital Inflation will produce Profit Inflation, which, according to Keynes, will in turn cause Income Inflation 'through the eagerness of entrepreneurs to secure the services of the factors of production', and so on (1930, I, p. 282).

Of course, the phase of the crisis or the collapse of the economy, or even simply its sliding toward recession was the aspect of the cycle which was most troubling to Keynes and, in 1936, the one most in need of attention. When prices are falling faster than costs, entrepreneurs are faced with few options: to absorb losses or to cut costs, either by reducing output and employment or by maintaining employment and reducing the wage-bill. For the sake of limiting the discussion here solely to the welfare benefits and losses of inflation and deflation, attention is drawn to Keynes's awareness that cyclical gains and losses do not fall symmetrically and are not absorbed by everyone in society in the same proportion. 'From the standpoint of distributive justice it may be preferable to rob the entrepreneur for the benefit of the consumer than to rob the consumer for the benefit of the entrepreneur' (1930, I, pp. 273–4), but the facts show it to happen otherwise. In the upswing, the factors of production are paid less, and proportionally less than the entrepreneurs' earnings, while on the downswing, the factors of production, including labour, are paid more, yet they are also in a period of unemployment and underutilization of capital. What now about the monetary mechanisms?

On policy intervention, two remarks about Keynes's recommendations might be made here. On the one hand, Keynes was fairly confident that in general monetary policies for avoiding or mitigating credit fluctuations do exist. Like Wicksell, Keynes thought that the manipulation of the money-rate of interest could be used for policy intervention. In his case, intervention would be designed to prevent the Marginal Efficiency of Capital from diverging too widely in the directions of over- or under-expansion. As long as the cyclical fluctuations have not gone too far or as long as some kind of policy remedy is keeping the cycle within reasonable inflationary and deflationary bounds, controls can be effective.

Keynes even felt that monetary controls could be useful when the economy is in recession. In this instance, Income Inflation might be used as a way to jumpstart an upturn in the cycle. He noted the necessary distinction between

> a change in bank-rate which is intended to prevent a Profit Inflation (or Deflation) and one which is intended to cause an Income Inflation (or Deflation); for the former operates to preserve equilibrium by adjusting the market-rate of interest to the natural-rate, whereas the latter operates *via* disequilibrium by forcibly divorcing the market-rate from the natural-rate. (1930, I, p. 273)

Of course, more could be said about these complications, but the point here is to illustrate at the very least how, set in this context, Keynes's discussion of inflation and deflation was much more complicated than Wicksell's theoretical construct.

In the most difficult case of depression, however, the answer to the question of what could be done to counter the deflation that leads to the situation in which the Marginal Efficiency of Capital is dangerously low for an economy to rebound was less obvious. It might be thought that, if the monetary authority were capable, without restriction, of setting the money-rate of interest, something could be done. Keynes quickly pointed out at the start, however, that in practice there are several limitations on the monetary authority to establish rates of interest across the whole range of possibilities. These difficulties are of special interest as pertains to the deflationary phase of the cycle. In *The General Theory* in chapter 15, 'Incentives to Liquidity' (1936; 1970, pp. 207–8), Keynes listed four reasons why full control of the interest rate by the monetary authority is impossible.

1. Like Wicksell, Keynes observed that there is a certain amount of credit offered privately which escapes the monetary authority, for

whatever reasons – refusal of the banks to lend because of high risk, availability of private deals between individuals, such as mortgages, less constraining borrowing conditions, and so on. These go on independently of what the monetary authority does and could offset or accentuate its actions, depending on the expectation and will of those who are engaged in such arrangements.

2. When the money-rate of interest is so low that the general public prefers holding cash to lending, it has become insensitive to the interest rate and cannot be tempted to part with its cash. This is Keynes's 'absolute liquidity preference'.

3. When there is a breakdown in confidence or in the stability of the currency, and by extension, for Keynes, in the rate of interest, Keynes saw an instance of individuals' not being willing to hold either currency or debt on any terms of interest. Some would turn to holding 'liquid goods' instead, for example, land, art, or gold. As long as the expectation would last that the currency will not regain strength and perhaps fall even more, little could be done, and, as had happened historically in Russia and Central Europe after the war, a 'high and rising rate of interest was unable to keep pace with the marginal efficiency of capital' (1936; 1970, p. 207).

4. There is a certain minimum rate below which the money-rate cannot fall. There are expenses inherent to the banking operation, the cost of which has to be paid, if the banking system is to operate. The limit is determined by 'the intermediate costs of bringing the borrower and the ultimate lender together' (1936; 1970, p. 208).

Keynes also acknowledged, like Wicksell, that in an open economy, the monetary authority of a single country would suffer major limits on control, even of its own national economy, especially in light of the four limitations noted above, if it did not coordinate its efforts with those of other countries:

> We come finally to what is in the world of to-day the insuperable limitation on the power of skilled monetary management to avoid booms and depressions, – a limitation which it would be foolish to overlook or to minimise. No national Central Bank which is a member of an international system, not even the Federal Reserve System of the United States, can expect to preserve the stability of its price-level, if it is acting in isolation and is not assisted by corresponding action on the part of the other Central Banks. (1930, II, p. 374)

Partly because of all these limitations of the banking system, the situation that Keynes treated with utmost seriousness was the slump:

I am doubtful, therefore, whether those are right who believe that a period of deflation generally does less harm than a period of inflation . . . The warmest advocates of the value of leisure would scarcely prefer the leisure of severe unemployment to the over-stimulated activity of a boom, and enthusiasm about a high level of real-wages may be cooled by a realisation that the increment of real-wages is being paid at the expense of the accumulation of wealth by the community (1930, I, p. 274).

According to him, circumstances of the slump may demand some action. While, however, Wicksell had relied entirely on the policy of stabilizing the value of money, to correct for the discrepancy between the money-rate and the natural-rate of interest, manipulation of the interest rate was only one option for stabilization in Keynes. Given his much more complicated model, Keynes suggested other alternatives, all to increase the volume of investment as the ultimate, appropriate outcome.

In the early part of the slump, although obviously inflationary, one incentive for investment might be rising prices. An increase in price will shift the Marginal Efficiency of Capital upward, which would trigger an increase in investment in the factors of production, including employment. 'The cure of unemployment involves improving business profits. The improvement of business profits can come about only by an improvement in new investment relative to saving. *An increase of investment relative to saving must also, as an inevitable by-product, bring about a rise of prices* . . .'(1973b, p. 362, emphasis added). Rising prices would both correct for Commodity Deflation initially and do nothing more than 'bring the price-level back again to equilibrium with the existing level of income' (1930, I, p. 297). In other words, Keynes thought that not to let prices rise or rather 'to stabilise prices at the bottom of a Commodity Deflation would be a stupid thing to do' (1930, I, p. 298).

'[A]ny policy which at this stage of the credit cycle is not directed to raising prices also fails in the object of improving business profits', Keynes announced in 'The Road to Recovery', the third of three lectures he gave in June 1931 for the Harris Foundation series in Chicago, entitled *in toto* 'An Economic Analysis of Unemployment' (Keynes, 1973b). He there noted three corrective measures which could be used to bring about improvements in new investment, all of which he considered 'bankers' business', whether implemented through the usual private endeavours or public expenditure:

When I have said this [cited above], I have, strictly speaking, said all an economist as such is entitled to say. What remains is essentially a technical banking problem. The practical means by which a business can be increased is, or ought to be, the bankers' business, and pre-eminently the business of the central banker. But you will not consider that I have completed my task unless I give some indication of the methods which are open to the banker. (1973b, p. 363)

Keynes went on to identify 'three lines of approach': 'the restoration of confidence both to the lender and to the borrower', 'new construction programmes under the direct auspices of the government or other public authorities', and 'reduction in the long term rate of interest' (1973b, pp. 363–5). A few comments will be added here on the subject of public expenditure as an economic stimulus strategy since it is one that became so distorted as a part of Keynesian policy. Keynes had clear reservations about 'extensive programmes of public works', which were, he felt, appropriate only when 'the cheap-money stimulus to investment cannot be applied' (1973b, p. 112). For Keynes, such 'a government programme is calculated to improve the level of business profits and hence to increase the likelihood of private enterprise again lifting up its head' (1973b, p. 364); its sole *raison d'être* is to be a stimulus to private investment.

There was for Keynes, also a part of the slump in which the profit margin can be restored without external corrective measures being needed. It is when deflation has progressed to the point of touching income and unemployment has become widespread, that is, when the decrease in factor costs is greater than the decrease in prices. This case implies Wage Deflation. In both the *Treatise* and *The General Theory*, Keynes saw, however, Wage Deflation as less than practicable. In the *Treatise*, he wrote that he would rather 'hope for an increase in efficiency by which lower money-earnings per unit of output might be compatible with unchanged money-earnings per unit of the factors of production' (1930, I, p. 184).

For Keynes even when policy means are required, manipulation of the money interest rate was only one option in the process of economic stabilization and not necessarily the one that was always appropriate or needed. Keynes suggested other policy means, identifying wage deflation and increased factor efficiency, as well as public spending and currency strengthening. 'The problem resolves itself, therefore into the question as to what means we can adopt to increase the volume of investment, which you will remember means in my terminology the expenditure of money on the output of new capital goods of whatever kind' (1973b, p. 362). In sum, while both Wicksell and Keynes were concerned with equilibrating the forces needed to dampen price fluctuations and both resorted to interest rate policy and appeal to monetary intervention, in terms of macroeconomic implications of their respective approaches, there remains a gulf of difference between them.

Nonetheless, the Keynesian textbook suggestion, based on the IS-LM – that the monetary authority should intervene to raise/lower interest rate as inflation/deflation develops, now the rule-of-thumb practice[9] blindly followed by central bankers – and further the belief that when inflation is controlled the problems of inequity resulting from it are solved are ironically more the ideas of Wicksell than Keynes. Even though, as mentioned above with reference to Figure 6.1(c), Keynes did distinguish the extreme of the full employment of resources from the rest of the spectrum of situations below that point, the skewed asymmetry between the former particular situation, which he refers to as 'true inflation', and the rest must still be emphasized. Only when true inflation starts to materialize is a rise in the rate of interest called for, as indicated by his response to Henderson above at the beginning of the chapter. That situation, in fact is rather rare, since the squeeze in the full employment of resources and subsequently of profits generally will cause a reversal in sensitive expectations, which will in turn cause an overturn at the height of the cycle or at full equilibrium, in Keynes's sense. Any increase in the interest rate before that particular point would only precipitate crisis. Inflation and deflation is for Keynes not a characteristic of the extremes, as seems to have been being perpetuated for decades now in the IS-LM textbook presentation of Keynes. Inflation and deflation can and do occur at any phase during the course of the cycle.

6.5   SHIFTS OF RESOURCES, INCOME REDISTRIBUTION, AND STABILIZATION POLICY

Keynes concluded his *General Theory* with some notes on the social philosophy towards which his theory might lead. This book was written during an exceptional economic period and directed at alleviating a specific problem, the preoccupying high unemployment of the 1930s. Keynes was predominantly concerned in the work with the short-term analysis of an economy in a state of underemployment. He nonetheless attempted, in general terms, in its chapter 24, to expand on his views on the growth of capital and wealth, and full employment, and to project some long-run implications, directions towards which his general *General Theory* might lead. From the perspective of a long-term assessment of *The General Theory*, Keynes was concerned, in general, with two major economic problems: (1) the economy's failure to provide for full employment and (2) the arbitrary and inequitable distribution of wealth and income within the domestic economy.

Although Keynes conceived *The General Theory* theoretically for a closed economy, he did nonetheless in his concluding remarks, discuss its international implications. He identified two economic causes of inter-national friction: population pressure and the competitive struggle for markets. The ultimate expression of friction among nations is war. It was the bellicose struggle for markets, which he recognized as particularly germane to the policy implications of *The General Theory*. Under laissez-faire approaches and an international gold standard, there were no means for governments to mitigate economic distress at home, except through a successful competitive struggle for markets abroad.

Unemployment and disproportionate income disparity were, for Keynes, the traditional results of scarcity of land and driven scarcity of capital. Although he was in *The General Theory* more preoccupied with unemployment, by extension he believed that the policies he advocated for bringing about full employment would also lead to greater equity in the distribution of national income. Shortage of land and capital provides high rent and high interest to the rentiers and financiers, eager to preserve their privileges.

It is clear that, for Keynes, unemployment and income distribution go hand in hand and cyclical fluctuations are by definition a reallocation of resources, whether through shifts in the factors of production from one sector to another, in financial liquidities from one form of money to another, and in the level and/or composition of output. There are bound to be movements in prices corresponding to these reallocations. When Inflation/Deflation of the general price level is decomposed into the various Inflations/Deflations of Figure 6.2 above, changes of relative prices and earnings or relative purchasing power are revealed to be occur-ring at every phase of the cycle across an economy. In relation to one vari-able or another, income redistribution is thus a permanent feature of the trade cycle.

To advocate, as Wicksell did, a stabilization of the currency does not entirely respond to Keynes's concern for equity, since keeping the general level of price constant does not guarantee at all that its components are remaining unchanged. In the *Treatise*, he showed that unless inflation is decomposed into its various components, the overall price does not reveal much and can be misleading. He ran his analysis through several scenarios and explained how intricate inflation/deflation can be throughout the phases of the cycle, where different varieties of Inflation/Deflation run ahead or behind one another, and thus offset one another or accumulate to create acceleration/deceleration. Figures 6.1(a), (b), and (c) are illustra-tions of how Inflations/Deflations can result in the Slump, Stagflation, or True Inflationary phases of the cycle. Figure 6.1(b), Stagflation is of par-ticular interest here, since it reveals that to experience (not an equilibrium) but Inflation/s and/or Deflation/s, the economy does not have to be at

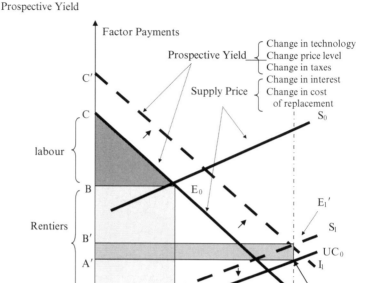

Figure 6.3   Prospective yield and income distribution

either of the extremes: the Slump or a state of high unemployment or True Inflation, or full employment. Furthermore, even at the extreme highs and lows of the cycle, Inflations will coexist with Deflations.

While Keynes believed that a policy of a low money rate of interest could stimulate the inducement to invest, he never maintained that this interest rate policy would directly create constancy in the price level. As can be seen in Figure 6.3, as investment **I** is induced, and the Equilibrium point **E$_0$** moves toward **E$_1$**, a shift of at least either the Supply Price curve downward or the Prospective Yield curve upward is required. A shift of both in the noted respective directions is, however, also possible. The Supply Price curve is affected when there is change in the interest rate and/or in the cost of capital replacement (downward in the case of a drop in either or both). The Prospective Yield curve is affected when there is a change in technology and/or in the prices of the output, and/or in taxation.

In Figure 6.3, remembering that each level of the Marginal Efficiency of

Capital corresponds to a given level of employment, for any level of the Marginal Efficiency of Capital on the Prospective Yield curve, the distribution of the earnings of the economy can be read, from the designated areas under the curve. The earnings are divided into the returns to Labour, Rentiers, and User Cost or replacement cost. The residual triangle, $\mathbf{BCE_0}$, represents the wage bill, the rectangle $\mathbf{ABE_0E'}$, the income share of the investors, and the rectangle $\mathbf{OAE'I_0}$, what is needed to cover User Cost. It is easy to see how, with a sustained low interest rate policy, which makes more financing available for investment, together with the encouragement of the propensity to consume, it is possible to shift the economy from the Equilibrium $\mathbf{E_0}$, which corresponds to the level of investment $\mathbf{I_0}$, given a level of employment $\mathbf{N_0}$, toward $\mathbf{E_1}$, which corresponds to a higher level of investment and a higher level of employment. Notice, as investment financing becomes more available, the rate of return diminishes.

The wage-bill of labour (corresponding to triangle $\mathbf{B'CE_1'}$ in Figure 6.3) gets larger relative to the total profits (represented now by rectangle $\mathbf{A'B'E_1'E_1}$). Thus, the shift of the Equilibrium point reduces the relative share of the earning of the rentiers in favour of labour. High interest rates might 'diminish the propensity to consume', while lower interest rates might well 'stimulate the propensity to consume', 'by redistributing incomes or otherwise' (1936; 1970, p. 321). Keynes's ultimate goal for a more equitable society was to reduce inequality by decreasing the relative share of the earning of the rentiers in favour of employment.

To Keynes's mind, the propensity to consume through aggregate demand is the driving force by which an increase of investment might ensue. Its rise brings about a chain reaction of an increase in production, leading to an increase in employment, or a decrease in unemployment. He believed that economies left to themselves do not have mechanisms that will necessarily automatically foster the propensity to consume and encourage the growth of capital. Therefore, when the market fails to provide adequate stimulus, the State has to intervene and make the needed increase in capital possible. The intervention of the State has, however, to be done carefully, so as not to trigger negative reactions from taxpayers and/or investors.

Keynes saw in forms of direct taxation an instrument which, over the years, had been successful in reducing domestic income disparity to some extent, although not yet, to his mind, to an acceptable level. 'I believe that there is social and psychological justification for significant inequalities of incomes and wealth but not for such large disparities as exist today' (1936; 1970, p. 374). He was, however, persuaded that advocacy of ever heavier taxation might lead taxpayers to enhance their efforts at tax evasion and entrepreneurs to be discouraged in their acceptance of risk. Another argument against tax increase was also current with Keynes's writing: that a reduction in the income of the rich through taxes on inheritance and/or income would, in reducing their savings, thwart the growth of capital in the economy at large. He did not deny that the rich could have an effect on the growth of an economy's wealth; a negative impact would come about by the class's abstinence from consumption, however, not by its being submitted to higher death duties or income taxes.

Keynes did believe, however, that increased taxation could quite severely threaten the growth of capital, if it caused a reduction in an entrepreneur's willingness to accept risk for potential stakes of return. '[T]here are valuable human activities which require the motive of money making and the environment of private wealth ownership for their full fruition' (1936; 1970, p. 374). He saw the addiction to money-making as the lesser of many human foibles: 'It is better that the man should tyrannize over his bank balance than over his fellow citizens' (1936; 1970, p. 374). Running against the general assertion that if consumerism is high, capital is low, Keynes presented his point of view that the growth of capital depends on a high marginal propensity to consume. The propensity to consume functions as an essential stimulus to investment, under conditions of less than full employment. Should capital still be somewhat scarce, savings by institutions and sinking funds (monies set aside to compensate for amortization) would be adequate to maintain the growth of capital during such periods. *Keynes also notes that at full employment, the growth of capital depends on a low marginal propensity to consume* (1936; 1970, p. 373, ch. 3–4).

However much taxation was a focus of *The General Theory*, the main implication of the work on future inequalities of wealth was for Keynes, most simply put, his interest rate theory. Traditionally, a moderately high interest rate had been considered an inducement to save, but for him, effective savings depends on the scale of investment, which is determined by a low rate of interest (under conditions of less than full employment). According to Keynes therefore, to reduce the interest rate to the level of the marginal efficiency of capital would be compatible with the goal of bringing about full employment, provided that the aggregate propensity to consume does not increase radically. Demand for capital is strictly limited by what the economy can absorb.

The main player in Keynes's interest rate theory was the rentier, he who, for supplying capital, earns a living from the combination of interest rate and dividend returns. Abundance of capital would mean the 'euthanasia' of the rentier and the end of the financier's power that derives from scarce capital. Keynes saw the rentiers' return in the form of the interest rate as a reward for no genuine sacrifice, in the sense that rentiers suffer no need to tighten their belts when capital is scarce; in fact tight capital affects them in exactly the opposite way. To Keynes's mind, there was no reason for an intrinsic scarcity of capital in the long run, except in conditions of full employment when the propensity to consume exceeded net savings. Even then, he thought, it would always be possible for the State to reduce the scarcity of capital through communal saving.

The key to devising forms of direct taxation to aid in income distribution, a socially equitable taxation policy, would be to allow the financiers' services to be rewarded on reasonable, but not excessive, terms. The rentier, whom Keynes called the 'functionless investor', would thus no longer receive a 'bonus' from capital. The aim of making capital abundant is to bring the marginal efficiency of capital to a reasonable level where its return must at least cover exhaustion by obsolescence and by wastage, as well as risk and the premium for expertise and supervision. While his long-term aims were clear, Keynes found himself, in the 1930s, faced with the short-term problem of stimulating capital. He wondered, in terms of pursuing the aim of depriving capital of its scarcity value, just how far State policy should be directed toward increasing and supplementing the inducement to invest, and how far it would be safe to stimulate the average propensity to consume.

Keynes argued that to achieve the proposed policy goals, the State has to exercise a guiding influence on the propensity to consume. An orchestrated drop in interest rates would cause consumption to rise so easily that, Keynes believed, near full employment would be attainable with a rate of accumulation of capital little greater than was current. Under such conditions, higher taxation for large incomes would probably not even be needed. On the other hand, high consumerism and low savings could lead dangerously back to a scarcity of capital and the need, therefore, to restrict consumerism. Three types of State policies were proposed by Keynes to cause, among other things, the propensity to consume to move in the right direction: taxation, setting the interest rate, and 'other means', interpreted by Minsky as 'consumption financed by transfer payments, along with increased output of public goods' (1975, p. 156).

Keynes envisaged a role for the State in determining (and inducing) a rate of investment optimal for near full employment. The influence of State banking policy on the rate of interest alone may be insufficient, Keynes believed, to achieve the desired investment level. He advocated that State stimulation of investment be done with cooperation and compromise with private initiatives, with the State assuming a dual role. 'Common will', or State policy, would (1) 'determine the aggregate amount of resources devoted to augmenting the instruments' of production and (2) determine 'the basic rate of reward to those who own them' (1936; 1970, p. 378). These two goals could be introduced gradually, he felt, with ultimately the establishment of 'an aggregate volume of output corresponding to full employment, *as nearly as is practicable*' (1936; 1970, p. 378, emphasis added).

In the policy context of *The General Theory*, Keynes's stimulation of investment entails simply the means that allow for adjustments between the inducement to invest and the propensity to consume, which are both compatible with near full employment. The State is not to be involved in production itself, but rather with indicating 'the nature of the environment which the free play of economic forces requires if it is to realize the full potentialities of production' (1936; 1970, p. 379). 'Free play' may need to be curbed or guided tightly. The form of government intervention Keynes envisaged was, while institutional, legislative not bureaucratic. Keynes was persuaded, however, that so long as the large number in society is addicted to money making, the 'search-for-profit' game will continue to be played, in accordance with and not withstanding appropriate rules and regulations.

NOTES

1. Fleming's belief that for Keynes's understanding of inflation one should look at the work of Barro-Grossman and Malinvaud, among others, is, however, not helpful.
2. In this case, the Aggregate Supply, in the neoClassical interpretation, is vertical.
3. See 1936; 1970, fn i, p. 319.
4. Also defined as 'over-investment': 'a state of affairs where every kind of capital-goods is so abundant that there is no new investment which is expected, even in conditions of full employment, to earn in the course of its life more than its replacement cost' (1936; 1970, p. 320–21).
5. It presumably stemmed from Wicksell's article published in the *Economic Journal* (1907).
6. Keynes defined the Credit Cycle, as earlier noted, as 'the alterations of excess and defect in the cost of investment over the volume of saving and the accompanying see-saw in the Purchasing Power of Money due to these alterations' (1930, I, p. 277).
7. It is presumably also possible to imagine situations in which demand for Financial Circulation is not being met in the Banking System. When the demand for a form of money, so secure as to be usable for precautionary purposes, is not available, entrepreneurs, like consumers may turn to gold or another commodity which serves as an excellent store of value – thus to a non-monetary or credit component of the economy. As far as when excessive demand for speculative purposes is not satisfied, some money is funnelled, in an open economy, toward national and international securities purchases as well as other types of new investment outside national boundaries. A positive state of windfall profits, showing to what extent the earnings of financial investments are above their normal levels, might well induce speculation in any available stock market. Purchases of land, art, and so on also serve as non-monetary ways to meet speculation, when excessive demand calls for it.
8. See the equation for p on p. 44 of *The General Theory*, $p = Z_r + U_r / O_r$, which can be made to be identical with this equation (1936; 1970, p. 45).
9. Whether as Taylor rule or otherwise.

Conclusion

This book, however academic, is actually a straightforward reconsideration of the ideas of one of the most important authors to have written in the field of economics, John Maynard Keynes. One of its main objectives has been to analyse anew two related texts of Keynes's ideas, first, *A Treatise on Money*, published in 1930, in which Keynes summarized his liquidity theory and trade cycle, and second, *The General Theory* (1936). The purposes were twofold: to fuse *The General Theory* with the credit cycle model of the *Treatise*, and to affirm the position that *The General Theory* is the discussion of but one phase of Keynes's whole trade cycle. This analysis has constituted the focus of the volume, within which several themes have been developed: Keynes's theory of money, his theory of cycles and prices, his capital theory, his theory of employment, and his policy on inflation and deflation. Keynes's ideas in relation to those of, for example, Wicksell, Hayek, and Hicks have been highlighted.

A rereading of the actual words of Keynes has been found to be absolutely necessary because one of the most unfortunate outcomes of the early debates over his two most important theoretical works was to have deflected attention away from the true novelty and uniqueness of their offerings. Right after publication of the *Treatise*, the exchanges with Friedrich von Hayek and Dennis Robertson led to the quick disappearance from view of the substance of the work, without the significant matters of the economists' disagreements having been resolved. Upon release of *The General Theory*, two reviews by John Hicks reduced the scope of this second major work of Keynes into a single, narrow problem: unemployment in the slump. Rereading the *Treatise* and *The General Theory* now together and in terms of Keynes's own corpus reveals that whether due to the inflammatory rhetoric or simplification found in the immediate defaming reviews they received, in their light the actual contents of Keynes's works were largely neglected, and almost immediately following the appearance of each one.

Why, it has been asked here, did Hayek, as author of *Prices and Production*, focus so completely on what he found to have been the enormously difficult vocabulary of Keynes's *Treatise*? Why did Hicks see immediately only the left side of the apparatus of his IS-LL lurking in the chapters of *The General Theory*? Both took seemingly great pains to grapple with a particular work, and Hicks with the *Treatise* as well, but neither was apparently able to separate his own theory from that of Keynes. The analysis here has thus attempted to reexamine, not the impatience of Hayek or Hicks to understand Keynes, but rather the preoccupations of each with his own specific vision of the dynamics of the economy as well as his prescriptions for its proper working. While Hicks was at least still searching, even after 30 years, for who was right, Keynes or Hayek, the discipline alas long ago ceased to ask the question of who could better express Keynes's ideas, he himself or his reviewers. It had opted immediately for the latter! It is argued that the very positions taken by Hayek and Hicks as reviewers prevented them, and hence many generations of economists thereafter, from grasping the details and the subtleties of Keynes's theory.

It has been elucidated here how, despite early and continuing assessments to the contrary, Keynes had arrived at a full theory of the trade cycle from the perspective of the *Treatise* and its study of the impact of credit on the economy. Refocus on the theoretical aspects of that early contribution of Keynes has been in order, to explain how money and investment impact prices, income, and employment to create his trade cycle. His theory of the trade cycle is shown to be extremely rich and extends far beyond analysis of the single phase or two the profession has retained for him.

Most economists since Keynes, whether pro- or anti-Keynesian, have primarily focused on only parts of *The General Theory*. Generation after generation of followers of Keynes has, partly for this reason alone, held to an erroneous understanding of Keynes. Ensuing theories, even if linked to Keynes in name, resemble very little Keynes's own. This book at its core is an exposition of the actual model of Keynes's theory, ensuing from a fusion of *A Treatise* and *The General Theory*. The generalized General Theory of Keynes is laid out according to the wide variety of its components, from his *Treatise* to its extension into *The General Theory*. In addition to an analysis of Keynes's fundamentally important ideas on money and credit, this book reveals the EC-SP model his theory encapsulated.

There is a second main objective of the book: if successful, it has made accessible a new way of conceiving Keynes's contribution and offers thus the possibility of a re-evaluation of the implementation of Keynes's policies. The book is, it is hoped, of interest to historians of economic thought, but even more importantly to economics's macro-theorists. Ever since Keynes's ideas were published and the concept of a macroeconomics began, few economists have not taken a position with respect to their understanding of Keynes. This work is therefore aimed, with the historical perspective as a starting point, at bringing a fresh appreciation to Keynes's remarkable contributions.

It was September 3, 2008, as the last paragraphs of this Conclusion were initially being written. The first term of the university year was beginning. 'Macroeconomics' was newly in my mind as one of the required fundamental courses that every economics student must take. The question naturally presented itself: given that Keynes's theoretical contributions were first and foremost in macroeconomics, how were all the controversies, discussions, and Keynes's macroeconomics itself, discussed in the present book, relevant to what is taught in the classroom today? Then, however, the disturbance of the financial crisis came crashing into this largely pedagogical environment, and there was real cause for a thoughtful answer!

For Keynes, as has been many times noted throughout this book, entrepreneurs' profits are the source of the creation of wealth and of inequitable distribution. They must be protected, to induce the investment necessary to sustain the level of output. They might, however, also be channelled, through ways devised to encourage that their fostering of employment in their use of liquid and working capital investment is also an improvement in the relative earnings return to the large number. In short, for Keynes, well-employed entrepreneurs' profits can lead to a more equitable distribution of the national wealth among the incomes of all of society. Keynes intended his vision to encourage an economy of value-added *entrepreneurial production* rather than one of monopolies, big finance, and speculation.

To this end, 'government intervention', the spectre that has scared so many into the anti-Keynesian camp, was, in Keynes's mind, simply the evocation of a very narrow spectrum of centralized duties and responsibilities, those of the institution of the monetary authority. It encompassed primarily the healthy management of the money wealth of the nation, resulting from his determination that, through a policy of low interest rates, in the short run, producers' marginal efficiency of capital could be sustained and, in the long run, capital could be made abundant to increase the competitiveness of its marginal efficiency and to diminish excessive relative returns to rentiers, investors or speculators.

The assertions in this book about the original Keynes are landing at the moment when the discipline of economics, relatively barren in theory and policy ideas, could hardly be considered enlightened in terms of analysis or understanding about the current economic environment. As the historical story has gone, reigning Keynesianism, albeit one strain of neoClassical economics, was so vulnerable in the 1970s that it took but the articulation of 'expectations' (rational ones!) by anti-Keynesians not only to disorient it but also to bring about co-option. While Smith's Invisible Hand and its guise as the market spontaneity of Hayek, taken each in context, allude to the outcome of subtle, social interactions in the economic activity of a free-market economy, the new 'expectations' programmed as rational, whatever the complexity attached to their calculations, do not. Nonetheless, under the influence of anti-Keynesians, society, even for Keynesians, came to be made up of rational consumers and producers, who know what they want and are always capable of bringing output to its natural level. Thus, the speculation of 2008, for example, interpreted in current macroeconomics as the free-market environment which preserves freedom of choice – with all the rhetoric of individual rationality attached – is the same speculation to have fostered the *consumer demand* which has resulted in current disproportionate income disparity and market collapse.

Updated Smithian and Hayekian concepts describing the harmonious forces of the market have some significance in a small-is-beautiful world, where there are a large number of consumers and producers, with individuals having little influence on price formation, but the world of today is not that one. It is instead the world of Keynes, one of corporate finance and monopolies, in which the economic forces are in the hands of entrepreneurs and investors, whose behaviour is guided by the competitive search for profits from sales to consumers, however rational or irrational they may be. At the same time, Keynes's approach is ironically the very one that would dissuade that concentration of the much in the hands of the few that jeopardizes the world of small-is-beautiful. This work's content could be, therefore, a stimulus for researchers who are interested in a theoretical foundation from which to re-evaluate economics today, in terms of trade cycle, banking, and monetary theories as well as financial policy, not to mention the history of economic thought. It should interest those concerned with credit, money, and business today, both within and totally removed from their historical context.

Despite the fact that the main attention given to Keynes over the years has been focused on the scope of *The General Theory*, his wider interests, which came through in his *Treatise* and in the later chapters of *The General Theory*, were, as has been affirmed through this study, in money, credit, and the trade cycle. His own interest in credit and economic cycles was part of the already strong presence of such ideas in the literature of the Banking School in England, on the Continent, and in the United States, as, for example, in the works of Thornton and Tooke, and continuing into the twentieth century with the work of Hawtrey, and to some extent into that of Hayek, on prices and production, and of Hicks, on credit and institutions. Clearly the role of credit and the interest rate have recently become central to the explanation of deflationary or inflationary phenomena worldwide, and awareness of the richness of Keynes's views on this and any number of other issues could enhance the theories applied to current debates. Michael Woodford and the economists from the World Bank are using, they think, Wicksell's theory of cumulative process and the interaction between real and monetary rates of interest and the price level. The current approach – witness Woodford's book on money and interest, considered, for example, one of the more recent developments in economic theory – is, however, so locked into analysis of the demand side of the economy that what Keynes has to offer has been completely missed.

Looking forward, it is important to recognize that there has been a considerable amount of empirical research done since Keynes wrote his two major works, an accumulation of data and some analysis that could be a huge asset to theoretical rethinking of Keynes. Empirical research in the area of income distribution, for example, is revealing, just as does Keynes's own theory alluded to above, that the causes and corrections for inequity are much more complicated and pertinent than any perceptions of them Keynesians or anti-Keynesians have offered thus far. Keynes's concern in chapter 24 of *The General Theory* was explicitly on the role and impact of investment on distribution in an economy in a situation other than that of under-employment. Some of Keynes's recommendations as to alleviating disparity and stabilizing the economy at an adequate level of employment have already been explained in Chapter 6.

The main concluding point here is that with the increasing participation of investors at all income levels in the stock market and in speculation in general, whether via mutual funds, pension plans, house purchases, and so on, income distribution theory has become much more thorny for both pro- and anti-Keynesians. Economists and business people, no matter how socially conscious, can take quite distinct stands as to what to do about the impact of economic changes. Keynes's euthanasia of the rentier, predicted in chapter 24, although perhaps more than ever the needed route to pursue, is far from being realized, particularly given the distorting policies currently undertaken in the name of Keynes. However distorted, echoes of the profound differences in the economic policies of a 'Hayek' or a 'Keynes' reside hidden in the many current persuasions about the government and the current banking system, whether they are part of the cause or of the solution of economic fluctuations. Present Keynesian policies simply do not square with Keynes whose entrepreneurs, through their efforts, create the value-added, while the investors provide funds in exchange for a 'rent' which, when capital is rare, becomes exorbitant.

Many of the interpretations of Keynes in this book will probably be controversial in that they will come as a surprise or even a shock to both Keynesians and anti-Keynesians alike. It is hoped that the jolts – that producer–consumer symmetry, at the heart of the IS-LM, is simply not a part of Keynes's picture, that Keynes was definitely not the all-time advocate of expansionary effective demand that he has come to be believed to have been, that Keynes advocated government intervention *only* in very special circumstances and *only* for very specific periods of time, and most importantly that most, if not all, of what really were Keynes's ideas are still relevant at both the national and international scale[1] – are well timed. Although the summary of economics after Keynes would belie this, perhaps the task of making new sense of Keynes is somewhat easier now, with the waning of his being considered exclusively in light of Walrasian equilibrium theory. Keynes's ideas, in being freed from Hayek, Hicks, and their successors, could perhaps be more able to be understood on their own merits.

It would be presumptuous to say that Keynes was a prophet and would have had a solution to everything to come, but he was an exceptional theorist, who was also an astute historian, banker, and thinker, extremely involved in the problems and remedial policies of his time. He was among the most important economic theorists to have given a role to credit in the trade cycle. His contributions ought to have given a jumpstart to the studies of monetary business cycles, even as his name became immediately attached to solely one particular part of the cyclical pattern, the recessionary phase. He had a good sense of what was happening in his time, but also of what might come. It is the way he foresaw and theorized economic problems that serves as the basis for this book's reconstruction of his generalized General Theory. It is hoped that this offering has gone much of the way toward unstifling the very Keynes who originated macroeconomics.

NOTE

1. The international component of Keynes's ideas has been almost completely neglected in this book, as the focus here was on the core of his theory. Much could still be written about Keynes's theory in relation to international economics.

Appendix: False novelties

John Maynard Keynes proposed an economic theory fundamentally different from those of the Classicals and the neoClassicals. In his sustained use, however, of a basic set of terms known to his predecessors, little difference is to be found; his was a vocabulary composed of virtually the same words of either one or the other school: equilibrium, production, competition, market clearing, the monetary economy, and many others. There is nonetheless much that is distinct in the respective meanings of some of these concepts. Again, there is a lot which is not so different in the understanding of the premises of their theories: the laws of supply and demand, of marginal productivity, utilization of cost–benefit analysis (profit maximization, cost minimization), the quantity theory of money, and so on. Nonetheless, the key premises regarding society's macroeconomic goals and the motivation and rationality of the behaviour governing decision-making are, however, different. How different was Keynes's methodology,[1] by which we mean the way he went about showing what he wanted to show and what purpose he gave to his theorizing? It is not so much a general awareness of scientific objectivity in his methodology, through its use of mathematics or probability, which made it different, but Keynes's theorizing of decision-making around expectations[2] and uncertainty, which called for a unique notion of probability, his concept of non-numeric, non-comparable probabilities.

Keynes's theory had a particular approach to the study of production and market mechanisms, in relation to the spontaneity of supply and demand in the marketplace and the probabilistic aspects of future outcomes, unique to him. When the various elements of economic vocabulary, premises, and method which make Keynes different are understood in the way he plainly laid them out, and not reinterpreted or placed within a different framework, there emerges an economic theory that is distinct from those of the Classicals and the neoClassicals in its dynamics, in which time, incomplete knowledge, differing decisions based on differing future expectations, and the uncertainty about what is to come are taken into account. Once an assessment of the way Keynes is different from his predecessors is done in retrospect, then it should be possible to see, in the light of these differences, how Keynesianism has actually failed to see the distinctiveness of Keynes's theory in relation to those of both the

Classicals and the neoClassicals. Comprehending Keynes's theory on its own ground produces an understanding of the mechanism of the cause-and-effect workings of a market economy that is different from those of the Keynesian models.

One cannot grasp Keynes's novel, overall theoretical contribution found in *A Treatise on Money* and in *The General Theory* without placing it in perspective and contrasting it to the existing canons of Classical and neoClassical economics. From the theoretical setting, there is a clear distinction between the Classical economics of Smith–Ricardo and the neo-Classical economics of Walras–Jevons. Keynes's theory, even if it appears to have a foot in both Classical and neoClassical economics, is neither. To become immersed in the details of the distinctive originality of Keynes's theory, some clarification is required as to what the general relationship and thrust of these alternative theories of economics are, in terms of what makes them different in their basic conception: who are the 'players', who are the 'decision-makers' in each setting, what is the goal, what are the means and 'tools' by which it is achieved, and what is the 'dynamic' process which permits such achievement.

It might help to reiterate that the concern common to all economics is the study of the creation and distribution of wealth, the agenda taken from Adam Smith. Of main interest is how through a market mechanism of exchanges of flows of goods, services, and mediums of payment, factors of production are combined to yield products. In a macroeconomic setting of multiple exchanges, an institutionalized process of flows of production and exchange can be addressed through theory only if it is among commensurables; the constituents, that is, the goods, the products, and the services, have to lend themselves to some sort of common measurement, thus the importance of the concept of Price. To discuss prices, one has to begin with a theory of value. What then are the respective theories of value and the working framework for the three alternative theories here: (1) the neoClassicals', (2) the Classicals', and (3) Keynes's?

A.1   NEOCLASSICAL (OR NEOWALRASIAN) THEORY

NeoClassical or neoWalrasian theory creates a world[3] or setting in which flows of goods and services from households, on the one side, to firms, on the other, are balanced by flows of payments between households and firms. All of these flows are an expression of supplies and demands. The sets of prices of goods/services and wages are determined by the decision of the household, to choose its time preference for labour or leisure, and that of the firm, to choose its preference for employing labour or capital. It is the dynamics of this relationship in which no one's freedom of choice is forced which yields the market outcome. Households adjust their choices among various goods according to their marginal utilities (MU). The marginal utility between work and leisure is equal.

Firms adjust their various productions such that the marginal product (MP) between goods and services is equal.[4] Prices, or more precisely **relative prices** (which are an expression of the exchange of how much of one good or service is given, or substituted, in order to receive another), are determined by marginal utility and marginal productivity:

$$\frac{Pa}{Pb} = \frac{MUa}{MUb} \quad \text{and} \quad \frac{Pa}{Pb} = \frac{MPa}{MPb} \tag{A.1}$$

All relative price ratios are the monetary equivalent of the ratio of the marginal utilities and marginal productivities. Money is a unit of account. The dynamics of the workings of an economy as a whole consist in an interaction of supply and demand for goods and services resulting from selling and buying, with a total outcome represented, such that the total value of all transactions is equal to the total amount paid for those transactions, which gives the equation of the well known Quantity Theory of Money:

$$MV = \sum P_i x_i = PT \tag{A.2}$$

(where M is the total amount of Money, V, its velocity of circulation; P_i and x_i, the corresponding individual prices; P, the overall Level of Price, and T, the total of all transactions).

A neoWalrasian world is a monetary setting in which money is a unit of account as well as the medium of exchange. The model of its whole economic system consists then, as Hicks encapsulated it, in 'nothing else but equations of supply and demand for goods and services of every sort, for securities and for money' (1939, p. 245).

The macroeconomic setting of the neoWalrasian world derives from the sum total of micro-components. Spontaneity of the market mechanism is conceived in this economic model as a system of simultaneous equations from which macroeconomic variables such as P, M, and T are derived. In a harmonious environment, where the major players in the model are households and firms, the outcome of their interactions, when unhindered by any imperfections (such as monopoly power, restricted information, imposed rationing or any other rigidities), yields, in a welfare sense, a first-best solution (Paretian solution), and such a solution can be interpreted in a macroeconomics sense as a full-employment situation. As Lerner put it, 'it was supposed that a similar adjustment [to the equalization of supply and demand for a particular commodity] would equalise overall supply and demand by an automatic movement of the general price level to a point where it would produce full employment'.[5] This is a situation such that what is produced corresponds to what is desired to be produced.

A Paretian solution is possible, but only on a basis of perfect flexibility in the substitution of the two factors of production used to produce goods and services, labour and capital, and in the equality of the amount of goods and services demanded and supplied in exchanges. In other words, there has to be perfect substitution between goods and services exchanged and the factors of production used in producing those goods and services, in such a manner that full advantage is taken of any remaining reallocation of resources, which can result in additional gain to make everyone better off without making anyone worse off. Efficiency in this context means full use of resources to attain the maximum levels of satisfaction and production given available endowment.

From a macroeconomic perspective, the neoWalrasian macroeconomic model exhibits the following characteristics:

1. It is a **stock analysis**, in the sense that the outcome of what is produced and what is exchanged is constrained by a given endowment.
2. What is produced and what exchanged are all desired quantities; since they are all desired, **markets clear**.
3. The dynamics of the **substitution** of factors in production and of goods and services in exchange, which allows for efficiency in the attainment of an ultimate **equilibrium, is virtual and ahistorical** (this is also true of its inter-temporal model).
4. By 'entrepreneur' is meant the firm, namely, the institution in the model which undertakes the act of producing, with given capital, technology, and available labour, as represented in the production function. By the institution of the 'household' is meant the individuals who decide to engage in labour or leisure. It is the total amount of labour offered by individuals, which becomes the determinant factor for how much will be produced. The total payment for that labour will in turn buy the total amount of goods and services produced. Technology being exogenous and given, it is the individuals through their decision to offer labour in anticipation to get goods and services in return that is aggregate demand. In a sense, the aggregate demand anticipates and thus determines the aggregate supply. By construction of the model, what is desired to be produced is what is produced. Every product will find a 'débouché', and, as a corollary, **supply creates its own demand**.[6]

5. Factor payments, expressed by their relative marginal productivity, are uniquely and simultaneously determined, as aggregate supply equates aggregate demand. Efficiency in **production** and determination of the **distribution of income** are two facets of the **same issue** in the optimization process.

6. To every production corresponds a money income, and that income is always fully expended on consumer goods and services (consumption) and on capital goods and services (Investment). Since money does not have utility in itself and serves only as a medium of exchange, what is not consumed is saved (S) and what is saved is, by definition, invested (I): **I = S** always. Both I and S are components of the expenditure side; that is to say, they form one part of **Aggregate Demand** (I is the flip side of S, emanating from the same decision).

7. Since there is a one-to-one correspondence between production and income, and between expenditure and the supply of both consumption and investment goods and services, **money,** the intermediary *numeraire* that facilitates exchanges, **is neutral.**

8. **Aggregate Supply** is exclusively determined by the production function and the labour market.

9. The equilibrium between Aggregate Demand and Aggregate Supply determines both the overall level of price and the level of employment that corresponds to full employment.

This model, as encapsulated in Hicks's *Value and Capital*, represents the theoretical working of the forces of the market economy when they are completely unhindered. It serves as a reference for the market's best, most efficient performance. Reference to the real world shows, however, that the forces of the market economy do not always operate smoothly and that many complications can prevent attainment of the 'best' outcome – for example, price rigidities,[7] just to mention one example of interest here. How do these complications affect the idealistic world of the model; how do they alter the model? It is a neoWalrasian model, in macroeconomic form, with its characteristics (1) through to (9), which Hicks had in the back of his mind and against which he assessed and reviewed Keynes's *General Theory*. It is this model which led to his IS-LL synthesis, which in turn became the IS-LM, the bare-bones framework of Keynesianism.

A.2 THE CLASSICAL THEORY

What about the model that predates the Walrasian, the model of the Classical theory? The Classical model of Smith and Ricardo[8] is also an analysis of market forces. Like their successors of the neoClassical school, the Classicals were interested in the wealth of a nation deriving from the goods and services that are produced. Their primary focus was, however, on how the total product is distributed among the three participating classes: workers, entrepreneurs, and landowners. The determination, on the one hand, of relative prices in exchange, and on the other, of individual prices in the production sphere, as derived from their factor payments (wages and profits, with rent residual), are essential in explaining who gets what out of the total product and how the accumulation of capital occurs.

In the guise of Smith's concept of the Invisible Hand, the dynamics of price formation (the relative prices of products and of factors), in a free market economy, is the outcome of market forces, balancing within individual firms and between firms the use of factors and what is paid for their use, under the given condition that the flow of the factors of labour and capital is constantly wherever their respective return is highest.[9] The dynamics of price formation makes reference to production as well as to demand and supply. In the Classical setting, all prices, whether of commodities or of services (wages and profits), have two expressions: a long-term price, '*natural price*', and a short-term price, '*market price*'. The terms 'natural' and 'market' each refer to a same variable, which determines, although in relation to different forces, what they become, either in the short or long term. In the case of the prices of commodities, Ricardo identifies the forces determining their short-term prices by market supply and demand, while he sees their long-term prices as depending on cost of production: 'It should be recollected that prices always vary in the market and in the first instance through the comparative state of demand and supply' (1817; 1952, II, p. 139), but

> it is the cost of production which must ultimately regulate the price of commodities and not, as has been often said, the proposition between the supply and demand: the proposition between supply and demand may indeed for a time, affect the market value of a commodity . . . but this effect will be only of a temporary duration. (1817; 1952, IV, p. 382)

Prices in a market economy are in perpetual movement. The dynamics of the behaviour of each pair of prices is conceptualized as *market prices gravitating around natural prices*. The understanding is that the former will tend to converge to the latter, but 'this tendency, this gravitation as it were of profits, is happily checked at repeated intervals by the improvements in machinery . . . as well as by discoveries' (Ricardo 1817; 1952, II, p. 140). When market forces are unhindered and left to themselves, there is, however, no substitution of factors. The natural wage and the natural rate of profit depend on the natural price of a commodity.[10] That natural price is determined by the cost of production of the individual commodity, whose wages and rates of profit are predetermined, or given, by supply and demand at the market level. It is thus clear that in the long run, while it is the cost of production that determines natural commodity prices, it is still market forces, and gravitational dynamics, which bring about those very prices.

There is striking similarity between the neoClassical and Classical models. Both theories attribute ultimate equilibrium to the outcome of the forces of the market economy. For the Classicals, additionally, market forces allocate resources in the most *efficient* way, in the sense that *resources move where the return is highest*. Ultimately an equilibrium occurs when the flow of labour and capital between firms and sectors reaches a point where there is *equalization of wages and rates of profit*, respectively, albeit with market forces unhindered and left to themselves. This equilibrium is one of *full employment*.

There are, however, major differences between the neoClassical and the Classical theories. In the neoClassical world, it is labour through household choice (leisure or work) that is the kernel from which everything else develops. Through the interaction of market supplies and demands, an equilibrium emerges to yield 'full employment', which is really only the full employment of labour. For the Classicals, the key factor is capital; it is the driving force in the market, invested in both the manufacturing and agricultural sectors, the latter constrained by the availability and productivity of land. Equilibrium for the Classicals derives from the flow of capital, going where it is the most advantageously invested,[11] which in the long term settles the economy also into 'full employment', the full employment of available capital. Labour, while not fully employed, as in the neoClassical theory, is considered abundant, and therefore non-constraining.

The Classicals' was a supply-side approach.[12] A rigorous microeconomic analysis of market demand and supply, by its omission, was clearly not their concern. For them, the root cause of the dynamic working of market forces was the price of commodities deriving from their cost of production. In terms of each individual commodity, its cost, which comes before production of the final product, determines its price. Ricardo saw natural, not market, cost components as the more relevant to the calculation of the prices of commodities. Since, however, market prices are observable and natural prices are not, the latter are purely conceptual to establishing the correlation between production cost and prices of commodities.[13]

Since, for Ricardo, the goal of economic theory is '[T]o determine the laws which regulate . . . distribution' (1817; 1952, II, p. 5) and it is the cost of factor payments that determines distribution, the main focus of economic theory must be the cost of production. For example, says Ricardo, 'a rise in wages would raise the price of commodities, but would invariably lower profits; and secondly, if the price of all commodities could be raised, still the effect on profits would be the same' (1817; 1952, II, p. 127). As a general rule, distribution changes with the demographic pressure to produce more. Such pressure in turn causes diminishing profits, due to the diminishing marginal productivity of land: 'in proportion to the increase of capital will be the increase in the demand for labour' (1817; 1952, II, p. 95), as 'population presses against the means of subsistence' (1817; 1952, II, p. 99) with wages uncompressible at their subsistence level. Further, the profit from land regulates the profits of all other trades, so with the decreasing marginal productivity of land, 'the natural tendency of [all] profit then is to fall' (1817; 1952, II, p. 120). Ricardo was of the opinion that the only 'happy' remedy to this reduction in profits was the introduction of machinery, which would yield a situation in which 'all classes will improve' (1817; 1952, IV, p. 392).

It is the entrepreneurs who decide how much to produce, how much capital to invest, and how much labour to employ to match that capital. Their decisions determine how much to produce and the quantity of production sets the price. The relative prices determine what is exchanged for what. The entrepreneurs' decisions, as to where and how resources are allocated, depend, for the Classicals, on their own interests, which are different from those of the landowners and workers. The balance of forces which, for the Classicals, determines distribution at the production level, yields different results from the balance of forces of the market in the neoClassical theory. For the Classicals, relative prices and relative productivity are determined by competition among entrepreneurs.

Total profit depends on the wage-bill; the rate of remuneration, whether as profit or wages, is calculated according to a labour theory of value. In the very first paragraph of his *Principles*, Ricardo stated the labour theory of value: 'The value of a commodity, or the quantity of any other commodity for which it will exchange, depends on the relative quantity of labour which is necessary for its production, and not on the greater or less compensation which is paid for that labour' (1817; 1952, II, p. 11). Simply stated mathematically, commodity a produced with direct and indirect labour, La will sell at price, Pa, and similarly for b, such that their relative prices can be determined as follows:[14]

$$\frac{Pa}{Pb} = \frac{La}{Lb} \qquad (A.3)$$

Aware of the difficulty of finding an invariable measure of value, Ricardo opted for labour, rather than a specific currency, as the standard, even though money was the reigning medium of exchange. For Ricardo,

It is of no importance in elucidating correct principles in what medium value is estimated. Only that the medium itself is invariable. Money–corn, labour are all equally good . . . An alteration in the value of money has no effect on the relative values of commodities, for it raises or sinks their price in the same proportion. (1817; 1952, IV, p. 396)

Furthermore, '[T]he variation in the value of money however great makes no difference in the rate of profits' (1817; 1952, II, p. 50). This Classical world, as a matter of fact, assumes money as neutral; it does not need money, since value can be explained in the real terms of the real economy.

From a macroeconomic perspective, a Classical model exhibits the following characteristics:

1. It is **flow analysis**, comprised of three different dynamics: (a) a flow of resources searching for the highest return, which has a tendency to cause market prices to move toward their natural equilibrium value, (b) pressure from population increase and diminishing return from land, which causes diminishing profits, and (c) the introduction of machinery, which halts a diminution of profits by establishing a new capital–labour ratio. Market prices are constantly being jolted away from their tendency to move toward a natural level in an economy that never has time actually to settle into a stationary-state equilibrium.
2. What is produced is what it was decided by the entrepreneurs to produce. As 'demand is only limited by production' (1817; 1952, II, p. 290), **markets clear**; every product will find a 'debouché', since **supply 'creates' its own demand**.
3. The dynamics of the **substitution** of factors in production, that is, labour by machines, keeps disturbing the tendency of market prices toward natural prices, even as the projected, ultimate **equilibrium is virtual**.
4. By 'entrepreneur' is meant one class 'of the community', the one which decides production. It is distinct from another class, the workers, who conform in offering their labour services. Production is realized according to a fixed labour–capital ratio for a given technology. It is the total amount of **capital** provided which becomes **the determinant factor** in how much will be produced; the return to **labour is determined**.
5. For a given wage-bill and a given capital–labour ratio, distribution is given, and relative prices are only dependent on the amount of direct and indirect labour needed to produce the respective commodities, not on the rates of wages and profits. With pressure from the wage-bill, even with a given capital–labour ratio, distribution will be changing.

There is a tendency toward the most efficient use of resources, and resource use and the **distribution of income** are two facets of the **same issue** when market values converge to their natural values.

6. To every production corresponds an income. 'To save is to spend',[15] so there cannot be a glut of all commodities[16] or all money.[17] Therefore, labour being a unit of account, **money**, as a medium of exchange,[18] is **neutral**, and investment equals saving, **I = S** always. Both I and S are components of the expenditure side, that is to say, they form one part of **'effectual' Demand** (I is the flip side of S).

7. **Aggregate Supply** is exclusively determined by capital in a fixed coefficient production function.

8. The equilibrium between (effectual) Aggregate Demand and Aggregate Supply determines the employment of capital. Taken in terms of full employment, if there is full employment, it is that of capital, not that of labour. Although the overall level of price could be easily inferred, it was not of concern for the Classicals.[19]

The above characteristics, (1) through to (8), are obviously very compressed gists of the highly theoretical model of the Classicals, in this case as read through Ricardo. They would not all be considered representative, either by some of the adherents to Classical economics or by some historians of thought as interpreters of the Classical economists.[20] The labour theory of value has admittedly gone through many different transformations and sophistications, especially in the hands of Mill, Marx or Sraffa, although also by others. One member of the Classical school, Malthus, a contemporary of Ricardo's, was most critical of Say's law and of the roles Ricardo gave to money and to investment and savings; his views would be inconsistent with some aspects of the above characteristics. What is of concern here is not the various controversies internal to the Classical School, surrounding the issues of the wage-fund, the machinery effect, gluts, and so on, however crucial they are to understanding the labour theory of value, but rather what is common to the Classical School of thought: labour is used as measure of value and as unit of account. The dynamics of the market economy has to do with market values in relation to their natural values and the decision and interests of the entrepreneurs as individuals or as a group as different from those of the workers. The analysis of equilibrating forces by the Classicals has decidedly different implications, in terms of production, employment, and income distribution, from that analysis by the neoClassicals.

Comparing the amount of research and writing that has been produced over the years on the development of the Classical and the neoClassical theories, a truly disproportionate sum has been allocated to analysis of the neoClassical School. If the refinement of the types of the respective schools is also considered, there is no comparison between the two in terms of attempted mathematical applications. The overwhelming amount of work done on the neoClassical theory has undoubtedly aided its claim to superiority and greater scientificity and brought it to overshadow the Classical School. By virtue of the law of large numbers, there seems to be a consensus among economists today that on theoretical grounds the neoWalrasian approach is the more general, from which everything else can be derived. Although it is virtually the only theory taught to them, they have adopted the assumption that it subsumes every other.

Paul Samuelson, among the few eclectic and the most influential of the post-war defenders of the neoClassical or neoWalrasian model, calls the Classical theory 'one-legged' (Samuelson 1991), in that it can account only for the production side of the economy and does not take into account the demand side.[21] From a macroeconomic perspective, the Classical description of a market economy is more realistic than the neoClassical, in terms of its seeing market values gravitating around natural or real values. The theoretical aspects of the labour theory of value concern themselves with the long-term equilibrium, that is, when undisturbed, if sufficient time is allowed, prices will converge to the cost of production. It is this ultimate effect that was of concern to the Classicals. The theory is consistent and coherent in that it is capable of explaining prices, distribution, and accumulation, all in terms of *real* variables. If one restricts oneself to the time of Smith, Ricardo, and Malthus, the emphases in the theory may even seem understandable, in light of a mostly agrarian economy.[22] Given, however, that its complete independence of money derives from the fact that its value theory is based on labour, the Classical approach, as it was conceived, can explain capital accumulation without reference to money.

What is striking, however, from a purely theoretical perspective, is that when both the Classical and neoClassical theories are stripped down to their bare-bones core, as in characteristics (1) through to (8/9) above, the neoWalrasian or neoClassical theory also appears to be 'one-legged', for the opposite reason: production, or the supply side, remains unaccounted for – it is just a reflection of demand. The neoClassical theory is a sophisticated equilibrium theory, which concentrates on exchange relations as led by demand with supply as its reflection. Unlike the Classical theory, it cannot do without money. Since the only type of money that is consistent with making the system of supply and demand coherent is a neutral medium of exchange, a *numeraire*, this theory cannot, except in an artificial manner, incorporate the complexities of money, finance, and credit, as well as the implications of those on the production process. For the neoClassicals, there is a dichotomy between the real and the money sectors.

The allusion to 'one-leggedness' rings quite true in the cases of both the Classical and neoClassical approaches, as to the scope of their theories. It is in this context, with the help of Samuelson's allusion to the 'one-legged' theory of the Classicals, now applied by parallel extension here to the neo-Classical theory as well, that the question is now posed: could such a thing as a 'two-legged theory' ever exist? In relation to explaining employment and unemployment, the Classical labour theory cannot be of much help because of the already mentioned characteristics. Its premise of an elastic supply of labour might, nonetheless, shed some light on the existence of sustained unemployed labour, which neoClassical theory cannot. The neo-Classical theory is built on the premise that the household labour-leisure choice is voluntary and therefore that any unemployment that might creep in is voluntary, [23] rather than possibly being interpreted, as it might by the Classicals, as structural involuntary unemployment. Keynes, who took up the focus on employment and unemployment in the second quarter of the twentieth century, from a macroeconomics perspective, thought that neither the Classical nor the neoClassical theory, which he saw as one, 'the classics', at least in connection to some of the characteristics above – namely, the neutrality of money,[24] the implications they drew from Say's law, and their treatment of the labour market – could deal with the problems of unemployment in the *monetary* market economy of his time. It is asserted in this book that he and only he brought a truly 'two-legged' theory into being.

A.3   KEYNES'S THEORY

In light of the previous sketches of the two earlier theories, the immediate focus here is to encapsulate the nature of Keynes's economic dynamics, by identifying who the players, who the decision-makers, and what the sources of his theory's causal dynamics are. Like in the case of the other theories, Keynes's starting point had to be a theory of value, which is found in the Fundamental Equations of *A Treatise on Money*, which, as the underlying core of his economic theory, became[25] the underpinnings of his general theory of price and employment. In *A Treatise*, Keynes provided a third, truly alternative theory of value for sector prices, in embryonic form:

$$P = \frac{E}{O} + \frac{I - S}{R} \qquad\qquad (A.4)$$

$$\Pi = \frac{E}{O} + \frac{I - S}{O} \qquad\qquad (\text{FEII A.5})$$

where P is the price level of consumer goods, R, P, the price of investment goods, C, and Π, the overall level of price of output, O. E is the cost of the factors of production, I, investment, I', the cost of producing C, and S, savings out of income. (More has been said about the equations and the definitions of their terms in previous chapters.)

In his equations, Keynes presented a novel theory of value, but it went completely unnoticed by the profession, for a lot of reasons, among them too much emphasis was placed on his use of symbols and the truism of his equations rather than on the substance he wanted them to convey. First, in an unusual way of proceeding, the theory was conceived from an exclusively macroeconomic perspective. His prices were indices, not individual prices. They did not depend exclusively on a labour theory of value (as in the Classical 'one-legged' theory), and yet they were still related to labour as part of the cost of production. Nor did prices for Keynes depend on marginal utility or marginal productivity,[26] as in the neoClassical theory (the other 'one-legged' theory), but on average productivity. Most importantly, for Keynes, the market component, supply and demand makes its impact on prices through investment and savings, and on windfall profits (losses). In an ingenious way, by grafting into his equations the impact of market changes $(I - S/O)$, Keynes related prices to both cost of production, and supply and demand (to yield a 'two-legged' theory).

Keynes's equations have embedded in them both a long-term and a short-term component. As in the theory of the Classicals, if, hypothetically, an economy is left to itself, unhindered competition will tend to equalize Savings and Investment, in which case prices will converge to the cost of production and thus to some kind of long-term equilibrium. Unlike in the Classical dichotomy between the long-term cost of production and the short-term supply and demand of the market, however, where market prices gravitate around natural prices, in Keynes, both the short-term and the long-term components are embedded together, and price is a reflection of both.[27]

In Keynes's theory, more interestingly, relative prices, the expression of exchange, are, however, determined neither by the ratios of marginal utilities, as in the neoClassical model, nor by the ratios of labour values, as in the Classicals. They are instead determined by combinations of average costs and sectoral windfall profits (losses). It is through the channel of prices being linked to investment and savings that the rate of interest impacts on the level of prices. Monetary effects thus make an impact on prices through both an as-it-were long-term component, the amount of money needed as payment for E, and a short-term component, the profitability and loss impacts on liquidity preference, and I, I', and S, as a reflection of interest rates.

One can grasp with greater ease Keynes's having been terribly perplexed in the 1930s as to how to create a truly 'two-legged' theory which could deal with the dynamics of the market economy: the *conflicting interests and interactions* of both the two parties to production, *employers*, who decide production, and *workers*, who provide labour, and the two parties in the market, *entrepreneurs*, who are constantly seeking funds, and *rentiers*, who provide those funds. It is with regard to these two conflicting pairs that the pivotal role of the entrepreneur becomes central in Keynes's theory: he is constantly weighing his returns against both the cost of production, which links him to the worker, and the cost of funding, which connects him to the rentier. It is the entrepreneurs' expectation of returns that will ultimately determine how much production will be undertaken.

How now do the characteristics of Keynes's bare-bones model from a macroeconomics perspective compare with those of the Classical and the neoClassical macroeconomic models above?

1. It is **flow analysis**, in which it is the flow of resources searching for the highest return, which has a tendency to cause market prices to move toward a balanced equilibrium. Due to the conflicting interests of the three classes in the economy, the rentiers, the entrepreneurs, and the workers, and given that it is the entrepreneurs who decide production, it is their decisions that ultimately determine the overall market equilibrium. The labour market is not determinant in entrepreneurs' decisions: the level of employment is an outcome of their decisions about production; the ensuing equilibrium may or may not be a full-employment equilibrium.
2. What is produced is what it was decided by the entrepreneurs to produce. That level of production is set dependent on expected sales. **Markets may or may not clear**, however; unlike in the neoClassicals, not every product will necessarily find a 'débouché'. The production of goods and services and their availability are not spontaneous or simultaneous,[28] and expected buying depends on different decisions from expected sales. There is no guarantee that what is produced will be sold or what will be demanded will be met. Keynes's model allows for gluts as well as shortages of production.
3. Keynes's analysis of **factor substitution** is unlike both the Classicals' population–machinery interactions and the marginalism of the neo-Classical theories. Since production for Keynes is a process in which one part of labour is used to produce capital goods and the other part, making use of those capital goods, is used to produce consumer goods, 'production should be so organized as to produce in the most efficient manner compatible with delivery at the dates at which

consumers' demand is expected to become effective' (1936; 1970, p. 215). For Keynes, capital is regarded as an asset that as a 'yield over the course of its life' (ibid.), whose **use value** is determined by market return, not by its physical marginal productivity.[29] It is thus the market that determines both the allocation of capital through time, or **efficiency** (having nothing to do with Pareto's definition), and also therefore the substitution of factors between labour and capital.

4. Keynes regards labour, including both 'the personal services of the entrepreneur and his assistants' and the workers, 'as the sole factors of production'. Since, however, the entrepreneur is the one who decides production, the workers operating 'in a given environment of technique, natural resources, capital equipment and effective demand' (1936; 1970, pp. 213–14), are as if as passive as their environment in the short term.[30] In the market arena for capital, however, the entrepreneur is but one of two deciding classes in the community; the other is the rentier. It is the amount of **capital** needed or available for production that is **the determinant factor** for the economy's overall production.

5. Real wages are determined by the marginal productivity of labour, but money wages depend on the market level of investment and saving, which determines the overall prices. It is the marginal efficiency of capital, which determines the appropriate level of investment, which determines the level of employment to which a real wage then corresponds.[31] The **distribution of income** is an outcome of market decisions depending on entrepreneurs' expected return and the interest rate; wages are residual. It is uniquely determined, in so far as the expectation of yield, the propensity to consume, and the attitude to liquidity are given, but as shifts in one or more of these psychological states occur, the distribution of income will also change.

6. To every production corresponds an income, and that income corresponds to an amount of money. For the economy as a whole the value of total production at cost price (Gross Domestic Product) is equal to total income (Gross National Income), expressed in money, but the level of Price is also dependent on investment and saving, the second component of Fundamental Equation II (FEII A.5 above). For Keynes, **saving** and **investment**, which are the decisions of two distinct individuals, entrepreneurs and rentiers, effect shifts in liquidity, which affect interest rates and in turn investment and saving. It is thus possible for the price to change even in the case in which there is no change in money supply. **Money**, as a medium of exchange and as a store of value, in Keynes's model, is **not neutral**.[32]

7. In Keynes's terminology, the Aggregate Demand and Aggregate Supply do not relate the level of output to the level of price but the level of employment to the expected proceeds, and both are conceived from the entrepreneurs' standpoint, as they perceive them. Aggregate **Supply** represents factor costs plus profits resulting from given amounts of employment. Aggregate **Demand** relates employment to expected return from the labour output. It is the intersection of the two, which gives the *effective demand*, which can be interpreted as the point where marginal aggregate revenue equals marginal aggregate cost. The equilibrium between Aggregate Demand and Aggregate Supply determines employment. Taken in terms of return to the entrepreneur, there is maximization of expected proceeds; taken in terms of employment, however, this is not necessarily the level of the full employment of labour.[33]

It is clear from these sets of characteristics that Keynes's theory, at least in its specification and the meanings attributed to its vocabulary, is different from those of both the Classicals and the neoClassicals. By linking prices to cost of production, by making capital the determinant factor of production, and by giving the pivotal role to the entrepreneur, Keynes had a foot in the Classicals' camp, in the sense that he was a supply-side economist. By relating relative prices to market forces as they interact through saving and investment instead of labour values, and thus putting emphasis on supply and demand, he also had a foot in the neoClassicals' side. His can thus be seen as a hybrid theory of value, different from either of the others. The richness and the complexity embedded in Keynes's simple price equations are far more intricate than those of either of the other theories. He clearly distinguished the roles and decisions of the various classes involved in the macro-dynamics of production in an economy and separated the economic forces related to the organization of production from those of the market finances that support it, in other terms the ownership of capital.

To develop an original and coherent overall theory of employment, interest, and money for an *entrepreneurial economy*, Keynes resorted to the use of unusual symbols, notations, and vocabulary. He introduced unconventional definitions for concepts, such as income, investment, unit of measure, and so on. To counter and convince his critics who did not grasp his terms, he kept trying to re-express elements of his theory by modifying terminology, and readjusting and re-clarifying some of his arguments, all of which made his efforts look like he was being indecisive and changing his mind. That led to an unwarranted, exaggerated belief in the economics profession that in part Keynes's own re-examination of the

Quantity Theory of Money and of his Fundamental Equations, as well as his reinterpretation of Wicksellian interest rates, to name a few facets of his thinking, was a rejection of his theory of *A Treatise on Money*, for that of *The General Theory*. The impatience and rapidity with which the profession, in its interpretation of Keynes, shunted his writings back into the traditional way of thinking left both his original contributions unexploited and his struggle and suggestions as to how to deal methodologically with a dynamic analysis of cyclical fluctuations as well as with particular situations, such as slumps, by moving away from the traditional method based on a tautological concept of equilibrium, ripe for assessment.

Furthermore, the assertion that Keynes did not read his predecessors, based on the observation that he lumped them all together as 'classicals', has not been substantiated. It is argued here that to the contrary; Keynes had a deep understanding and awareness of the controversial theoretical issues that divided not only the Classical from the neoClassical School, but also members within a same school. For him, there was nonetheless a chief common failure of both the Classical and neoClassical theories: their inability to deal with money and to integrate it into their models, principally other than as a *numeraire*, to encapsulate the dynamics of the capitalist market economy. Keynes argued, 'the classical theory, as exemplified in the tradition from Ricardo to Marshall, appears to me to presume that the conditions of a neutral monetary economy are fulfilled' (1933; 1979, p. 675).

In an early draft of *The General Theory* (1933; 1979, p. 68–73), Keynes made a clear distinction between his theory, which he described as one of an entrepreneurial economy, and those of his predecessors, which he labelled theories of a *real-wage economy* or *cooperative economy*. It is the implications of the neutrality of money on prices, saving, investment, and so on which made their models most appropriate to a *cooperative economy* and inappropriate for an *entrepreneurial economy*. To Keynes's mind, this was as true for Ricardo as for Walras, who, as Keynes observed, wrote in Appendix I (III) of his *éléments d'Economie pure*:

> 'l'échange d'épargnes contre capitaux neufs', argues expressly that, corresponding to each possible rate of interest, there is a sum which individuals will save and also a sum which they will invest in new capital assets, that these two aggregates tend to equality with one another, and that the rate of interest is the variable which brings them to equality; so that the rate of interest is fixed at a point where saving, which represents the supply of new capital, is equal to the demand for it. Thus he is strictly in the classical tradition. (1933; 1979, pp. 176–7)

Historians of thought juxtapose the labour theory and the marginal theory of value, to draw a demarcation line between Classical and neoClassical theory, as described above. There is, however, another way of categorizing the development of economic theories. Hicks alluded rightly to that alternative, centred on the role of money and its transmission, in the opposing theories of the Banking and Currency Schools. The Banking School ran from Thornton to Tooke and Wicksell, and its rival, the Currency School thrived from Ricardo to Marshall to Robertson. Keynes's labelling his predecessors, including Marshall and Pigou, as Classicals might well be at odds with certain traditional demarcations but can quite easily be understood in the light of the second type of classification based on monetary theory. They, like many before them, were adherents to a continuing Currency School. On the other hand, 'Malthus, as a contemporary of Ricardo, and Wicksell as a contemporary of Marshall, are obviously to be cited as the leading accredited economists who were discontented with the limitations of classical theory as an explanation of the real world and laboured towards extending its boundaries' (1933; 1979, p. 67). These other economic thinkers, in the tradition of the Banking School, were, for Keynes not Classicals, and it is definitely with them rather than with the whole line of Classicals that Keynes's idea of a monetary theory of production germinated.

One more general remark about his theory in relation to those of the Classicals might yet be made. Just as in Smith and in the Classicals, who, in inquiring into the causes of wealth of a nation, made the distribution of income central to their investigation, Keynes too, in analysing the macroeconomic aspects of a monetary theory of production, made the distribution of income a focus of analysis, on which employment and prosperity depend.

A.4 KEYNES'S THEORY OF INCOME DISTRIBUTION

From the distribution of income perspective, Keynes sympathized with the Classical approach.[34] It seems, however, that Keynes reversed the Ricardo–Malthus analysis of income distribution. In their theory of the diminishing marginal productivity of land, the total shares of the factors of capital and labour, for a given particular land, are determined by the factors' combined marginal productivity, while the rent is assumed residual. These Classicals further assumed wages to be constant (in the long-run) at subsistence level, in order to disentangle the labour shares from those of capital. For both Malthus and Ricardo, the long-term pressure of population would lead to an increased use of the combined factors of capital and labour.

Figure A.1, a very simplistic, schematic model of the Classical theory,

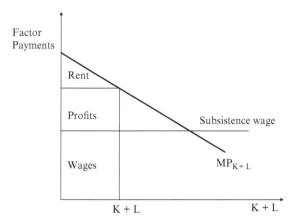

Figure A.1   Ricardo–Malthus theory of income distribution (given land)

shows that both labour and capital simultaneously determine production. While labour wages remain at their irreducible level (equivalent to the marginal disutility of employment), under the pressure of population expansion, profits are squeezed in favour of rent. Both Malthus and Ricardo, in their analysis, were aware of an economic implication: the squeeze of the entrepreneur's profit to the benefit of the rentier. Both advocated a policy of avoiding reaching an ultimate stationary-state where the entrepreneur would be obliterated. Thus, to ease the strain on domestic agricultural production caused by population increase, Ricardo proposed unrestricted imports of corn, while Malthus, a slow-down in population growth.

In Keynes, since it is the entrepreneur who determines the volume of investment, his expectation alone determines the level of production. This idea can be represented in a diagram, analogous to the one above representing Malthus and Ricardo. In Figure A.2, the diminishing marginal productivity of capital determines the payment to capital, which includes both the profit of the entrepreneurs and the rent of the rentiers, combined, the providers of investment funds. It assumes wages residual. These relationships are described in Marshall's theory of distribution of which Keynes was well aware.

As can be seen from the very simple picture of Figure A.2, if the net cost of capital is assumed constant, an increase in the capital fund for a given value of the marginal product of capital produces **a squeeze in the share of capital**. The ultimate result is the complete extinction of windfall profits. Since gross return to capital includes its 'replacement cost', if investment is pushed to the point where the value of the marginal product of capital

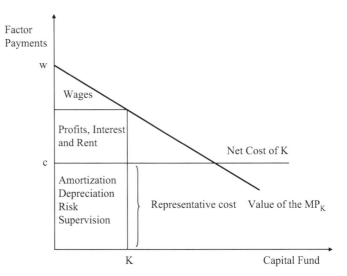

Figure A.2   Keynes's ultra simplified theory (with given technology)

is just equal to its net cost and there are no profits, there will be zero net payment on capital, signalling the disappearance of the rentier. While Malthus's and Ricardo's policies were designed to prevent the economy's theoretically reaching this critical steady-state equilibrium, Keynes's theory attempted to bring the economy pre-emptively to an equilibrium tied to near full-employment.

In the latter scenario, as rent and profit are squeezed, the wage-bill, however, increases. **NB:** In the Ricardo–Malthus diagram (Figure A.1), the ultimate stationary-state point corresponds to the maximum population that can be sustained by the full exploitation of resources under given technology. In Keynes's Figure A.2, as capital is exploited to its maximum for a given technology, that point is the maximum return for those engaged in production, the entrepreneurs and workers, as opposed to the rentiers. Of course, in Keynes's *The General Theory*, the analysis and definition of terms are more complicated than those represented by the depiction in Figure A.2. The much more sophisticated representation, using Keynes's actual terminology and definitions, focused on the level of capital and its prospective yield, is developed in Chapter 5, in the discussion of the framework of his *The General Theory*.

NOTES

1. It is not the purpose here to go into the philosophical aspects of Keynes's methodology, for example, his uses of deduction/induction, objectivity/subjectivity, means and ends, which are discussed by A.M. Carabelli (1988) and R.M. O'Donnell (1989).

2. Hicks, in his first review of Keynes, pointed out that the introduction of expectations into Keynes's *General Theory* was 'the most revolutionary thing about this book', although he felt he had to point out that this peculiar but 'very significant type of analysis' was 'not altogether a new discovery'. (1936; 1982, II, p. 86).

3. Taken in the senses found in utilitarianism and marginalism, as developed by Walras, Menger, Jevons, and their successors, but also understood as a general equilibrium, as encapsulated in Hicks's *Value and Capital* (1939).

4. All this is found encapsulated in Hicks (1939, ch. XX).

5. Lerner (1974, p. 38).

6. This is what is usually referred to as Say's law. Say's time predates the neoWalrasian formulation, and one makes the argument that in the descriptive world of a market economy 'creates' refers to a causal relation. In the neoWalrasian setting, it would be more logically correct to say 'supply meets its own demand'.

7. More will be said about price rigidities below.

8. By the Classical school is meant here those who participated in the elaboration of the labour theory of value. It is understood that this theory went through tremendous changes between Smith and Ricardo, with Ricardo's work representing the most developed state of the core of the theory. After Ricardo, the theory went through transformations in the hands of Mill, Marx, and others. For the modest purpose here of simply sketching the Classical theory of value, it is its exposition in Ricardo which is retained.

9. Capital 'will naturally seek for it that employment which is most advantageous' (Ricardo 1817; 1952, II, p. 111). '[R]estless desire on the part of all the employers of stock, to quit a less profitable for a more advantageous business . . . has a strong tendency to equalize the rate of profits' (ibid.).

10. '[I]t appears then that wages are subject to a rise or fall from two causes: 1st the supply and demand of labourers. 2nd the price of the commodities on which wages of labour are expanded' (1817; 1952, II, p. 97).

11. '[R]estless desire on the part of all the employers of stock, to quit a less profitable for a more advantageous business' (Ricardo, 1817; 1952, II, p. 111).

12. The Classical supply-side economics is different from the modern neoWalrasian supply-side economics. To the Classicals, it meant the study of a market economy through its structure of production, which subsumes the element of demand. The neoWalrasian approach depends on a clear dichotomy between aggregate demand and aggregate supply. One aggregate is the flip side of the other.

13. The very exceptional situation in which the former actually converges into the latter can, however, occur.

14. There has been, and continues to be, lots of controversy as to how to reduce the cost of production to a simple expression of labour, using concepts such as dated-, abstract-, incorporated-, command-labour. The issue here is to express relative prices as formulated in the theory of value in the most simple terms, so they can be compared with those of the neoWalrasian formulation.

15. Ricardo (1817; 1952, II, p. 449).

16. Ricardo (1817; 1952, II, p. 292).

17. Ricardo (1817; 1952, III, p. 383).

18. Ricardo (1817; 1952, II, p. 292).

19. Since the distribution between profits and wages was the main focus, and any change in the money wage affects the rate of profit, and the money wage was itself dependent on the price of the subsistence commodity, it was the price of corn which retained attention. Also, exchange was conceived as a relative amount of labour rather than a relative amount of money, hence the total amount of money related to the total value

of transactions (directly deducible as per the Quantity Theory of Money) is of less relevance to the labour theory of value.

20. For example, Dobb, Myrdhal, Sraffa, Samuelson, and Hollander.
21. See Samuelson (1991). From a neoWalrasian perspective, Samuelson has been perhaps understandably unable to see how price could be determined by cost of production without taking market supply and demand into consideration. What he does not appreciate is the Classicals' embeddedness of market supply and demand in factor pricing on the production side.
22. The debates about credit were in their infancy, and credit itself as a component of a more sophisticated financial realm was just beginning to develop.
23. See Pigou (1968) and Malinvaud (1977).
24. 'The classical theory, as exemplified in the tradition from Ricardo to Marshall, appears to me to presume that the conditions of a neutral monetary economy are fulfilled . . . Malthus, as a contemporary of Ricardo, and Wicksell as a contemporary of Marshall, are obviously to be cited as the leading accredited economists who were discontented with the limitations of the classical theory as an explanation of the real world' (extracts of typed notes of drafts of *The General Theory*, 1933, in Keynes, 1979, p. 67).
25. Even though implicit in *The General Theory*.
26. Although marginal productivity can creep in for different reasons, see Keynes, 1979, p. 72.
27. Although Keynes did not write an equation for P' in his notation, Hayek did. It is explained in Chapter 3 why Hayek's equation for P' does not convey Keynes's definition of investment goods.
28. From the neoWalrasian tautological spontaneous realization of exchange, that is, that for every sell there is an instantaneous buy (what is given is exactly what is received; it cannot be otherwise). Keynes's context is, however, a state of the world in which the 'givers' (sellers, firms, investors, and so on) are constantly wondering whether their transactions will be completed according to contractual obligation and whether their commitments, which have an embedded time-margin, will allow them still to be viable, given the myriad possible changes in intervening circumstances.
29. 'If capital becomes less scarce, the excess yield will diminish without its having become less productive – at least in the physical sense' (1936; 1970, p. 213).
30. Even when the environment changes in the long run.
31. 'Thus the volume of employment is not determined by the marginal disutility of labour measured in terms of real wages, except in so far as the supply of labour available at a given real wage sets a maximum level to employment. The propensity to consume and the rate of new investment determine between them the volume of employment, and the volume of employment is uniquely related to a given level of real wages – not the other way around' (1936; 1970, p. 215).
32. The concern for Keynes was the reality of the fact that when non-barter transactions are conducted, frequently what is given now has only the promise of a counterpart, something which will be received later, and even if it is already quantified, there is no guarantee that its 'store of value' will remain unaltered. The 'givers' (sellers, firms, investors, and so on) exist in a money-based credit economy in which their ongoing actions are also dependent upon the promissory payments of the 'receivers' (buyers, consumers, borrowers, and so on).
33. In fact Keynes's Aggregate Supply and Aggregate Demand refer to employment and expected proceeds, not to two terms relating Price to Production as became the widely used understanding of them in macroeconomics.
34. See his Chapter 16, 'Sundry Observations on the Nature of Capital', section II (1936; 1970, pp. 213–17).

Select bibliography

The literature dealing with Keynes is voluminous, authored in virtually every language in which modern economics is discussed. This bibliography encompasses only a subset of these works, relatively small to the whole and mainly works in English. There is, however, in this vast collection so much recycling of words and quotations from the same works and correspondence that here a great deal of these works not directly related to Keynes's theory can be left aside.

Not all the works on Keynesianism and Keynesian economics could be considered pertinent to this study, which is devoted exclusively to the development of Keynes's own ideas, but any omission among those which might be considered important is not intentional. The goal here is not to review the literature, but to concentrate on the small number of authors who at the start derailed Keynes's theory. The bibliography is organized along the following lines. The first section contains the very few authors whose works are key to this study and considered in depth. In the second is a selection of reviews of both the *Treatise on Money* and *The General Theory*. Specific themes are addressed in the next three sections, related especially to the transition from the *Treatise* to *The General Theory* and to the theoretical aspects which are key to both works, the Fundamental Equations and the Aggregate Demand and Aggregate Supply. The remainder of the bibliography is comprised of works which might have relevance to specific chapters in this book or ones which are grouped in a general category at the end. Of course, the four-volume collection edited by J.C. Wood (1984) *John Maynard Keynes. Critical Assessments* contains many more essays not mentioned below.

Some of the works cited are significant to one or more of the bibliographic sections, but for the sake of avoiding repetition, any work is noted only once. Also, not all of the contents of these references are pertinent to the present study; therefore, in many cases, it is only the portions that deal with Keynes *per se* that are of interest.

Given the enormous literature on Keynes and Keynesianism and the flippant way in economics in which consensuses are formed to become the truth, there is need for a concordance to be undertaken to compare, in the light of this book, what was said at the source, what was ascribed first-hand as having been said, and then what was made second-hand of those accounts, multiplied over and over. There is a delightful abundance of aberrations: witness Caldwell, 'The barebones model of the *Treatise* is simply Marshall with a Wicksellian twist' (Hayek 1931; 1995, p. 26), Klein, 'Keynes apparently thought that he was bringing out the heart of his theory in the exposition of his pretentious "fundamental equations," but the "fundamental equations" were not the essential contribution of the book' (1966, p. 17), or Stiglitz, 'It is widely recognised that the assumption that wages are rigid is central to Keynes' explanation of the persistence of unemployment' (1986, p. 153). Having said this, it is not claimed that everyone, everytime, everywhere should always run back to the sources nor, as Hicks once said, that the source should be taken as divine, but when a claim is made, it must be able to stand, as few presently do.

THE AUTHORS AND THEIR WORKS KEY TO THIS STUDY

Hamouda, O.F. (1993), *John R. Hicks. The Economist's Economist*, Oxford and Cambridge, MA: Blackwell.

Hayek, F.A. (1931), *Prices and Production*, London: Routledge.

Hayek, F.A. (1931), 'Reflections on the Pure Theory of Money of Mr. J.M. Keynes', *Economica*, **33** (August), 270–95; reprinted (1995), in F.A. Hayek, *Contra Keynes and Cambridge. Essays, Correspondence*, B. Caldwell (ed.), in *The Collected Works of F.A. Hayek*, S. Kresge (ed.) London: Routledge, vol. IX, pp. 121–46.

Hayek, F.A. (1932), 'Reflections on the Pure Theory of Money of Mr. J.M. Keynes (continued)', *Economica*, **35** (February), 22–44; reprinted (1995), in F.A. Hayek, *Contra Keynes and Cambridge. Essays, Correspondence*, B. Caldwell (ed.), F.A. Hayek, *The Collected Works of F.A. Hayek*, S. Kresge (ed.) London: Routledge, vol. IX, pp. 174–97.

Hayek, F.A. (1963), 'The Economics of the 1930s as seen from London', reprinted (1995), in F.A. Hayek, *Contra Keynes and Cambridge. Essays, Correspondence*, B. Caldwell (ed.), in *The Collected Works of F.A. Hayek*, S. Kresge (ed.) London: Routledge, vol. IX, pp. 49–73.

Hayek, F.A. (1966), 'Personal Recollections of Keynes and the Keynesian Revolution', reprinted (1995), in F.A. Hayek, *Contra Keynes and Cambridge. Essays, Correspondence*, B. Caldwell (ed.), in *The Collected Works of F.A. Hayek*, S. Kresge (ed.) London: Routledge, vol. IX, pp. 240–246.

Hayek, F.A. (1983), 'The Keynes Centenary: The Austrian Critique', *The Economist*, June 11, 45–8; reprinted (1995), in F.A. Hayek, *Contra Keynes and Cambridge. Essays, Correspondence*, B. Caldwell (ed.), in

The Collected Works of F.A. Hayek, S. Krege (ed.) London: Routledge, vol. IX, pp. 247–56.

Hicks, J. (1939), *Value and Capital*, Oxford: Clarendon Press.

Hicks, J. (1950), *A Contribution to the Theory of the Trade Cycle*, Oxford: Clarendon.

Hicks, J. (1974), *The Crisis of Keynesian Economics*, Oxford: Blackwell.

Hicks, J. (1979), 'On Coddington's interpretation: a reply', *Journal of Economic Literature*, **17** (3), 989–75, reprinted (1989) in J.C. Wood and R.N. Woods (eds), *Sir John R. Hicks. Critical Assessments*, London: Routledge, vol. III, pp. 209–16.

Hicks, J. (1935a), 'Wages and interest: the dynamic problem', *Economic Journal*, **45** (178), 156–68; reprinted (1982) in J. Hicks, *Money, Interest and Wages*, Cambridge, MA: Harvard University Press, pp. 64–79.

Hicks, J. (1936), 'Mr Keynes's Theory of employment', *Economic Journal*, **46** (182), 238–53; reprinted (1982), 'The General Theory: a first impression', in J. Hicks, *Money, Interest and Wages*, Cambridge, MA: Harvard University Press, pp. 83–99.

Hicks, J. (1980), '*IS-LM*–an explanation', *Journal of Post-Keynesian Economics*, **3** (2), 139–51; reprinted (1982) in J. Hicks, *Money, Interest and Wages*, Cambridge, MA: Harvard University Press, pp. 318–31.

Hicks, J. (1982b), 'Mr. Keynes and the Classics', 1937, in J. Hicks, *Money, Interest and Wages*, Cambridge, MA: Harvard University Press, pp. 100–115.

Keynes, J.M. *The Collected Writings of John Maynard Keynes*, D. Moggridge (ed.) and E. Johnson (ed.), London: Macmillan, New York: St. Martin's Press, for the Royal Economic Society:

(1971) *A Tract on Monetary Reform*, vol. IV, 1923.

(1971) *A Treatise on Money, 1, The Pure Theory of Money*, vol. V.

(1971) *A Treatise on Money: 2, The Applied Theory of Money*, vol. VI.

(1973a) *The General Theory of Employment, Interest, and Money*, vol. VII.

(1973b) *The General Theory and After: Pt. 1, Preparation*, vol. XIII.

(1979) *The General Theory and After: A Supplement*, vol. XXIX.

(1983) *Economic Articles and Correspondence*: *Investment and Editorial*, vol. VIII.

(1987) *The General Theory and After: Pt. 2, Defence and Development*, vol. XIV.

(1989) *Bibliography and Index*, vol. XXX.

Keynes, J.M. (1930), *A Treatise on Money*, 2 vols, New York: Harcourt, Brace.

Keynes, J.M. (1931a), '"Mr. Keynes" Theory of Money: a rejoinder', *Economic Journal*, **41** (163), 412–23.

Keynes, J.M. (1931b), 'The Pure Theory of Money. A reply to Dr. Hayek', *Economica*, **34** (November), pp. 387–97.

Keynes, J.M. (1937), 'The "Ex-Ante" Theory of the Rate of Interest', *Economic Journal*, **47**, (188), 663–9.

Keynes, J.M. (1970), *The General Theory of Employment, Interest, and Money*, London: Macmillan, 1936.

Robertson, D.H. (1931), 'Mr. Keynes' Theory of Money', *Economic Journal*, **41** (163), 395–411.

Robertson, D.H. (1936), 'Some notes on Mr. Keynes' *General Theory of Employment*', *The Quarterly Journal of Economics*, **51** (1), 168–191.

Robertson, D.H. (1938), 'Mr. Keynes and "Finance"', *Economic Journal*, **48** (191), 555–6.

Rymes, T.K. (1989), *Keynes's Lectures, 1932–35, Notes of a Representative Student: A Synthesis of Lecture Notes Taken by Students at Keynes's Lectures in the 1930s Leading Up to the Publication of The General Theory*, Ann Arbor, MI: University of Michigan Press.

Sraffa, P. (1932), 'Dr. Hayek on money and capital', *Economic Journal*, **42**, 42–53; reprinted (1995), in F.A. Hayek, *Contra Keynes and Cambridge. Essays, Correspondence*, B. Caldwell (ed.), in *The Collected Works of F.A. Hayek*, S. Kresge (ed.) London: Routledge, vol. IX, pp. 198–209.

Wicksell, K. (1907), 'The influence of the rate of interest on prices', *Economic Journal*, **17** (June), pp. 213–20.

Wicksell, K. (1934, vol. I; 1935, vol. II). *Lectures on Political Economy*, L. Robbins (ed.) and E. Classen (tr.) London: Routledge and K. Paul.

Wicksell, K. (1936), *Interest and Prices* [(1898) Geldzins und Güterpreise], R.F. Kahn trans., London: Macmillan.

Wicksell, K. (1999), *Selected Essays in Economics*, 2 vols, B. Sandelin (ed.), London: Routledge.

REVIEWS OF *A TREATISE ON MONEY*

Hardy, C.H. (1931), '[Review of] *A Treatise on Money* by John Maynard Keynes', *The American Economic Review*, **21** (1), 150–55.

Hawtrey, R.G. (1931), '[Review of] *A Treatise on Money* by John Maynard Keynes', *Journal of the Royal Statistical Society*, **94** (4), 618–23.

Hicks, J. (1967), *Critical Essays in Monetary Theory*, Oxford: Clarendon Press.

James, F.C. (1931), 'The insecurity of industry', *Annals of the American Academy of Political and Social Science*, **154** (March), 173–4.

Mitchell, G. (1931), '[Review of] *A Treatise on Money* by John Maynard

Keynes', *International Affairs* (*Royal Institute of International Affairs 1931–1939*), **10** (3), 397–9.

Simmons, E.S. (1933), 'Mr. Keynes's control scheme', *The American Economic Review*, **23** (2), 264–73.

Stamp, J.C. (1931), 'Mr. Keynes' Treatise on Money', *Economic Journal*, **41** (162), 241–49.

Theobald, D. (1932), '[Review of] *A Treatise on Money* by John Maynard Keynes', *The Journal of Land & Public Utility Economics*, **8** (1), 110–12.

Williams, J.W. (1931), 'The monetary doctrines of J.M. Keynes', *Quarterly Journal of Economics*, **45** (4), 547–87.

REVIEWS OF *THE GENERAL THEORY*

Beckhart, B.H. (1936), '[Review of] *The General Theory of Employment, Interest and Money* by John Maynard Keynes', *Political Science Quarterly*, **51** (4), 600–603.

F[lux], A.W. (1936), '[Review of] *The General Theory of Employment, Interest and Money* by John Maynard Keynes', *Journal of the Royal Statistical Society*, **99** (2), 383–8.

Hansen, A.H. (1936), 'Mr. Keynes on underemployment equilibrium', *Journal of Political Economy*, **44** (5), 667–86.

Hardy, C.O. (1936), '[Review of] *The General Theory of Employment, Interest and Money* by John Maynard Keynes', *American Economic Review*, **26** (3), 490–93.

Harrod, R.F. (1937), 'Mr. Keynes and traditional theory', *Econometrica*, **5** (1), 74–86.

Knight, F.H. (1937), 'Unemployment: And Mr. Keynes's revolution in economic theory', *Canadian Journal of Economics and Political Science/ Revue canadienne d'economique et de science politique*, **3** (1), 100–23.

Landauer, C. (1937), 'A break in Keynes's theory of interest', *American Economic Review*, **27** (2), 260–6.

Leontief, W.W. (1936), 'The fundamental assumption of Mr. Keynes' Monetary Theory of Unemployment', *Quarterly Journal of Economics*, **51** (1), 192–7.

Meade, J.M. (1937), 'A simplified model of Mr. Keynes' system', *Review of Economic Studies*, **4** (2), 98–107.

Pigou, A.C. (1936), 'Mr. J.M. Keynes' General Theory of Employment, Interest and Money', *Economica*, New Series, **3** (10), 115–32.

Robertson, D.H. (1936), 'Some notes on Mr. Keynes' General Theory of Employment', *Quarterly Journal of Economics*, **51** (1), 168–91.

Schumpeter, J.A. (1936), '[Review of] *The General Theory of Employment,*

Interest and Money by John Maynard Keynes', *Journal of the American Statistical Association*, **31** (196), 791–5.

Viner, J. (1936), '[Review of] *The General Theory of Employment, Interest and Money* by John Maynard Keynes', *Quarterly Journal of Economics*, **51** (1), 147–67.

More reviews are to be found in Backhouse, R. (1999), *Keynes, Contemporary Response to the General Theory*, South Bend, IN: St Augustine's Press.

STUDIES OF THE TRANSITION FROM THE *TREATISE* TO *THE GENERAL THEORY*

Dimand, R.W. (1988), *The Origins of the Keynesian Revolution: The Development of Keynes' Theory of Employment and Output*, Stanford, CA: Stanford University Press.

Hirai, T. (2008), *Keynes's Theoretical Development: From the Tract to the General Theory*, London: Routledge.

Khan, R. (1978), 'Some aspects of the development of Keynes's thought', *Journal of Economic Literature*, **16** (2), 545–59.

Klein, L.R. (1966), *The Keynesian Revolution*, 2nd edn, New York: Macmillan.

Laidler, D.E.W. (1999), *Fabricating the Keynesian Revolution: Studies of the Inter-war Literature on Money, the Cycle, and Unemployment*, Cambridge: Cambridge University Press.

Lerner, A. (1974), 'From the Treatise on Money to the General Theory', *Journal of Economic Literature*, **12** (1), 38–42.

Patinkin, D. (1976), *Keynes' Monetary Thought: A Study of its Development*, Durham, NC: Duke University Press.

Patinkin, D. (1982), *Anticipations of the General Theory and Other Essays on Keynes*, Chicago, IL: University of Chicago Press.

Patinkin, D. and J.C. Leith (eds) (1978), *Keynes, Cambridge and the General Theory: The Process of Criticism and Discussion Connected with the Development of the General Theory*, Toronto: University of Toronto Press.

SPECIFIC PUBLICATIONS ON KEYNES'S FUNDAMENTAL EQUATIONS

Adarkar, B.P. (1933), 'The 'Fundamental Error' in Keynes's *Treatise*', *American Economic Review*, **23** (1), 87.

Hansen, A.H. (1932), 'A fundamental error in Keynes's *Treatise on Money*', *American Economic Review*, **22** (3), 462.

Keynes J.M. (1932), 'Keynes's fundamental equations: a note', *American Economic Review*, **22** (4), 691–2.

Rubner-Petersen, K. (1934), 'The error in the "Fundamental Equations": a new interpretation', *American Economic Review*, **24** (4). 595–602.

SPECIFIC WORKS ON KEYNES'S AGGREGATE DEMAND AND AGGREGATE SUPPLY

Anderson, B.M. (1945), 'Equilibrium creates purchasing power; a refutation of Keynes' attack on the doctrine that aggregate supply creates aggregate demand – basic fallacies in the Keynesian system', *The Chase Economic Bulletin*, New York: The Chase National Bank.

Casarosa, C. (1984), 'The microfoundations of Keynes's aggregate supply and expected demand analysis: a reply', *Economic Journal*, **94** (376), 941–45.

Chick, V. (1983), *Macroeconomics after Keynes: A Reconsideration of the General Theory*, Oxford: Philip Allan.

Encarnación, J. (1993), *On Keynes' Aggregate Supply Function*, Quezon City: University of the Philippines, School of Economics.

Garello, J. (1966), *Le Contenu de la courbe keynesienne d'offre globale*, Paris: CUJAS.

Hawtrey, R.G (1954), 'Keynes and supply functions', *Economic Journal*, **64** (256), 834–39.

Hawtrey, R.G. (1956), 'Keynes and supply functions', *Economic Journal*, **66** (263) 482–84.

Holmes, J.M. (1972), 'The Keynesian aggregate supply function for labor', *Journal of the American Statistical Association*, **67** (340), 797–802.

King, J. (1993), *Aggregate Supply and Demand Analysis since Keynes: A Partial History*, Bundoora, Australia: La Trobe University, School of Economics and Commerce.

Neissen, H. (1961), 'Keynes' aggregate supply function: a comment', *Economic Journal*, **71** (284), 849–852.

Robertson, D.H. and H.G. Johnson (1955), 'Keynes and supply functions', *Economic Journal*, **65** (259), 474–8.

Torr, C. (1984), 'The microfoundations of Keynes's aggregate supply and expected demand analysis: a comment', *Economic Journal*, **94** (376), 936–40.

Weintraub, S. (1957), 'The micro-foundations of aggregate demand and supply', *Economic Journal*, **67** (267), 455–70.

Wells, P. (1960), 'Keynes' aggregate supply function: a suggested interpretation', *Economic Journal*, **70** (279), 536–42.

Wells, P. (1961), 'Mr. Wells' aggregate supply function – a further comment', *Economic Journal*, **71** (283), 636–7.

Wells P. (1985), 'The aggregate supply curve: Keynes and downwardly sticky money wages', *Journal of Economic Education*, **16** (4), 297–304.

PREFACE, INTRODUCTION, AND CONCLUSION

Blanchard, O. (2005), *Macroeconomics*, 4th edn, Eaglewood Cliffs, NJ: Prentice Hall.

Boland, L.A. (2003), *The Foundations of Economic Method: A Popperian Perspective*, London: Routledge.

Carabelli, A.M. (1988), *On Keynes's Method*, Basingstoke: Macmillan.

Clarke, P.F. (1988), *The Keynesian Revolution in the Making, 1924–1936*, Oxford and New York: Clarendon Press/Oxford University Press.

Hamouda, O.F. (2005), '[Review of] *The Foundations of Economic Method: A Popperian Perspective* by Lawrence A. Bolland', April, http:// eh.net/ bookreviews/lbrary/0924.

Hayek, F.A. (1995), *Contra Keynes and Cambridge: Essays, Correspondence*, B. Caldwell (ed.), vol. IX, in *The Collected Works of F.A. Hayek*, S. Kresge (ed.), London: Routledge.

Hutchison, T.W. (1977), *Keynes versus the 'Keynesians': An Essay in the Thinking of J.M. Keynes and the Accuracy of its Interpretation by his Followers*, London: Institute of Economic Affairs.

Kahn, R.F. (1984), *The Making of Keynes' General Theory*, Cambridge: Cambridge University Press.

Leijonhufvud, A. (1968), *On Keynesian Economics and the Economics of Keynes: A Study in Monetary Theory*, New York: Oxford University Press.

Marzola, A. and F. Silva (eds) (1994), *John Maynard Keynes: Language and Method*, R. Davies (tr.) Aldershot, UK and Brookfield, VT, USA: Edward Elgar.

O'Donnell, R.M. (1989), *Keynes: Philosophy, Economics and Politics. The Philosophical Foundations of Keynes' Thought and their Influence on his Economics and Politics*, Basingstoke: Macmillan.

Pasinetti, L.L. (2007), *Keynes and the Cambridge Keynesians: A 'Revolution in Economics' to be Accomplished*, Cambridge: Cambridge University Press.

Robinson, J. (1988), 'What has become of the Keynesian revolution?', in Milo Keynes (ed.), *Essays on John Maynard Keynes*, Cambridge University Press, pp. 123–31.

Woodford, M. (2003), *Interest & Prices*, Princeton, NJ: Princeton University Press.
Worswick, G.D.N. and J.A. Trevithick (eds) (1983), *Keynes and the Modern World: Proceedings of the Keynes Centenary Conference, King's College, Cambridge*, Cambridge: Cambridge University Press.

CHAPTER 1 AND APPENDIX: CLASSICALS, NEOCLASSICALS, AND KEYNES

Ahiakpor, J.C.W. (1998), *Keynes and the Classics Reconsidered*, Boston, MA: Kluwer Academic.
Bernanke, B. (2009), 'The Crisis and the Policy Response', Josiah Charles Stamp Lecture, London School of Economics, January 13, available at http://www.lse.ac.uk/collections/LSEPublicLecturesAndEvents/events/2008/20081203t1159z001.htm
Böhm-Bawerk, E. von (1890), *Capital and Interest*, London: Macmillan.
Böhm-Bawerk, E. von (1891), *The Positive Theory of Capital*, London: Macmillan.
Böhm-Bawerk, E. von (1895), 'The positive theory of capital and its critics', *Quarterly Journal of Economics*, **9** (1), 113–31.
Caspari, V. (1989), *Walras, Marshall, Keynes*, Berlin: Duncker and Humbolt.
Convert, B. and F. Héran (2000), *L'entrepreneur chez Keynes*, Paris: Harmattan.
Corry, B.A. (1959), 'Malthus and Keynes – a reconsideration', *Economic Journal*, **69** (276), 717–24.
Ferguson, N. (2008), 'The age of obligation', FT Comment and Analysis, *Financial Times*, December 19.
Fischer, S. (1972), 'Keynes-Wicksell and neoclassical models of money and growth', *American Economic Review*, **62** (5), 880–90.
Fisher, I. (1963), *The Purchasing Power of Money*, 2nd edn, New York: Kelley.
Gerrard, B. (1995), 'Keynes, the Keynesians and the Classics: a suggested interpretation', *The Economic Journal*, **105** (429), 445–58.
Hamouda, O.F. (2001), 'The Neoclassical Classical fallacy', *International Journal of Applied Economics and Econometrics*, **9** (2), 147–69.
Hamouda, O.F. (2002), 'The history of economic thought of the last 200 years through its schools and its canons', *International Journal of Applied Economics and Econometrics*, **10** (1), 55–68.
Hollander, S. (1979), *The Economics of David Ricardo*, Toronto: University of Toronto Press.

Jevons, W. S. (1957), *The Theory of Political Economy*, 5th edn, New York: Kelley and Millman.

Marshall, A. (1966), *Principles of Economics: An Introductory Volume*, 8th edn, London: Macmillan.

Marshall, A. (1991), *Money, Credit & Commerce*, Fairfield, NJ: A.M. Kelley.

Menger, C. (1981), *Principles of Economics*, New York: New York University Press.

Mill, J.S. (1965), *Principles of Political Economy*, in J.M. Robson (ed.), *Collected Works of John Stuart Mill*, vols II and III, Toronto: University of Toronto Press.

O'Leary, J.J. (1942), 'Malthus and Keynes', *Journal of Political Economy*, **50** (6), 901–19.

Pareto, V. (1927), *Manuel d'économie politique*, 2nd edn, Paris: M. Giard.

Phelps, E. (2008), 'Keynes had no sure cure for slumps', FT Comment. Opinion, *Financial Times*, November 5.

Pigou, A.C. (1951), *Keynes's 'General Theory'; a Retrospective View*, London: Macmillan.

Pigou, A.C. (1960), *The Economics of Welfare*, 4th edn, London: Macmillan.

Pigou, A.C. (1968), *The Theory of Unemployment*, New York: A.M. Kelly.

Ricardo, D. (1952; 1817), *On the Principles of Political Economy and Taxation*, in vols II–IV of P. Sraffa (ed.) with M.H. Dobb, *The Works and Correspondence of David Ricardo*, Indianapolis, IN: Liberty Fund.

Rutherford, R.P. (1987), 'Malthus and Keynes', *Oxford Economic Papers*, New Series, **39** (1), 175–89.

Samuelson, P.A. (1991), 'Sraffa's other leg', *Economics Journal*, **101** (406), 570–574.

Walras, L. (1900), *Éléments d'économie politique pure, ou théorie de la richesse sociale*, 4th edn, Lausanne: Rouge.

Walras, L. (1965), *Elements of Pure Economics or The Theory of Social Wealth*, W. Jaffé (tr.), Homewood, Il: R.D. Irwin for the American Economic Association and the Royal Economic Society.

CHAPTER 2: PERSPECTIVES ON MONETARY THEORY, KEYNES, AND OTHERS

Ahmad, S. (1970), 'Is money net wealth?', *Oxford Economic Papers*, New Series, **22** (3), 357–61.

Ahmad, S. (1975), 'The "Paradox of Bliss" and money as net wealth: comment', *Journal of Money, Credit and Banking*, **7** (3), 385–90.

Ahmad, S. (1977), 'Transactions demand for money and the quantity theory', *Quarterly Journal of Economics*, **91** (2), 327–36.

Andrew, A.P. (1899), 'What ought to be called money', *Quarterly Journal of Economics*, **13** (1), 219–27.

Blaug, M. (1995), *The Quantity Theory of Money from Locke to Keynes and Friedman*, Aldershot, UK and Brookfield, VT, USA: Edward Elgar.

Bridel, P. (1987), *Cambridge Monetary Thought: The Development of Saving-Investment Analysis from Marshall to Keynes*, Basingstoke: Macmillan.

Brunner, K. and A.H. Meltzer (1988), 'Money and credit in the monetary transmission process', *American Economic Review*, May, 446–51.

Buiter, W.H. (2002), 'The fiscal theory of the price level: a critique', *Economic Journal*, **112** (481), 459–80.

Buiter, W.H. (2005), 'New developments in monetary economics: two ghosts, two eccentricities, a fallacy, a mirage and a mythos', *Economic Journal*, Conference Papers, **115** (502), C1–C31; given as Royal Economic Society 2004 Hahn Lecture.

Cantillon, R. (1931), *Essai sur la nature du commerce en general*, H. Higgs (ed. and tr.), London: Macmillan, 1755.

Ceva, G. (1711), *De re nummaria, quoad Fieri potuit geometrice tractata, ad illustrissimos et excellentissimos dominos Praesidem Quaestoresque hujus arciduaclis Caessaraei Magistratus Mantuae*, Mantua: Albertum Pazzonum.

Cochran, J.P. and F.R. Glahe (1999), *The Hayek–Keynes Debate: Lessons for Current Business Cycle Research*, Lewiston, NY: Edwin Mellen Press.

Dice, C.A. and P. Schaffner (1939), 'A neglected component of the money supply', *American Economic Review*, **29** (3), 514–20.

Dillard, D. (1942), 'Keynes and Proudhon', *Journal of Economic History*, **2** (1), 63–76.

Dillard, D.D. (1948), *The Economics of John Maynard Keynes: The Theory of a Monetary Economy,* New York: Prentice-Hall.

Dow, S.C. and P.E. Earl, (1982), *Money Matters. A Keynesian Approach to Monetary Economics*, Oxford: Martin Robertson.

Eshag, E. (1964), *From Marshall to Keynes. An Essay on Monetary Theory of the Cambridge School*, Oxford: Basil Blackwell.

Fisher, I. (1963), *The Purchasing Power of Money: Its Determination and Relation to Credit, Interest and Crises*, New York: Macmillan.

Gilbert, J.C. (1982), *Keynes's Impact on Monetary Economics*, Sevenoaks: Butterworth.

Goodhart, C.A.E. (1987), 'Why do banks need a central bank', *Oxford Economic Papers*, **39**, 75–89.

Goodhart, C.A.E. (2002), 'The endogenity of money', in V. Chick, P. Arestis, M. Desai, S.C. Dow (eds), *Money, Macroeconomics and Keynes*, London: Routledge.

Hamouda, O.F., R. Rowley and B. Wolf (1989), *The Future of the International Monetary System*, Aldershot, UK and Brookfield, VT, USA, Cheltenham: Edward Elgar.

Harrod, R. (1969), *Money*, London: Macmillan.

Hawtrey, R. (1930), 'Money and index numbers', *Journal of the Royal Society*, **93** (1), 64–85.

Hicks, J. (1935b), 'A suggestion for simplifying the theory of money', *Economica*, New Series, **2** (3), in 1–19; reprinted (1982) in J. Hicks, *Money, Interest and Wages,* Cambridge, MA: Harvard University Press, 46–63.

Hicks, J. (1969), *A Theory of Economic History*, London: Oxford University Press.

Holtrop, M.W. (1929), 'Theories of the velocity of circulation of money in earlier economic literature', *Economic History* (Supplement to *Economic Journal*), **1**, 503–24.

Hume, D. (1752), 'Of money', *Political Discourses*, in S.G. Medenna and W.J. Samuels (eds) (2003), *The History of Economic Thought: A Reader*, London: Routledge, pp. 135–39.

Knapp, G.F. (1973), *The State Theory of Money*, Clifton, NY: Augustus M. Kelley, 1924.

Laidler, D.E.W. (1977), *The Demand for Money. Theories and Evidence*, New York: Dun-Donnelley, 1969.

Laidler, D.E.W. (1999), *Fabricating the Keynesian Revolution: Studies of the Inter-war Literature on Money, the Cycle, and Unemployment*, Cambridge: Cambridge University Press.

Marget, A.W. (1931), 'Leon Walras and the "Cash-Balance Approach" to the problem of the value of money', *Journal of Political Economy*, **39** (5), 569–600.

Meltzer, A.H. (1990), *Keynes's Monetary Theory: A Different Interpretation*, Cambridge: Cambridge University Press.

Pigou, A.C. (1917), 'The value of money', *Quarterly Journal of Economics*, **32** (1), 38–65.

Pigou, A.C. (1949), *The Veil of Money*, London: Macmillan.

Shackle, G.L.S. (1938), *Expectations, Investment and Income*, London: Oxford University Press.

Tooke, T. (1844), *An Inquiry into the Currency Principle; The Connection of the Currency with Prices, and the Expediency of a Separation of Issue from Banking*, London: Longman, Brown, Green and Longmans; (reprinted 1959), Series of Reprints of Scarce Works on Political Economy, No. 15 London: The London School of Economics and Political Science.

Wilson, E.B. (1948), 'John Law and John Keynes', *Quarterly Journal of Economics*, **62** (3), 381–95.
Woodford, M. (2003), *Interest and Prices. Foundations of a Theory of Monetary Policy*, Princeton: Princeton University Press.

CHAPTER 5: *THE GENERAL THEORY*

Asimakopulos, A. (1983), 'Anticipations of Keynes's General Theory?', *Canadian Journal of Economics / Revue canadienne d'economique*, **16** (3), 517–30.
Asimakopulos, A. (1991), *Keynes's General Theory and Accumulation*, Cambridge: Cambridge University Press.
Brenner, B. (1979), 'Unemployment, justice, and Keynes's General Theory', *Journal of Political Economy*, **87** (4), 837–50.
Coddington, A. (1982), 'Deficient foresight: a troublesome theme in Keynesian Economics', *American Economic Review*, **72** (3), 480–87.
Coddington, A. (1983), *Keynesian Economics: The Search for First Principles*, London: G. Allen and Unwin.
Curtis, M. (1937), 'Is money saving equal to investment?', *Quarterly Journal of Economics*, **51** (4), 604–25.
De Vroey, M. (1997), 'Le concept de chômage involontaire, de Keynes aux nouveaux keynésiens', *Revue économique*, **48** (6), 1381–408.
De Vroey, M. (2004), *Involuntary Unemployment: The Elusive Quest for a Theory*, London: Routledge.
De Vroey, M. (2006), 'Keynesian theory and involuntary unemployment. A reply to Hamouda', *History of Economic Ideas*, **14** (2), 127–31.
Drobny, A. (1988), *Real Wages and Employment: Keynes, Monetarism, and the Labour Market*, London: Routledge.
Ellsworth, P.T. (1936), 'Mr. Keynes on the rate of interest and the marginal efficiency of capital', *Journal of Political Economy*, **44** (6), 767–90.
Fanning, C., D. O'Mahony and J. Campling (1998), *The General Theory of Profit Equilibrium: Keynes and the Entrepreneur Economy*, Basingstoke: Macmillan Press and New York: St. Martin's Press.
Fender, J. (1981), *Understanding Keynes: An Analysis of 'the General Theory'*, New York: Wiley.
Froyen, R.T. (1976), 'The aggregative structure of Keynes's general theory', *The Quarterly Journal of Economics*, **90** (3), 369–87.
Gordon, S. (1982), 'A paraphrase version of Keynes' General Theory', Working Paper #476, Kingston, Ontario: Queen's University, Institute for Economic Research.

Hajela, P.D. (1952), *Keynes' 'General Theory' Trade Cycle and Foreign Exchange*, Allahabad: Pothishala.

Hamouda, O.F. (1986), 'Beyond the IS-LM device: was Keynes a Hicksian?', *Eastern Economic Journal*, **12** (4), 370–82.

Hamouda, O.F. (1997), 'The General Theory of Employment, Interest and Money and Prices', in P. Arestis, G. Palma and M. Sawyer (eds), *Capital Controversy, Post-Keynesian Economics, and The History of Economic Theory. Essays in Honour of Geoff Harcourt*, vol. I, London: Routledge, 226–34.

Hamouda, O.F. (2006a), 'The Era of "Ex Falso Quodlibet"': An Example, [Review of] De Vroey, Michel, *Involuntary Unemployment. The Elusive Quest for Theory'*, *History of Economic Ideas*, **14** (1), 136–45.

Hamouda, O.F. (2006b), 'Keynesian theory without Keynes: a reply to Michel De Vroey', *History of Economic Ideas*, **14** (2), 133–5.

Hansen, A.H. (1946), 'Keynes and the General Theory', *Review of Economics and Statistics*, **28** (4), 182–87.

Hansen, A H. (1953), *A Guide to Keynes*, New York: McGraw-Hill.

Hayes, M. (2006), *The Economics of Keynes: A New Guide to the General Theory*, Cheltenham, UK and Northampton, MA: Edward Elgar.

Heckscher. E.F. (1946), 'Något om Keynes' *General Theory* ur ekonomisk-historisk synpunkt', *Ekonomisk Tidskrift*, **48** (3), 161–83.

Hicks, J.R. (1986), *Towards a More General Theory; Managing without Money?* Nankang, Taipei: Institute of Economics, Academia Sinica.

Hudson, J. (1988), *Unemployment after Keynes: Towards a New General Theory*, Hemel Hempstead: Harvester Wheatsheaf and New York: St. Martin's Press.

Johnson, H.J. (1976), 'Keynes's General Theory: revolution or war of independence?', *Canadian Journal of Economics / Revue canadienne d'economique*, **9** (4), 580–94.

Kaldor, N. (1983), *Limitations of the 'General Theory'*, London: British Academy.

Lerner, A.P. (1938), 'Alternative formulations of the theory of interest', *Economic Journal*, **48** (190), 211–30.

Maclachlan, F.C. (1993), *Keynes' General Theory of Interest: A Reconsideration*, London and New York: Routledge.

Malinvaud, E. (1977), *The Theory of Unemployment Reconsidered*, Oxford: Basil Blackwell.

Pearce, I.F. (1977), *The Pathology of Keynes' General Theory*, Kingston, Ontario: Queen's University, Institute for Economic Research.

Perelman, M. (1989), *Keynes, Investment Theory, and the Economic Slowdown: The Role of Replacement Investment and q-Ratios*, Basingstoke: Macmillan Press.

Robinson, J. (1938), *Introduction to the Theory of Employment*, London: Macmillan.

Robinson, J. (1979), *The Generalisation of the General Theory, and other Essays*, 2nd edn, New York: St. Martin's Press.

Rueff, J. (1947), 'The fallacies of Lord Keynes General Theory', *Quarterly Journal of Economics*, **61** (3), 343–67.

Samuelson, P.A. (1946), 'Lord Keynes and the General Theory', *Econometrica*, **14** (3), 187–200.

Schmitt, B. (1971), *L'analyse macro-économique des revenus; révision des multiplicateurs de Keynes*, Paris: Dalloz.

Seth, M.L. (1957), *An Introduction to Keynesian Economics: the Modern Theory of Employment*, Agra: L.N. Agarwal.

Somers, H.S. (1941), 'Monetary policy and the theory of interest', *Quarterly Journal of Economics*, **55** (3), 488–507.

Stiglitz, J.E. (1986), 'Theories of wage rigidity', in J.L. Butkiewicz, K.J. Koford, and J.B. Miller (eds), *Keynes' Economic Legacy*, New York: Praeger, pp. 153–206.

Tarshis, L. (1939), 'Changes in real and money wages', *Economic Journal*, **49** (193), 150–54.

Tarshis, L. (1941), 'Real and money wage rates: further comment', *Quarterly Journal of Economics*, **55** (4), 691–7.

Tily, G. (2007), *Keynes's General Theory, the Rate of Interest and 'Keynesian' Economics: Keynes Betrayed*, Basingstoke and New York: Palgrave Macmillan.

Tobin, J. (1948), 'The fallacies of Lord Keynes' General Theory: comment', *Quarterly Journal of Economics*, **62** (5), 763–70.

Young, W. (1987), *Interpreting Mr. Keynes: The IS-LM Enigma*, Cambridge: Polity Press.

CHAPTER 6: EMPLOYMENT AND INCOME DISTRIBUTION

Ball, R.J., and P. Doyle (eds) (1969), *Inflation; Selected Readings. [Contributions by J.M. Keynes and others]*, Harmondsworth: Penguin Books.

Hart, A. (1933), 'An Examination of Mr. Keynes's price-level concepts', *Journal of Political Economy*, **41** (5), 625–38.

Humphrey, T.M. (1981), 'Keynes on Inflation', *Economic Review*, January–February, 3–13.

Humphrey, T.M. (1992), 'Price level stabilization rules in a Wicksellian model of the cumulative process', *Scandinavian Journal of Economics*, **94**, 509–18.

Trevithick, J.A. (1975), 'Keynes, inflation and money illusion', *Economic Journal*, **85** (337), 101–13.
Worswick, D. and J. Trevithick (eds) (1983), *Keynes and the Modern World*, Cambridge: Cambridge University Press.

GENERAL

Abraham-Frois, G. (1993), *Keynes et la macro-économie contemporaine*, 4th edn, Paris: Economica.
Allan, W. (ed.) (1993), *A Critique of Keynesian Economics*, New York: St. Martins Press.
Backhouse, R. and Bateman, B.W. (eds) (2006), *The Cambridge Companion to Keynes*, Cambridge and New York: Cambridge University Press.
Baldassarri, M. (ed.) (1992), *Keynes and the Economic Policies of the 1980s*, New York: St. Martin's Press.
Barrère, A. (ed.) (1988), *The Foundations of Keynesian Analysis: Proceedings of a Conference held at the University of Paris I-Panthéon-Sorbonne*, Basingstoke: Macmillan.
Baumol, W. and R. Turvey (1951), *Economic Dynamics*, New York: Macmillan.
Biven, W.C. (1989), *Who Killed John Maynard Keynes? Conflicts in the Evolution of Economic Policy*, Homewood, IL: Dow Jones-Irwin.
Burton, J. (1986), *Keynes's General Theory, Fifty Years on: Its Relevance and Irrelevance to Modern Times*, London: Institute of Economic Affairs.
Cairncross, A. (1983), *The Relationship between Monetary and Fiscal Policy*, London: British Academy.
Cottrell, A. and M.S. Lawlor (1995), *New Perspectives on Keynes*, Durham, NC: Duke University Press.
Davidson, P. (2007), *John Maynard Keynes*, Basingstoke: Palgrave Macmillan.
Dostaler, G. (2007), *Keynes and his Battles*, Cheltenham, UK and Northampton, MA, USA: Edward Elgar.
Dow, S.C. (1996), *The Methodology of Macroeconomic Thought*, Cheltenham, UK and Brookfield, VT, USA: Edward Elgar.
Dutt, A.K. and E.J. Amadeo (1990), *Keynes's Third Alternative? The Neo-Ricardian Keynesians and the Post Keynesians*, Aldershot, UK and Brookfield, VT, USA: Edward Elgar.
Forstater, M. and L.R. Wray (2008), *Keynes for the Twenty-First Century: The Continuing Relevance of the General Theory*, New York: Palgrave Macmillan.
Hamouda, O.F. (1990), 'Hicks' changing views on economic dynamics', in

D.E. Moggridge (ed.), *Perspectives on the History of Economic Thought*, Aldershot, UK and Brookfield, VT, USA: Edward Elgar.

Hamouda, O.F. (1991), 'Joan Robinson's Post Keynesianism', in I. Rima (ed.), *The Economics of Joan Robinson*, New York: M.E. Sharpe.

Hamouda, O.F. and B.B. Price (1998), *Keynesianism and the Keynesian Revolution in America*, Cheltenham, UK and Lyme, NH, USA: Edward Elgar.

Hamouda, O.F. and J. Smithin (eds) (1987), *Keynes and Public Policy after Fifty Years*, vol. I: *Economics and Policy*, vol. II: *Theories and Method*, London: Gower.

Hamouda, O.F., M. Colonna and H. Hagemann (eds) (1994), *Capitalism, Socialism and Knowledge. The Economics of F.A. Hayek*, vol. II Aldershot, UK and Brookfield, VT, USA: Edward Elgar.

Harris, S.E. (1960), *The New Economics; Keynes' Influence on Theory and Public Policy*, London: D. Dobson.

Hawtrey, R. (1928), *Trade and Credit*, London: Longmans.

Hazlitt, H. (ed.) (1960), *The Critics of Keynesian Economics*, Princeton, NJ: D. Van Nostrand.

Johnson, E.S., and H.G. Johnson (1978), *The Shadow of Keynes: Understanding Keynes, Cambridge, and Keynesian Economics*, Oxford: Basil Blackwell.

Kates, S. (1998), *Say's Law and the Keynesian Revolution: How Macroeconomic Theory Lost its Way*, Cheltenham, UK and Lyme, NH, USA: Edward Elgar.

Keynes, M. (ed.) (1975), *Essays on John Maynard Keynes*, New York: Cambridge University Press.

King, J.E. (2002), *A History of post Keynesian Economics since 1936*, Cheltenham, UK and Northampton, MA, USA: Edward Elgar.

Kurihara, K.K. (1955), *Post-Keynesian Economics*, London: G. Allen and Unwin.

Lavoie, M. (2006), *Introduction to Post-Keynesian Economics*, Basingstoke, Hampshire / New York: Palgrave Macmillan.

Lawson, T. and H. Pesaran (1989), *Keynes' Economics: Methodological Issue*, London: Routledge.

Mair, D. (1991), *A Modern Guide to Economic Thought*, Aldershot, UK and Brookfield, VT, USA: Edward Elgar.

Mankiw, N.G. and D. Romer (eds) (1991), *New Keynesian Economics: Imperfect Competition and Sticky Prices*, vol. I, and *Coordination Failures and Real Rigidities*, vol. II, Cambridge, MA: MIT Press.

Middleton, R. (1985), *Towards the Managed Economy: Keynes, the Treasury, and the Fiscal Policy Debate of the 1930s*, London and New York: Methuen.

Milgate, M. (1982), *Capital and Employment: A Study of Keynes's Economics*, London and New York: Academic Press.

Minsky, H.P. (1975), *John Maynard Keynes*, London: Macmillan.

Palley, T.I. (1996), *Post-Keynesian Economics: Debt, Distribution, and the Macro Economy*, New York: Macmillan Press and St. Martin's Press.

Pasinetti, L.L. and B. Schefold (eds) (1999), *The Impact of Keynes on Economics in the 20th Century*, Cheltenham, UK and Northampton, MA, USA: Edward Elgar.

Scazzieri, R., A. Sen and S. Zamagni (eds) (2008), *Market, Money and Capital. Hicksian Economics for the Twenty-first Century*, Cambridge: Cambridge University Press.

Shackle, G.L.S. (1974), *Keynesian Kaleidics; the Evolution of a General Political Economy*, Edinburgh: Edinburgh University Press and Chicago: Aldine.

Singh, V.B. and M.H. Dobb (eds) (1956), *Keynesian Economics; a Symposium*, Delhi: People's Publishing House.

Skidelsky, R.J.A. (2001), *John Maynard Keynes*, New York: Viking.

Skousen, M. (1992), *Dissent on Keynes: A Critical Appraisal of Keynesian Economics*, New York: Praeger.

Toye, J.F.J. (2000), *Keynes on Population*, New York: Oxford University Press.

Weintraub, S. (1978), *Keynes, Keynesians, and Monetarists*, Philadelphia, PA: University of Pennsylvania Press.

Wood, J.C. (1994), *John Maynard Keynes: Critical Assessments*, London and New York: Routledge.

Name index

Subject index

approximation 128, 129, 155, 179
Austrian theory 2, 8, 35, 54, 55, 56, 77, 79–80, 84, 90, 103, 123, 136

balance of payments 24, 28, 68, 70
balance of trade 68, 70
banking 6, 15, 20, 23, 45, 53, 70, 93, 109, 113, 167, 170, 171, 172, 173, 175, 176, 181, 182, 189, 190, 194, 195, 228, 230
  School 7, 27, 41, 56, 194, 214
boom 55, 78, 111, 113, 115, 116, 162, 166, 168, 169, 170, 175, 177, 181, 182
  curbing 165, 169
budget deficits 11
bullishness and bearishness 6, 20, 38, 47, 49, 50, 65, 71, 72, 74, 77, 89, 111, 113, 154, 176

Cambridge Quantity Equation *see* Quantity Equation, Cambridge
Cambridge, UK 4, 12, 14, 15, 54, 87, 88, 220, 222, 224, 226, 229, 230, 231, 233, 234, 235, 236
  USA 12, 14, 87, 221, 230, 235
capital 6, 8, 16, 22, 24, 41, 60, 61, 65, 69, 75, 76, 77, 79, 81, 82, 84, 86, 87, 89, 93, 105, 114, 116, 122, 123, 133, 137, 144, 145, 146, 149, 155, 167, 169, 175, 180, 184, 187, 188, 189, 199, 200, 201, 203, 204, 205, 206, 211, 212, 213, 214, 215, 216, 217, 220, 222, 227, 235, 236
  account 70
  as rented service 133, 145, 152, 179, 189, 198, 201, 216
  available 16, 40, 41, 61, 62, 66, 72, 75, 83, 84, 86, 89, 94, 106, 110, 113, 116, 118, 119, 121, 122, 138, 149, 150, 162, 166, 180,
185, 187, 188, 189, 193, 195, 202, 203, 205, 207, 211, 215, 218
  categories of *see also* Fixed, Liquid, and Working 63, 64–5, 73, 77, 108, 114, 118, 145, 147, 168, 218
  circulating 63, 78
  demand *see* demand for capital
  depreciation 59, 60, 66, 70, 86, 136, 138, 145, 149, 162, 216
  efficiency of 5, 13, 14, 17, 19, 50, 52, 53, 75, 116, 122, 135, 144, 146, 147, 150, 152, 154, 156, 162, 163, 164, 165, 166, 167, 168, 174–84, 187, 188, 189, 193, 211, 231
  Fixed 6, 10, 20, 24, 61, 62, 63, 68, 73, 77, 78, 84, 86, 92, 108, 114, 115, 116, 117, 118, 122, 124, 133, 165, 166, 167, 168
  goods, or equipment vii, 46, 55, 59, 60, 61, 62, 63, 67, 68, 69, 71, 72, 73, 74, 75, 77, 80, 81, 82, 83, 84, 86, 87, 88, 90, 91, 92, 93, 94, 95, 96, 97–9, 100, 101–4, 105, 107, 108, 109–14, 116, 117, 118, 122, 123, 124, 129, 133, 136–7, 153, 154, 165, 166, 168, 176, 179, 183, 190, 201, 209, 210, 211, 218
inflation *see* Inflation, Capital
intensive technology 24, 91–2, 93, 100, 101, 105
investment vii, x, 5, 6, 8, 15, 17, 18, 19, 20, 21, 22, 24, 25, 26, 29, 33, 34, 38, 39, 41, 46, 47, 48, 49, 52, 55, 57, 58, 59, 60, 61, 62, 64, 65, 66, 67, 69, 70, 71, 72, 73, 74, 75, 76, 77, 78, 80, 81, 82, 83, 84, 85, 86, 87, 88, 89, 92, 93, 94, 96, 97, 98, 99, 100, 101, 102, 103, 104, 105, 106, 107, 108–16, 117–24, 125, 127, 130, 131, 132, 133, 135, 136–90, 191–216